RISKS OF CONSEQUENCES

Freddie Thomas
Risks of Consequences

All rights reserved
Copyright © 2024 by Freddie Thomas

—

Published by - Spines
ISBN: 979-8-89569-193-9

Risks of Consequences

Freddie Thomas

Disclaimer

This book is a work of fiction. All characters, places, and events portrayed within are products of the author's imagination. Any resemblance to real persons, living or dead, or actual events is purely coincidental. The views and opinions expressed in this work are those of the fictional characters and do not necessarily reflect those of the author or any real individuals.

PROLOGUE

Here's what I've come to understand: life is an intricate tapestry of experiences that extends far beyond the commonplace occurrences many of us settle into. Life, inherently, is a gamble, a series of calculated risks even for those who find solace in the perceived safety of routine. It's easy to slip into mechanical existence, losing ourselves in the monotony of what I term "the common adaptation of social alignment."

In simpler terms: "becoming entangled in the game."

This entails being so engrossed in the routine tasks of life that we cease to live for ourselves, navigating existence solely for the benefit of others. It's a phenomenon I've observed throughout my life—individuals like my father dedicating over 30 years to daily labor for a cause that enriched others while leaving him vulnerable to premature dismissal. Thirty-one years of service and not even a severance package to cushion his retirement. No commemorative pen or plaque to mark where he spent most of his life. This stark reality solidifies my conviction: life is inherently risky, regardless of perceived stability. Everything is subject to the unpredictable winds of change.

This prompts crucial questions: What is change? When does it arrive? Why is it often unannounced, and why does it yield happiness for some and agony for others? Amid life's undulating journey, my enduring philosophy has been this:

A risk is nothing more than a leap of faith toward the pursuit of happiness, and change is inevitable.

Given this reality, rather than idly waiting for circumstances to unfold, I implore you to do as I did – seize control of the inevitable, step out on faith, and follow your heart. However, bear in mind that chasing your dreams may necessitate leaving others behind. Pose the question to yourself: "Are you willing to take the risk?" Because with risk, there's only ONE guarantee: after you've embraced it, change is inevitable, and the consequences of that decision initiate a cascade of reactions. Some are manageable, while others are not. Always remember, the risk is solely yours to undertake, with the potential for either benefit or fracture. The scary thing is that some of us walk away with both.

   ~Bobby Pope

"Whispers in the Wind"

The morning was draped in a soft, gray mist as Amelia and her mother, Clara, walked through the gates of the Willow Creek Cemetery. It was a quiet Sunday, the kind where the world seemed to pause and whisper. They were there to visit the grave of Grandma June, a ritual that marked each anniversary of her passing.

Amelia, at six, found the cemetery more fascinating than frightening. To her young mind, it was a garden of stories, each gravestone a doorway into another time. Today, she was particularly excited because her mother had promised she could practice her reading on the inscriptions that adorned the ancient stones.

Hand in hand, they walked down the pebbled path, Amelia's small fingers gripping her mother's hand. Her wide eyes scanned the sea of gravestones, each one different from the last. Some were ornate, others simple; some weathered by time and elements, others new and sharply etched.

"Mommy, why are there so many stones?" Amelia's voice was a gentle murmur, blending with the rustle of the leaves.

"They're like bookmarks, sweetie! Marking the stories of people's lives, where they rest the chapters of their earthly journeys," Clara explained softly, squeezing Amelia's hand reassuringly.

Encouraged by her mother's poetic description, Amelia let go and wandered a bit ahead, her small fingers tracing the contours of the gravestones, feeling the cold, hard edges. She stumbled upon a section of the graveyard that was bathed in the soft light breaking through the morning clouds. Here, two particularly beautiful stones caught her eye.

These stones stood proudly next to each other, their surfaces smooth and gleaming. Intricate engravings of flowers cascaded down the sides, meeting at a cross at the base. The craftsmanship was exquisite, making them stand out among the more modest markers in their vicinity.

"Look, Mommy, look at these two over here!" Amelia called out, her voice filled with excitement.

Clara walked over, her eyes following Amelia's pointing finger. She read the inscriptions aloud. Amelia was very smart and could read at a 12th-grade level, so the inscriptions were fun and interesting for her to test her reading skills. What does it say, baby? Clara asked Amelia, "'To have felt the risk of love is worth the consequences' - Bobby Pope." She paused and then moved to the next, "And this one is Brandy Pope." As Amelia began to finish reading the remainder of the writing on the stones, her mother interrupted her.

"Oh, those are beautiful stones, honey," Clara replied, her voice tinged with a mix of admiration and faint sadness.

Amelia looked up at her mother. "What does it mean, Mommy? The risk of love?"

Clara knelt beside her, brushing a loose strand of hair from Amelia's face. "It means that loving someone deeply can sometimes lead to pain, but experiencing love is precious, even with its challenges. It's saying that love, in any form, is worth the difficulties we might face."

Amelia pondered this, looking back at the stones. "Did they love each other a lot?"

"I think they must have," Clara said, her eyes lingering on the twin graves. "To be remembered together like this, they must have shared a very special bond."

The lesson wasn't lost on Amelia. As they continued their search for Grandma June's grave, Amelia held her mother's hand a little tighter. The gravestones no longer seemed just markers of what was lost but also reminders of what had been: love that dared, despite the odds.

Eventually, they found Grandma June's stone, laying their flowers down gently. They stood together, the breeze picking up as if carrying their words and love upward. Today, Amelia had learned about the chapters of life and love encapsulated in the whispers of the wind swirling through Willow Creek Cemetery.

"Good morning, baby," Brandy greeted Bobby with a smile as the morning light filtered through the curtains.

"How did you sleep?" Bobby asked as he stretched his arms, still feeling the remnants of last night's energy.

"Man, you know I slept like a baby last night after that session we had. Boy, you're something else. You got any horses in your bloodline?" Brandy teased, her eyes sparkling with mischief.

"Look, baby, I gotta go and head into work," Bobby said, leaning over to kiss Brandy while she lay relaxed in bed. Her face was fresh without makeup, and her hair cascaded over the pillow like a silken veil. Brandy's beauty was truly unparalleled, captivating not only Bobby but everyone who laid eyes on her. She possessed a natural allure that required no embellishment; even in her simplest, most unadorned state, she was a knockout. Her presence alone could turn heads and draw admiring glances, making her the center of attention effortlessly. Whether she was dressed up for a night out or just lounging at home, Brandy exuded a kind of radiance that made her unforgettable and deeply admired.

Bobby paused for a moment, just staring at her. "You have no idea how much I love you, woman," he confessed, his voice thick with emotion.

Brandy sat up on her knees in the bed, the sheets pooling around her waist, and leaned over to kiss him again. "I bet you don't love me as much as I love you. Cause I love you more than there are grains of sand in the Sahara Desert."

"Wow, that's love," Bobby exclaimed, his heart swelling.

"So, aren't you going to try and top that?" Brandy challenged playfully.

"If you can't see how deep you are in my heart, then I'll never be able to explain it in a million years," Bobby replied earnestly, his eyes deep and sincere.

"Damn, that's deep too. Get outta here, boy, with your big old self. You beast, got my back hurting and stuff," Brandy laughed, her voice light and teasing.

As Bobby grabbed his briefcase and prepared to leave for the office, Brandy's voice, sweet yet firm, called out to him from the kitchen. "Oh, baby, before you go, don't forget I have the show tonight. I'll be looking beautiful for you, so don't be late."

Bobby turned and walked over to her, placing a tender kiss on her forehead. "I wouldn't miss it for the world, Brandy. Seeing you perform is one of the greatest joys of my life."

Brandy smiled, her eyes twinkling with excitement. "There will be tickets at the door for you and Meeka. I can't wait to see you in the audience."

Bobby smiled back. "We'll be there, I promise. Break a leg, sweetheart."

Brandy's performances at the Cadillac Palace Theatre in downtown Chicago were nothing short of magical. She performed five shows a week and became the headliner for the production. Each night, her powerful voice filled the theater, captivating audiences with its rich, soulful timbre. It wasn't just about the notes she sang; it was about the way she made every word come alive, conveying deep emotion and connecting with every person in the audience.

Her talent was undeniable. Brandy had a unique ability to draw people in, to make them feel every joy and sorrow, every hope and heartbreak. Her voice had a magical quality, resonating with purity and strength that left audiences spellbound. She didn't just sing; she told stories, each performance a journey that took her audience to new heights and depths of feeling.

The theater was always packed, with fans eager to experience the enchantment of Brandy's voice. She had a stage presence that was both commanding and graceful, making every performance memorable. The way she moved, the expressions on her face, the passion in her eyes—all of it combined to create an unforgettable experience.

For the past few years, Brandy has steadily built her reputation, becoming quite recognizable for her voice and performance. She was more than just a singer; she was a performer who could transform a simple song into a powerful, emotional experience. Her dedication to her craft and her ability to connect with her audience had earned her a special place in the hearts of many.

As Bobby headed out the door, he couldn't help but think about the evening ahead. Watching Brandy perform was always a highlight for him. He loved seeing her on stage, where she seemed to belong, radiating confidence and joy. Her voice was like a beacon, guiding him through the complexities of life and reminding him of the beauty and magic that still existed in the world.

Later that evening, Bobby arrived at the Cadillac Palace Theatre with Meeka by his side. The anticipation was palpable as they picked up their tickets and found their seats. The lights dimmed, and the audience hushed, waiting for the show to begin.

When Brandy stepped onto the stage, a wave of applause greeted her. She stood tall, her dress shimmering under the spotlight, her smile bright and inviting. As the first notes of her song filled the theater, Bobby felt a familiar thrill. Her voice was as magical as ever, weaving through the air and wrapping around each listener, pulling them into her world.

The audience sat in rapt attention, completely mesmerized by her performance. Brandy's voice soared and whispered, danced and wept, each song a testament to her incredible talent. She was a force of nature, and the theater was her domain.

Bobby watched, his heart swelling with pride and love. He knew that Brandy was born to do this, to share her gift with the world. And as he listened to her sing, he felt an overwhelming sense of gratitude for having her in his life.

As the final notes of the evening's performance faded, the audience erupted into applause, standing to their feet in appreciation. Brandy bowed gracefully, her eyes seeking out Bobby in the crowd. Their gazes met, and she smiled, knowing that she had once again touched his heart with her magical voice.

After the show, Bobby and Meeka made their way backstage to congratulate Brandy. She was glowing with happiness, the thrill of the performance still fresh.

"You were amazing, as always," Bobby said, wrapping her in a tight hug.

"Thank you," Brandy replied, her eyes shining. "I'm so glad you were here."

"Wouldn't miss it for anything," Bobby said. "You're incredible, Brandy. Truly."

Meeka chimed in, "You have a gift, Brandy. Tonight was unforgettable."

Brandy beamed, surrounded by the love and support of those who mattered most to her. In that moment, she knew that no matter what challenges lay ahead, she would always have the strength and the magic of her voice to carry her through. And with Bobby and Meeka by her side, there was nothing she couldn't achieve.

As Brandy sat at the table in the breakfast nook in her home, she gazed out of the window, allowing her thoughts to drift into memories of her life, specifically her relationship with Bobby.

In the heart of downtown Chicago, nestled on the twentieth floor of a sleek high-rise condominium, Bobby and Brandy's home exuded modern elegance and urban charm. As the morning sun cast its golden hues across the skyline, the floor-to-ceiling windows offered panoramic views of the bustling city below.

Stepping into the foyer, guests were greeted by a chic blend of polished marble floors and tasteful contemporary art pieces adorning the walls. A soft, ambient glow from designer light fixtures created an inviting atmosphere that complemented the natural light flooding in from the expansive windows.

The living area, seamlessly connected to the dining space, featured plush furnishings in muted tones of cream and charcoal, accented by pops of color from carefully curated throw pillows and a vibrant area rug. A state-of-the-art entertainment system, discreetly integrated into the minimalist décor, offered both comfort and entertainment.

The kitchen, a culinary enthusiast's dream, boasted sleek granite countertops and top-of-the-line stainless steel appliances. Reflective surfaces and minimalist cabinetry provided ample storage without compromising the airy, open feel of the space. A cozy breakfast nook by the window offered the perfect spot for Brandy to enjoy her morning coffee while watching the city come to life.

The master bedroom, a sanctuary of relaxation, was adorned with luxurious linens in calming shades of dove gray and azure. Floor-to-ceiling drapes framed the stunning cityscape outside, allowing Brandy to wake up to breathtaking views every morning. An en-suite bathroom featuring a deep soaking tub and a rain shower provided a spa-like retreat amidst the urban hustle.

Throughout the home, thoughtful touches such as abstract art pieces, curated bookshelves, and ambient lighting fixtures enhanced the contemporary aesthetic while reflecting Bobby and Brandy's sophisticated taste and lifestyle. Every corner of their home exuded warmth and sophistication, offering a serene oasis high above the dynamic energy of downtown Chicago.

As her thoughts shifted back to Bobby, it was clear to her how special he was. He was a strategic visionary, a dreamer who had an unwavering belief in his ability to turn his dreams into reality. If he set his mind to it, he could achieve it, and that's precisely what he did throughout his life. She fondly remembered the stories he used to share about his childhood.

From a young age, it was evident to everyone around him that Bobby was distinct. His momma used to say he was a charming boy right from the day he was born. He displayed a remarkable attention to detail, not just in his appearance but in the way he carried himself. His choice of clothing, his meticulous grooming, his hairstyle, and his ability to stay in tune with the ever-evolving fashion trends all set him apart.

As he transitioned into the world of business after college, his suits were tailored to perfection, radiating professionalism. Bobby's look remained timeless and elegant. When he strolled into his office, there was a certain confidence in his step that made it seem as though he knew precisely where he was headed and no one could stand in his way. Heads would turn when he entered a room, especially those who had their sights set on him, thinking he was a ticket to their dreams. "Hey, Bobby," yelled one of these admirers. "He's so fine. If he were mine, we'd be inseparable, like Siamese twins. I wouldn't ever... get off that ass... or let him out of my sight," they whispered, casting discreet glances at his departing figure. "Hey, ladies... how are y'all doing?" Bobby replied with that magnetic charm that suggested,

"Can I get some attention?" On more than one occasion, someone had to step in and keep the enthusiastic admirers at bay. "And, of course, that was me." Bobby was my man... and I wasn't having any of these thirsty-ass women trying to quench themselves with the flow that was coming off him. He frequented the gym two to five times a week, often sharing his mantra: "If you take care of your body, it will take care of you." Bobby possessed a magnetic charm that attracted women, young girls, and people of all ages. However, his most alluring trait was his mind. You could always tell in his conversation because he could go so deep. It was like he could paint the moment he was talking about so clearly you felt like he had taken you there, to that very place, "and that would turn me on." He was a master at phone sex, too. "If I was there, you know I would be tasting it, right? Yes, baby, aww, damn Bobby," she breathes heavily while touching herself with one hand and the phone in the other. Ohhh, she lets out a gasping sigh, "Damn, I don't like you, but I can't get enough of your ass." "You just wait till you get home." Any sister listening to him would have a hard time keeping her panties dry. Damn, he was a thinker.

Bobby always knew what to say to you to make you feel better, to motivate you. Not a day would go by that he wouldn't compliment me and make me feel like I was the most beautiful woman in the world. I ain't gonna lie. The way he held me up messed with my head and made me walk around like I was a queen bitch. I fault him for filling up my head, but truthfully, I loved it. That's why he was so good at his job working as a broker. Yeah, that's right; he started at Merrill Lynch as an intern fresh out of college and rose to VP of Accounts in less than three years. People trusted him because he made them believe in what he was selling. His momma always told him he could sell bibles to a nun and fake diamonds to a dope fiend.

Bobby's shoes were a point of pride, a lesson he learned from his uncle, who once said, "A true gentleman pays attention to his footwear; a dapper man's shoes must always be immaculate." Bobby took those words to heart, ensuring every aspect of his appearance exuded class. It wasn't just on the outside; he carried himself with poise and grace on the inside as well.

One elderly lady claimed he was the most exceptional visionary she had ever known. He possessed unparalleled creativity, and when he spoke, he had the ability to make things coherent that might otherwise remain confusing to those who were not in the know. His communication was articulate, his vocabulary extensive, and he excelled as a public speaker.

Bobby had a deep affection for people, but he remained an intensely private individual. His interests spanned poetry, philosophy, and theology, and writing was his abiding passion. Yet, it was a passion that would, at times, introduce challenges I wasn't quite prepared to embrace. He diligently maintained a daily diary and a poetry book, their contents closely guarded and known to no one. However, he would often send me the most exquisite poems through text messages. Every time I received one, it ignited a desire to return home and be as close to him as a rider on a horse's saddle.

On his cell phone and in his notebooks, Bobby meticulously recorded some of his profound and insightful remarks. Whenever he made a comment that resonated deeply, he would capture it by recording his own voice and repeating it. I would often tease him that if he ever passed away, his words would need to be shared, much like the wisdom of Gandhi or other great figures. Bobby was a remarkable conversationalist, not in an annoying way, but in a manner that encouraged you to embrace his wisdom.

He maintained a profound connection with God and had a deep spiritual relationship. Bobby possessed a unique gift for connecting with people from all walks of life. Striking up conversations with strangers, he had an innate ability to turn chance encounters into lasting friendships.

He possessed the art of leveraging his relationships to his advantage, using them as a powerful tool for his own success. He had a consistent habit of helping people, often going out of his way to provide assistance, even when it wasn't solicited. I recall one incident from our college days when we were out on a date.

A young lady approached him, requesting money to catch a bus, claiming she had fallen into hard times. There was something unusual about her demeanor. While her appearance didn't resemble that of a substance abuser, her approach had a certain resemblance. It didn't help that the area where she approached him was infamous for panhandlers and straight-out dope fiends seeking funds for illicit purposes.

Bobby informed her that he didn't have any money on him at the moment, although he had just received his paycheck from his part-time job. He got into his car and drove away as the lady continued walking down the street. However, it was an extremely cold day, with ten inches of snow from the previous night covering the ground.

As Bobby proceeded down the street, his conscience weighed heavily on him. Many people wouldn't have given a second thought to the plight of a homeless individual, but Bobby was deeply disturbed by not assisting her. He explained that there was something peculiar about the woman, even though she appeared to be trying to manipulate the situation to get her next fix. Bobby mentioned her striking sea-water blue eyes, surrounded by the purest white he had ever seen. He felt there was something unusual about her spirit.

About three miles down the road, Bobby decided to turn around and offer help, but when he returned, the lady was nowhere to be found. For two hours, Bobby tirelessly searched for the lady, driven by his commitment to help her. He returned to the exact spot where he had seen her, parked his car, and got out to investigate. He scrutinized the ground, and there, in the very place the lady had been standing, he spotted a gold coin. It was a puzzling discovery, as one might expect that even a desperate individual would have noticed this gleaming treasure. After all, they had an uncanny knack for sniffing out money from a mile away. Yet, there it lay, pristine and shimmering in the open parking lot, as if it had just been minted, casting a shine akin to the morning sun.

Bobby reached down to retrieve it, and his expression spoke volumes. He held in his hand a solid gold Saint Christopher coin, its size matching that of a silver dollar. It was notably weightier than the ordinary, and on the reverse side, it bore an engraved message: "God's grace." At that moment, Bobby realized he had missed an opportunity to be a source of blessing to the lady. However, he also understood that he would never again judge people based on their appearance, but rather by the godly responsibility he felt toward them.

From that day forward, wherever Bobby ventured, he made sure to carry silver dollars in his pocket, ready to offer them to anyone he sensed was in need of assistance. Later, he decided to have the coin appraised. To his surprise, he discovered that the coin was not silver but solid gold, with an estimated value of around $500. He never left his home without it, keeping it close, as he believed that one day, God would guide someone deserving of him.

Being a genuine people person, Bobby accrued more "I O U's" during his life than he could ever collect. His generosity knew no bounds, and in return, everyone wanted to do something kind for Bobby, a testament to the goodwill he had spread throughout his community.

"Triumphs and Memories"

Shortly after Bobby left for the office, Brandy stepped out of the hot shower, feeling a wave of panic and edginess wash over her. She decided to lie across the bed for a moment, a ritual she often turned to when she failed to take her trauma meds. As she sank into the mattress, the familiar, haunting tendrils of her past experiences began to creep back into her mind. Unable to fend them off, Brandy found herself once again drifting into the horror-filled prison of her memories, each one more vivid and terrifying than the last. Suddenly, she was there in the place where she lived as a little girl. Their home was a harsh realm of chaos, the walls forever echoing with screams and the sharp clinks of needles against glass. The apartment, nestled within a deteriorating building in a neglected neighborhood, bore the signs of long-standing wear—chipped paint and broken windows hinted at the neglect both outside and in.

Stepping inside, the disarray of their lives was mirrored in every corner. The living room was a jumble of old, mismatched furniture that had seen better days. The couch, stained and sagging, often served as a makeshift bed. The threadbare carpet was dirty, littered with empty takeout containers, cigarette butts, and remnants of drug paraphernalia. A small, outdated television sat on a rickety stand, often left on to provide background noise in an otherwise silent and suffocating space. The air was thick with the smell of smoke and stale air, as the windows were rarely opened for ventilation.

The kitchen, tiny and cramped, had peeling linoleum floors and countertops covered in grime. The sink overflowed with dirty dishes left for days, attracting pests. Empty bottles and cans were scattered around, alongside discarded food wrappers and broken appliances. The refrigerator, almost empty except for a few basic items, indicated a lack of regular meals.

Brandy's room was a small, dark space with a single bed covered in old, tattered sheets. Her personal belongings were strewn about haphazardly. Sylvia, her mother, and Carl shared the other bedroom, which was similarly cluttered. Their mattress lay on the floor, surrounded by piles of clothes and other miscellaneous items. Both rooms had minimal decorations —perhaps a few faded posters or photographs tacked to the walls.

The bathroom was grimy, with mold growing in the corners and a leaky faucet that dripped constantly. Towels and toiletries were scattered around, and the medicine cabinet was crammed with various prescription bottles, many of them empty. The hallways were narrow and lined with more clutter, creating an obstacle course of sorts. Any additional spaces, like closets, were overstuffed with junk, making it hard to find anything useful.

In this chaotic environment, Brandy navigated her days, each step a testament to the tumultuous life she and her family led. The physical state of their home was a constant, unyielding reminder of the battles they fought within.

Brandy, a mere child with innocence still etched on her face, bore witness to the nightly rituals of her mother and Carl as they danced on the precipice of oblivion. It was a deathly stroll, a performance that played out in the shadows of a dimly lit room. She escaped to the night that Carl, her father's impact, had left far-reaching scars that, no matter how hard she tried, continued to haunt her into her adulthood. She now became a little girl revisiting the vicious and rage-fuelled attack on Brandy's mother, Sylvia, which was a culmination of an escalating conflict in a night filled with horror. The root cause was a discovery that tore at the fragile fabric of their lives. Brandy's mother had unearthed the painful truth: Carl had impregnated another woman who lived in close proximity.

The dim light from a single bulb cast long shadows on the walls of the tiny, dilapidated apartment. The air was thick with the pungent smell of smoke, mingling with the acrid scent of old furniture and stale air. Brandy, a seven-year-old girl with wide, fearful eyes, sat quietly in her small, cluttered room. She clutched a worn-out teddy bear to her chest, listening to the muffled voices of her parents in the next room.

Carl and Silvia, both dope fiends, had settled into their nightly ritual. The coffee table, scarred and stained, held the tools of their trade: a tarnished spoon, a lighter, and a small bag of dope. Silvia, her hands trembling, carefully prepared the mixture, heating it until it bubbled and melted. She drew the liquid into a syringe and she became extremely skilled at prepping the works to get them ready for the hit. Carl, dripping with a thirst for the drugs, sat watching her do her thing and said, dam girl, you should have been a surgeon the way you do that hit. Silvia turned her head while prepping the works, looking around for the curious eyes of her daughter. BRANDY!!!...... she yelled. Stay yo ass in that room, baby. Don't come out here......, me and your daddy are busy...... YOU HEAR ME!!! Yeah, I hear you, Mommy, Brandy yelled in the distance. But by now, Brandy knew exactly what they were doing.

Carl sprawled on the old, torn-down couch, watched her

with glazed eyes. "Hurry up, Silvia. I need my fix," he muttered, barely able to keep his head up.

Silvia nodded, her movements mechanical, and injected herself first before handing the needle to Carl. He took it with a grunt, his eyes closing as the drug coursed through his veins. The tension in his body eased, and he sank deeper into the couch, the world around him fading into a distant hum.

For a moment, the apartment was quiet except for the occasional creak of the floorboards and the distant sounds of the neighborhood. Brandy stayed in her room, listening, her small heart pounding in her chest. She always hated the smell of the burnt drugs that invaded her little nostrils, but she was beginning to get used to it because it happened so often.

Silvia sat down next to Carl, her eyes red and swollen. The drugs would have different effects on different people, but Silvia always pulled out her inner emotions and removed her from her shy and acceptable-to-everything self. She became "voicetrous" and felt more emboldened when she was high. Those times were never good for Carl because, on occasion, she would beat him for things he had done to her before. He would be so high he couldn't fight back. She had been crying for days, ever since she discovered that Carl had impregnated another woman in their dope-infested neighborhood. Tonight, she could no longer hold back her anger and betrayal.

"Carl," she began, her voice shaking. "We need to talk."

Carl groaned, not wanting to be disturbed. "Not now, Silvia. You're messing up my high." "CARL!!! Wake your ass up," Silvia yelled as she kicked at him while he was lying down.

"I don't care about your high!" Silvia snapped, tears streaming down her face. "How could you do this to me? To us? You got another woman pregnant, Carl! How could you?"

Carl opened his eyes, his expression hardening. "What are you talking about?"

"You know exactly what I'm talking about!" Silvia yelled, her voice cracking. "I saw her, Carl. She told me everything. How could you betray me like this?"

Carl sat up slowly, his movements sluggish. "Silvia, you're overreacting. It's not a big deal."

WHAT DID YOU SAY???......, Silvia yelled. "Not a big deal?" Silvia screamed, standing up and glaring down at him. "You have another child on the way with another woman! How is that not a big deal?"

Carl rolled his eyes, leaning back against the couch. "Just calm down, Silvia. You're blowing this out of proportion."

Silvia's hands clenched into fists, her nails digging into her palms. "I'm not blowing anything out of proportion, Carl! This is our life, our family! And you just threw it all away for some cheap fling." With another bitch.

Carl's eyes narrowed, anger flaring in his drug-hazed mind. "Watch your mouth, Silvia. You don't know what you're talking about."

Silvia stepped closer, her voice dropping to a dangerous whisper. "Oh, I know exactly what I'm talking about. And I'm not going to stand here and let you ruin our lives anymore."

In a sudden, violent motion, Carl shoved Silvia hard. She stumbled back, crashing into the coffee table. The fragile wooden legs snapped, and the table collapsed under her weight, scattering their drug paraphernalia across the floor. Silvia's head had hit the table, and the glass fragments cut across her face. Blood was flowing everywhere.

Brandy, hearing the commotion, burst out of her room. "Daddy, stop it! Don't hurt Mommy!" she cried, her voice high and terrified.

Carl turned to her; his expression twisted with rage. "Get yo little ass back to your room, Brandy! This is none of your business!"

Brandy stood her ground, tears streaming down her face. "Please, Daddy, don't hurt her."

Silvia grabbed a towel that had been left on the floor and placed it on her face to stop the bleeding. Struggling to get up from the broken table, she looked at her daughter with desperation in her eyes. "Brandy, go back to your room. It's okay."

But it wasn't okay. Nothing about this was okay. The apartment seemed to close in around them, the shadows growing darker and the air heavier. Silvia managed to stand, her body shaking with both fear and rage.

"You see what you're doing, Carl?" she said, her voice breaking. "You're tearing this family apart. You're destroying us."

Carl still slumped on the couch, pointed a shaky finger at her. "You're the one making a scene, Silvia. You're the one causing all this trouble."

Silvia's eyes blazed with fury. "I'm causing trouble? You're the one who cheated. You're the one who can't keep his promises."

Carl tried to push himself up, but his legs buckled, and he fell back onto the couch. "I ain't done shit," he mumbled, though even he didn't believe his own words.

Silvia, seizing the moment, lunged at him. They struggled, grappling with each other as Brandy watched in horror. The room seemed to spin around them, their shouts and cries blending into a loudness of pain and betrayal.

"Daddy, stop! Mommy, please!" Brandy cried, but her small voice was barely heard over the chaos.

Carl managed to push Silvia off him, sending her sprawling onto the floor. He turned to Brandy with his eyes wild. "Get back to your room, now!"

Brandy hesitated, torn between fear for her mother and obedience to her father. Silvia, lying on the floor, looked up at her daughter with pleading eyes. "Brandy, please go to your room. Everything will be okay."

But Brandy knew it wouldn't be okay. She backed away slowly, tears blurring her vision as she retreated to the relative safety of her room. She closed the door; the sounds of her parents' struggle were muffled but still audible.

Inside, Brandy sank to the floor, clutching her teddy bear tightly. She rocked back and forth, trying to block out the noise, trying to pretend that everything would be all right. But deep down, she knew that her family was breaking apart, piece by painful piece.

This revelation became the catalyst for a devastating series of events. After the heated argument that followed the discovery, Brandy's mother left distressed and vulnerable, succumbed to the drugs Carl peddled to others. Tragically, she was later found dead, a victim of an overdose of cocaine laced with fentanyl—a lethal combination.

It was Brandy who stumbled upon the devastating scene the next morning. Hiding under her bed, she had finally managed to fall asleep, overwhelmed by the fear of the events she had witnessed and heard. As she cautiously approached her mother's room, now void of Carl, who had left after the violent assault, Brandy called out, her voice shattered by fear. "Momma... Momma... can I come in there with you?" There was no response.

As she pushed open the door, a chilling stillness hung in the air. The room, once a sanctuary, now bore the scars of a violent storm. Pieces of shattered glass glittered like ominous crystals on the floor, remnants of the chaos that had unfolded. The furniture, once familiar and comforting, now stood as silent witnesses to the brutality inflicted upon her mother.

Brandy's heart pounded in her chest as she made her way through the room. The pale morning light struggled to penetrate the heavy curtains, casting eerie shadows that danced across the walls. The air was thick with a stale, oppressive scent, a haunting reminder of the tragedy that had unfolded in those dark hours.

Her mother lay slumped over the bed, clothes torn, bearing

bruises on her back, face, and arms. Brandy was terrified, crying and shaking as if confronting a ghost. She called out again, her voice breaking, "Momma... Are you okay?"

Navigating through shattered glass and objects scattered by the previous night's abuse, Brandy reached the other side of the bed. It was there that she noticed a white substance on her mother's nose and face. Her mother were pale, her long black hair hanging over her head and partially covering her face, and her eyes were wide open—a haunting scene that would forever etch itself in Brandy's memory.

Overwhelmed by horror and shock, Brandy, a little girl, sat on the bed next to her lifeless mother, crying and lost in a moment that would shape the course of her life. The room, once a haven of safety, now echoed with the haunting remnants of a nightmare that refused to fade away.

Months later, Carl was eventually arrested and convicted of second-degree murder, sentenced to 25 years in prison without the possibility of parole. Brandy's life, forever altered by the devastating consequences of her mother's choices, was now on a trajectory of major change because of the risk her mother took in loving a man who never loved himself.

As the memory of her latest spell faded, Brandy slowly got up and walked into her expanded walk-in closet. Shaking and distorted from the spell, she found her medication, quickly swallowing a pill to stave off the lingering effects of her trauma. Determined to regain her composure, she began looking around, preparing for her departure. The routine was comforting, a familiar sequence of actions to ground her.

Moving around the room, Brandy busied herself with the tasks of the morning. As she did, her phone buzzed insistently on the nightstand. She glanced at the screen and saw Meeka's name flashing. A smile spread across her face as she answered the call, holding the phone between her ear and shoulder while continuing her routine.

"Hey, girl!" Brandy greeted me cheerfully.

"Hey, Brandy! How's my best friend doing this morning?" Meeka's voice was mischievous, as always.

Brandy chuckled, "Girl, let me tell you, I am full of love today. You hear me? Full! This man, Bobby... damn, girl. I just can't get enough of him. He drives me crazy!"

"Sounds like you had a good night," Meeka teased.

"Oh, it was more than good. It was perfect. He's just... everything. I mean, I wake up and feel like I'm on cloud nine." Brandy twirled around in her robe, her joy evident. She moved to her vanity and started brushing her hair, her smile never fading.

"Girl, don't you have to be at the theater for rehearsal?" Meeka asked.

"Nah, I called in and told them I'd be running late. I had to regroup and get myself together. Last night was... wow. Anyway, what are you up to?"

"I'm preparing a brief for a new case. And girl, you know it's about our people, right? Our people just don't seem to get it, girl. They just do the craziest stuff."

"Ain't that the truth? It's always something. But you know what, Meeka? You're out there fighting the good fight. You're making a difference." Brandy sighed, admiring Meeka's dedication as she rummaged through her closet, pulling out outfits and holding them up to herself in the mirror.

"Trying to, girl. It's not easy, but it's worth it. We've got to stand up for our community."

Brandy pulled out a red dress and held it up, admiring it. "That's why I love you, Meeka. You're always standing up for what's right. Speaking of which, I've got to make sure I'm looking right for my man tonight. What do you think: the red dress or the black one?"

"Red, definitely. Bobby won't be able to take his eyes off you."

"Red it is, then." Brandy smiled, laying the dress out on the bed and gathering her accessories.

Meeka's tone shifted slightly. "Brandy, you mentioned earlier that you had one of your memory spells. It sounded bad again. Did you take your meds?"

Brandy hesitated, feeling a twinge of guilt. "I... just took them."

"Girl, you know you can't skip those. They help keep you balanced. I scold you because I care. Please stay on top of it."

Brandy nodded, even though Meeka couldn't see her. "I know, Meeka. Thanks for looking out for me."

"Always. Anyway, I've got to get back to this brief. But let's catch up soon, okay?"

"Absolutely. Thanks for the chat, Meeka. Love you, girl."

"Love you too, Brandy. Talk soon."

Brandy hung up the phone, feeling a bit more centered. She took a deep breath and continued with her preparations, grateful for friends like Meeka, who always had her back.

Top of Form

Bottom of Form

As Brandy ended the call, she couldn't help but reflect on her friendship with Meeka. Meeka was a dynamo, both extremely smart and beautiful. With her dark chocolate complexion, dynamite curves, and striking features, she turned heads wherever she went. Yet, it wasn't just her looks that made her stand out. Meeka was a brilliant attorney known for her sharp mind and unwavering dedication to justice.

Meeka's passion for her work was matched by her loyalty to her friends. She had a no-nonsense attitude when it came to her career but was always there to lend a supportive ear or a word of advice to those she cared about. Brandy admired her for that— for the way Meeka balanced her demanding career with the same level of intensity she brought to their friendship.

Brandy glanced at the clock and realized she had to hurry.

She had spent too much time reminiscing and chatting. She quickly got dressed, slipping into the red dress that Meeka had approved. As she looked at herself in the mirror, she felt a surge of confidence. Today was going to be a good day; she was determined to make the most of it.

Her phone buzzed again, and she saw a message from Bobby. It was a simple text: "Thinking of you. Have a great day." She smiled, feeling the warmth of his love envelop her. Yes, life was good, and with friends like Meeka and a partner like Bobby, Brandy felt ready to take on whatever challenges came her way.

"The Seed of Corruption"

Morning light cascaded through the vast windows of the thirty-second floor of a shimmering tower in downtown Chicago, painting streaks of gold across the sleek, modern décor of Bobby Pope's office. Known among the circles of high finance for his meticulous sense of style and keen investment acumen, Bobby was a figure who commanded attention whenever he entered a room. His suits were always impeccably tailored, a reflection of his philosophy that details mattered, whether in fashion or finance.

As he reviewed the latest market trends on multiple screens, his phone buzzed with an incoming call. Glancing up, he saw Sarah, his trusted secretary, standing at the threshold of his office, her presence always marked by a blend of professionalism and warm cordiality.

"Morning, Bobby," she said, her eyes briefly sweeping over his attire with an approving smile. "That new suit really suits you—no pun intended! You've got Michael Madison of Genesis Global on line one. Sounds like he's pretty thrilled with something."

Bobby's lips curved into a smile, appreciative of Sarah's

compliment and intrigued by the prospect of good news. "Thanks, Sarah. Please put him through."

As the soft click signaled the transfer of the call, Bobby's demeanor shifted seamlessly from relaxed to razor-sharp focus.

"Bobby Pope speaking. Greg, how are you today?" he greeted, his tone both warm and professional.

"Bobby, I'm fantastic, and it's all thanks to you!" Greg's voice, crackling with excitement, filled the office. "Remember that portfolio we adjusted last quarter on your advice? Well, it's not just done well—it's tripled, Bobby. Tripled!"

"That's wonderful news, Greg!" Bobby replied, a genuine sense of satisfaction infusing his words. "I'm thrilled to hear the strategy paid off. It's all about playing the long game and trusting the process."

"Absolutely," Greg agreed. "Your foresight on this was incredible. I mean, I knew you were good, but this result is something else. It has made a significant difference."

"I'm very pleased to hear that, Michael. It's always our goal to exceed expectations," Bobby responded, his mind already flipping through the data and decisions that had led to this moment. "Let's set up a time to review and see where we can take it next. There's always more we can achieve."

"Definitely, I'll have my assistant set something up with Sarah. Thanks again, Bobby. You really are the best."

As they wrapped up the call with promises of further discussion, Bobby leaned back in his chair, allowing himself a moment to bask in the glow of a job well done. Yet, even as his professional life soared, a different kind of yearning tugged at his heart —a desire for something more, something different.

Despite the undeniable thrill of stock markets and investment returns, Bobby harbored a passion for something else, something he had long considered a mere hobby. Whether it was writing, philanthropy, or another venture entirely, the call to explore this latent desire had grown louder over the years. He wondered if, perhaps, amid these towering achievements, it was time to consider what could fulfil him not just financially but also spiritually and emotionally.

With a thoughtful frown, Bobby gazed out over the cityscape, contemplating the possibilities that lay beyond the financial graphs and shareholder reports. Maybe, just maybe, it was time to explore those dreams that had been waiting patiently in the wings of his meticulously planned life.

While awaiting an appointment with his new client, Bobby glances up from his desk as Jay T. Willabee nervously enters. They exchange handshakes, the atmosphere tense with anticipation.

Bobby gestures for Jay to take a seat, his mind already grappling with the ethical dilemma looming over them.

Jay, eager and adamant about investing his father's substantial estate in a microchip stock he's heard buzz about, dismisses Bobby's cautious warning about the high risk associated with it.

Bobby, aware of the volatile nature of the stock, knows the company has pressured him to push it, promising hefty rewards for bringing in clients. He hesitates, battling his internal struggle. He is committed to transparency but bound by the company's agenda.

In the end, Bobby resigned to the constraints on his honesty, facilitates the investment for Jay. As he executes the trade, the room seems to echo with the weight of undisclosed truths and hidden motives. The flickering lights in the office mirror the uncertainty of the market they are entering. "Okay, just a little more paperwork, and we can have this done. Jay T., if you don't mind, what is the 'T' for?" asked Bobby. Well, it's a sort of funny name, and I really haven't used it much since I was a kid in grade school, and the students used to tease me about it. So, let's just leave it at T. Thank you. Okay, no problem. It is Mister Jay T. Willabee. "I need you to understand this, though, Mr. Pope," said Jay, his voice tinged with urgency. "I've got a lot riding on this. And I mean a lot."

Mr. Pope leaned back in his chair, steepling his fingers thoughtfully. "Well, Jay, all I can tell you is that in life, everything we do, every step we take, is a mechanism of change. And change never happens unless we take some risks. But you should also know that with every risk, there can be consequences—sometimes good and sometimes not so good. It's completely up to the one who takes the risks."

Jay nodded; his brow furrowed with concern. "I understand that Mr. Pope. But this... this feels different. This could change everything for me – for better or for worse."

Mr. Pope regarded Jay with a sympathetic expression. "I get it, Jay. Taking risks can be daunting, especially when so much is at stake. But sometimes, you have to trust your instincts and take that leap of faith. Who knows? It might just be the best decision you ever make."

A flicker of determination crossed Jay's face as he absorbed Mr. Pope's words. "You're right, Mr. Pope. I can't let fear hold me back. I've come too far to turn back now."

With a reassuring smile, Mr. Pope clasped Jay's shoulder. "That's the spirit, Jay. Remember, fortune favors the bold. Now, go out there and seize the opportunity that's waiting for you."

Feeling emboldened by Mr. Pope's encouragement, Jay straightened his posture and squared his shoulders. With a newfound sense of purpose, he strode out of the office, ready to face whatever challenges lay ahead.

As he stepped into the bustling city streets, Jay couldn't help but feel a surge of excitement coursing through his veins. Yes, there were risks involved, but he was determined to see them through—no matter what the outcome. For in the end, he knew that true fulfillment could only be found by taking chances and daring to pursue his dreams. And with that thought guiding him, Jay set off toward his uncertain future, ready to embrace whatever adventures lay ahead.

As Jay expresses gratitude with a hopeful smile, Bobby can't shake the sense of foreboding. Unbeknownst to him, Jay is a seasoned hustler and conman, facing financial ruin and desperate to make amends. Bobby is completely unaware of Jay's troubled past, the people he owes, and the family he's struggling to take care of. This move, unbeknownst to Bobby, is Jay's last chance at redemption—an attempt to settle debts and make things right. Jay, with a strange sense of optimism, believes this risky investment is his final shot at turning things around. The room, now heavy with the weight of both their destinies, remains a battleground of hidden intentions and looming consequences.

Even at the mention of the words that Bobby spoke to Jay that day, his insides churned with unease. He couldn't shake the feeling of apprehension, knowing all too well about the volatility of the stock market and the risks involved. Yet, as a seasoned broker, he also understood that nothing was certain—what seemed bad might just turn out good, and vice versa.

Despite his own reservations, there was a sense of optimism in Bobby's heart for Jay. He genuinely hoped that the outcome would lean toward the positive rather than the negative. After all, he had seen his fair share of success stories born from risky ventures, and he believed in Jay's ability to navigate through the challenges ahead.

As Bobby sat at his desk, contemplating the conversation with Jay, he couldn't help but feel a surge of empathy. He knew what it was like to stand at the crossroads of uncertainty, grappling with the weight of important decisions. And although he couldn't predict the future, he was determined to offer Jay the support and guidance he needed to weather the storm.

With a renewed sense of purpose, Bobby picked up the phone, ready to reach out to Jay and offer his assistance. Whatever the outcome, he was committed to standing by his client's side, ready to lend a helping hand whenever it was needed. In times of uncertainty, it was the strength of Bobby's bond with his clients that would always help them see them through, guiding them toward a brighter tomorrow. Bobby's heart sank as he listened to the monotone of the voice on the other end of the line, informing him that the number he had dialled was disconnected. He furrowed his brow in frustration, his mind racing as he tried to recall if Jay had mentioned anything about changing his contact information. But try as he might, he couldn't remember Jay mentioning anything about a new number or address.

Panic began to set in as Bobby realized that he had no way of reaching Jay. He desperately searched through his contacts, hoping to find another number or email address that he could use to get in touch. But no matter how hard he looked, there was nothing—just a blank space where Jay's contact information used to be.

Frustration bubbled up inside him as Bobby cursed himself for not being more proactive in keeping in touch with Jay. He had been so caught up in his own life and work that he hadn't taken the time to check in with his client, and now it seemed like he had missed his chance to offer his support.

But Bobby refused to give up that easily. With determination burning in his chest, he made a mental note to keep an eye out for any news or updates about Jay. He would scour the internet, reach out to mutual friends, and do whatever it took to track down his client and make sure he was okay.

As he hung up the phone, Bobby made a silent vow to himself. No matter how long it took or how difficult the journey, he would find Jay and offer him the help and support he needed. Bobby was willing to go to any lengths to ensure that his client, Jay, knew he wasn't alone in facing whatever challenges lay ahead.

A couple of years later, Bobby discovers the devastating aftermath of the stock's collapse. Many people, including Jay, lost significant amounts of money. Bobby desperately tries to reach out to Jay, but he finds his phone is still disconnected. Concerned, he visits the address listed on the investment ledger, only to discover that the home has been foreclosed.

Bobby is consumed with regret, not just for the financial loss but for being a pawn in a scheme that went against his principles. The realization hits hard—company or no company, he played a role in a situation that hurt others. The weight of guilt settles heavily on his shoulders, a bitter reminder of the cost of compromising one's values for the sake of financial gain.

After the debacle involving Jay, the economic landscape began to deteriorate, a situation exacerbated when COVID-19 struck globally. Stock markets tumbled, triggering widespread panic across countries. In the midst of this chaos was Bobby, a financial advisor whose professional life was thrust into the storm's eye. Despite the turmoil, Bobby maintained a calm demeanor, advising his clients that the market downturn represented a unique opportunity to invest wisely and secure future gains. Bobby was sitting at his desk when Sarah knocked on his door. "Good afternoon, Bobby. Greg of Genesis Global is on line one. This time, he seems distressed." "Okay, Sarah, put him on." "Hello, Greg, how are you?" Bobby initiated, his voice laced with concern.

Michael's response was weary. "I've been better, Bobby. We took a massive hit—really massive. This stock market crash has shaken us to the core. I'm genuinely worried we might not recover. What should we do?"

Bobby, ever calm in the storm, reassured him, "Listen, Michael, you've got to trust me on this. I suggest we focus on two to three specific stocks. I have a few in mind that have been hit hard but are now at historically low prices—they won't stay this low for long. I'll send you the details after we hang up."

He continued, "These stocks are resilient. They've bounced back from dips before and will rise again. I promise you everything will rebound, but we need to act swiftly. Buy as much as you and your company can afford, and then hold steady. Once this storm passes, you'll see things improve."

Michael, filled with a mix of desperation and hope, replied, "Okay, Bobby. You've never let us down before. If this strategy works, I promise you, I'll make sure you're well compensated. You'll have made us a fortune, and for that, we won't forget you. Thanks, Bobby. Talk again soon." "You're welcome," said Bobby.

His advice paid off handsomely for a select group who heeded his counsel, yielding exceptional recoveries and, in some cases, generating millions in profits.

Privately, Bobby was living a lavish lifestyle, somewhat insulated from immediate financial pressures but concerned about the longevity of the economic recovery. His company, sensing the severity of the downturn, implemented severe cutbacks, slashing commissions and eliminating promised bonuses. Bobby himself quietly lost much of his investments and had some money remaining, but the atmosphere that surrounded him told him to lay low and stretch what he had left. Bobby, however, had anticipated such measures. Unlike his parents, who had been unprepared for financial hardship, Bobby had learned to be cautious and secretive about his finances, even with his wife, Brandy.

Unknown to Brandy, Bobby had amassed a significant nest egg from his astute dealings in the stock market, particularly from a lucrative bonus of approximately 1.5 million dollars stemming from his clients' strategic investments in microchip stocks; it was a kickback bonus from the same stock deal that took down Jay.

Amid whispers of turmoil within his company—a troubling mix of rumors suggesting both instability and involvement in questionable, if not outright illegal, activities—Bobby decided to take cautious measures. He recognized the signs early: the hushed conversations in shadowed corners of the office, the sudden, unexplained departures of senior staff, and the nervous glances exchanged during meetings. The air was thick with uncertainty and the stench of desperation.

In one particularly revealing incident, Bobby overheard a tense exchange between two executives as he passed by a slightly ajar conference room door. Their voices, low and urgent, spoke of "adjustments" and "necessary risks" that needed to be taken to keep the company afloat. The words "highly confidential" and "limit exposure" were mentioned more than once, setting off alarm bells in Bobby's mind.

This solidified his resolve. He knew he couldn't afford to leave his hard-earned bonus vulnerable to whatever storm might be brewing. With a practical, almost clinical precision, Bobby decided to secure his financial future. He contacted his bank and arranged for the transfer of his $1.5 million bonus into a separate, newly opened high-security account—one that offered enhanced privacy and limited access.

Later that evening, in the quiet of his home office, Bobby sat down to meticulously document his plan. He pulled out his personal ledger, a thick, leather-bound book that contained the details of all his financial maneuvers—hidden from the eyes of the world, including his wife, Brandy. As he recorded the transfer, he mulled over the decision, feeling the weight of keeping such secrets but knowing they were necessary. The pen scratched across the paper as he wrote, each line a silent testament to his determination to protect himself from potential fallout.

"I'm doing this to safeguard our future," Bobby whispered into the stillness, half-hoping Brandy would understand if she ever discovered what he had done. He leaned back in his chair, eyes fixed on the dim light of his desk lamp, and allowed himself a moment to imagine a more stable, prosperous future. But for now, he knew his actions, though heavy with secrecy, were justified in the face of such unsettling uncertainty at his company.

Moreover, Bobby harbored ambitions beyond his current role. He sensed impending trouble at his company and felt a growing urge to pursue his dreams of becoming a writer and film producer. This desire was not merely a flight of fancy but a deeply held life goal. However, the pandemic severely depleted his operational funds, and unbeknownst to Brandy, their financial situation had devolved into living paycheck to paycheck.

Despite these challenges, Bobby knew that if he was to make a significant change in his life, the time was now. He believed in his potential to succeed in the creative industry, trusting that his foresight in financial matters and his passion for storytelling would pave the way. Thus, with a mix of apprehension and excitement, Bobby prepared to navigate this uncertain phase, keeping his plans close to his chest until he was ready to make his move.

"Embracing the Dream"

One Year Later Yep, **that just** happened. Bobby Pope had always known what his true passion was. Yes, he wanted to make a great living and be able to afford the nicer things in life. He wasn't afraid of doing the work, and he had the brains to learn all the skills needed to be successful. He had charm and style that came to him naturally. He knew it, too, and used it to his advantage. You could dress nicely and sweet-talk all the way to the moon and back, but you had to be able to back that shit up. He had an innate sense when it came to people. He knew which ones to keep an eye on and not fully trust, and he could tell when a person had a sincere heart. There were even times when he just understood something was going to go his way. He could never explain to himself how he understood. It was as if he were being guided by something, and he truly believed it was because his intention for doing anything was done with grace and no expectation of anything in return. Somehow, a higher power was sending those good intentions back to him.

That is why he was so certain that this was the right step to take at this point in his life. He is one of the youngest and most successful financial brokers in Chicago. He's made a lot of money for his clients and a good amount of money for himself and Brandy. So, yeah, he was ready to pursue his dream. He was a bit nervous walking into his boss's office that morning. He waited until the end of the day, which rarely ended at five o'clock. He knocked on the door with three quick raps. His boss looked up and waved him in while he finished signing a document.

"Hey, Bobby! On your way out," his boss asked in a friendly voice.

"Um, yeah, but I need to talk to you about something, Dave," Bobby said as he gestured to a chair ok to ask if it was okay to sit. Dave waved his hand again, indicating that he should take a seat.

"So, what's up? Is there a problem with one of your accounts?" Dave asked, his tone turning serious.

"No, no, no, nothing like that," Bobby reassured him. He leaned forward in his chair, his elbows resting on the armrest, his hands clasped loosely in front of him. He was feeling a bit nervous, but nowhere close to how he thought he'd be feeling. He took that as a sign that this was the right move.

"Let me start by saying how much I appreciate you and all the experience I've gained while being here, working for you. But I feel like it's time for the next step in my life, and it's something that I have to dedicate more of my time and attention to." Bobby paused as he reached to pull out his resignation letter from the inside of his jacket and laid it on Dave's desk.

"Whoa, whoa, there, Bobby! Are you serious? Do you want a raise or some other perk or benefit? I thought you were happy here. You're one of our most successful brokers!" Not to mention our Vice President of Accounts. The look of shock on Dave's face was clear.

"No, Dave, it's nothing like that. Like I said, I think I've run my course for this stage of my life. I want to focus on another project, and this seems to be the perfect time to pursue that. Because of what I've learned working with you, I can comfortably focus on that since I'm in a great financial spot right now. I loved working at this firm, but I feel like it's time for a change, time to focus on something else while I'm still young. I really hope you understand," Bobby said sincerely.

Dave sat there looking at him for almost a minute. Bobby could sense the thoughts churning through his head. After what seemed like an eternity, Dave leaned back in his chair and let out a long sigh that sounded like defeat.

I want you to know... I didn't just walk up in here without going through a battle within myself. But it was something that someone said to me the other day that felt like they put a battery in my back... Here I am... a Black man, sitting on a podium that, in the world we live in, validates success at the highest level. No matter the accomplishments or accolades, I've come to understand that being a Brooker isn't who I am—it's what I do.

There is a vision in me, Dave—knowledge and wisdom beyond what I can contain. My cup is full. It's been filling up ever since the day I was put on this earth. Like many people with purpose inside them, waiting to be poured out, they don't feel like they'll ever get a chance or can muster the courage and confidence it requires to risk it all in pursuit of a dream.

It's not just about a transition from what I do; it's about an acceptance of what I was created to give out. In the common scenarios of life, some people see others' failures, faults, and faithlessness, but me? I see opportunity, direction, and an exit strategy for anyone who can witness those stories. I want to use my pen to push people into their purpose and to demonstrate through stories that the choices they've made are not theirs alone —others have made them, too.

If I can show them, through what I write, what struggle and victory look like for others, then maybe I can help them understand that the commonness of their crises can motivate them toward a victory they didn't otherwise believe they could accomplish.

"Well, Bobby, I can't tell you enough how much I hate to see you go. Hearing that makes sense, and that's a beautiful way of putting it. You might want to write that into some of the stuff you write. That can really work for some people. Listen, Bobby, you have been a great asset to this company, that's for sure. If there is nothing I can say or offer to get you to stay, I certainly won't stand in your way. As a matter of fact, I admire you for taking this step," he paused, thoughts flooding his eyes.

"Did I ever tell you that I wanted to become a professional fisherman?" Dave asked him, looking slightly embarrassed. Bobby chuckled softly and shook his head.

"Yep, yep, yep...that was my 'big' dream. But as you can imagine, doing that for a living is extremely hard to do. You have to have a pretty penny saved up to be able to spend hours on a lake or river, not to mention the cost of equipment and travel. But that never stopped me from dreaming about it. Now look at me. Thirty years later, at 57, I'm still sitting behind this desk, making money I don't really need. I guess I could retire and finally pursue that dream. However, it feels like it might be too late for me to try that at this point."

"But who says it's too late, Dave? Your wife, your kids? The CEO of this firm? That's entirely up to you, Dave. If you feel you have the means and you can make the time to do that without affecting your home, then why not? We're on this earth for a short time, so we should make the most of it. We've worked our asses off, man, and we are successful. Why not enjoy the rest of our years doing something we are passionate about," the earnestness in Bobby's voice surprised not only him but Dave, too. One of Bobby's greatest abilities and talents lay in his knack for peering into people's souls, sensing them in a way that unveiled their innermost selves and laid bare their true desires and abilities. This gift was inherent in him throughout his entire life. Those who had shared their concealed self with him, as Dave did in this case, would consistently express astonishment at how he could elucidate and reshape purpose in their world and life. It was a remarkable gift, and Bobby wielded it with the purest intentions, aiming to uplift others and instil confidence in the decisions they needed to make.

"I'm sorry, Dave, I didn't mean to overstep. It's just that I strongly believe that we should be able to pursue our dreams if, not...when we have the opportunity. That's all I'm saying." Bobby stood up and held out his hand to Dave.

Dave stood up in turn and shook his hand. Then he clapped his other hand over Bobby's as he looked at him and said, "You know, Bobby? Thank you for saying that. I think I just needed to hear from someone else that my dream wasn't 'corny' or 'crazy.'"

As Bobby turned to walk out of the office, Dave called after him, "So, are you going to tell me what your passion is, Bobby?"

He paused at the doorway before turning to look at Dave, not sure if he wanted to say it out loud. But then he said, "I want to be an author. I'm going to focus on publishing my book."

As a child, Bobby's days were colored by a vivid imagination and an insatiable curiosity. Even at a young age, he found solace and excitement in the world of words, captivated by movies and dramatic writings that transported him to different realms. An avid reader, his voracious appetite for stories fuelled his aspirations.

Deep within, a dream took root—Bobby knew he wanted to be a writer. It was a quiet longing but a persistent one. Despite his tender age, the passion burned within him. One day, a well-meaning principal at school approached him, posing the quintessential question, "Hey, kid, what do you want to do with your life?"

Bobby hesitated for just a moment before earnestly replying, "I want to be a writer." The principal, perhaps fuelled by practical concerns, responded with a dose of skepticism, cautioning, "Well, Bobby, you won't make much money doing that. Maybe think about something more financially lucrative first."

Little did the principal know that within the heart of that hesitant child resided a flame that no pragmatic advice could extinguish. Bobby's dream of becoming a writer was a compass guiding his journey, destined to shape the course of his life in ways both unexpected and extraordinary.

Years later, standing at the doorway of Dave's office, Bobby felt the weight of his convictions. The echoes of that childhood dream reverberated in his mind. The push of his inner passions was stronger than ever, urging him that now, more than ever, was the time to pursue his calling. Yet, as he faced this pivotal moment, a lingering uncertainty remained. How would he articulate this profound transitional phase to the woman he held so dearly—Brandy? The challenge ahead lay not only in pursuing his dream but also in navigating the delicate art of sharing it with those who mattered most in his life. It's not that Brandy was unaware of Bobby's aspirations to become a writer someday; rather, she didn't anticipate it unfolding at this particular moment in time.

As Bobby gathered his belongings from the office that had been his haven for over a decade, a space where he had not only successfully navigated his professional journey but also crafted a good life for himself, he stood on the precipice of closure and new beginnings. The door creaked shut behind him, echoing the finality of that chapter. Little did he know this moment would serve as the genesis of a new narrative—one that would simultaneously haunt and reshape his life in ways he could not yet fathom. The journey ahead was uncertain, but within that uncertainty lay the promise of transformation and the pursuit of a dream that had patiently waited for its moment to unfold.

As he walked out, his consciousness whispered to him, "A writer, Bobby? Are you serious? I hope you're doing the right thing. We made a lot of money there." The echoes of financial stability and the familiar comforts of his previous life taunted him, casting shadows of doubt on the path he had chosen. Yet, amidst the uncertainty, the flame of his long-held dream burned brighter, urging him to step into the unknown and embrace the potential for a richer, more fulfilling existence.

With a determined glint in his eye, Bobby responded to his inner doubts, "Yeah, a writer, and I'm gonna be a damn good one at that." The words carried the weight of conviction as he embraced the challenges and possibilities that awaited him on this uncharted journey. In the quiet recesses of his mind, he heard his mother's gentle whisper, "Bobby baby, you can do whatever you set your mind to if you just believe in yourself." The reassurance of her words became the steady anchor as he ventured into the uncertain seas of his dreams.

After years of toiling away in a job that suffocated his creativity, Bobby finally made the decision to pursue his passion for writing. As he drove through the familiar neighborhood, recognizing and waving at old friends headed toward his childhood home to give him and his thoughts the best chance of true, a sense of liberation washed over him. The weight of his resignation letter, once a burden, now felt like a ticket to freedom.

The sun was setting, casting a warm glow over the streets lined with trees shedding their autumn leaves. Bobby's footsteps echoed against the pavement as he approached the modest house where he grew up. The sight of it filled him with nostalgia, reminding him of simpler times when his biggest worry was completing his homework on time.

Pushing open the creaky gate, Bobby made his way up the front path, the anticipation building with each step. He paused for a moment to take in the familiar scent of his mother's cooking wafting through the air—a comforting aroma that never failed to make him feel at home.

Entering his mother's house, Bobby was greeted by her

bustling around the kitchen, her apron dusted with flour. "Bobby, darling, you're home! You got here earlier than I thought you would!" she exclaimed, her face lighting up with joy at the sight of her son.

"Yeah, I had some things to take care of," Bobby replied, unable to contain the excitement bubbling inside him.

His mother's eyes sparkled with curiosity. "Oh? What kind of things?"

Bobby hesitated for a moment, his heart pounding with anticipation. "I... I quit my job," he confessed, bracing himself for her reaction, anticipating a historical lecture like the one she gave to his father during the days when he himself talked about chasing his own dreams.

His mother's expression softened, a mixture of surprise and pride crossing her features. "Oh, Bobby, that's wonderful!" she exclaimed, enveloping him in a warm hug. "I always knew you were meant for something greater." "I prayed for it, you know."

As they pulled apart from their embrace, Bobby noticed the glint of unshed tears in his mother's eyes, reflecting both her joy and the culmination of her long-held hopes for him. He could see the years of worry and silent strength melt away in that moment of pure relief and satisfaction. "Mom, it was your belief in me that got me here," Bobby said, his voice catching with emotion. His mother brushed a tear from her cheek, laughing softly through her emotions.

"You always had it in you, Bobby. I just helped steer the ship from time to time," she replied, her hands resting on his shoulders as she looked at him, not just as her son but as the accomplished individual he had become. "Now, tell me everything. How did it happen? What did they say?"

Bobby began to recount the events that led to his significant achievement, watching as his mother absorbed every detail, her face alight with interest and bursting with questions. Each piece of the story seemed to weave them closer together, threading through their past struggles and sacrifices, highlighting the shared journey that had brought them to this pivotal point. As he spoke, it became evident that this accomplishment was not just his own—it was theirs, a testament to their resilience and unyielding hope.

Dinner was soon ready, but Bobby found himself unable to sit still. The thought of finally embarking on his journey as a writer filled him with an eagerness he couldn't contain. "I can't eat right now, Mom," he said apologetically. "Save some for me later. I need to get started on something—it's really important."

His mother nodded understandingly. "Of course, dear. I'll leave it in the fridge for you," she said, patting his hand affectionately.

With a grateful smile, Bobby made his way to his newly redesigned office—a space he had transformed into his creative sanctuary. It was quite different from his and Brandy's beautiful home near downtown Chicago. The walls were adorned with shelves filled with books that had inspired him, and his desk was cluttered with notebooks and pens, ready to capture his thoughts as they flowed.

Sitting down at his desk, Bobby opened up his laptop and took a deep breath. This was it – the moment he had been waiting for. For years, the story had been brewing inside him, its characters clamoring for a chance to be heard. Now, finally, he had the opportunity to give them life.

With a sense of purpose burning in his chest, Bobby began to type. Words spilled forth from his fingertips, weaving together to form the opening lines of his novel. With each sentence, he felt a weight lifting off his shoulders, as if he were finally setting free the stories that had been trapped inside him for so long.

As the night deepened, Bobby barely noticed the passage of time, engrossed in the intricate worlds unfurling under his fingertips. He was a creator, weaving narratives out of sheer will and imagination. However, as his eyelids began to droop with exhaustion, he acknowledged the need to pause. Tomorrow was another day ripe with unexplored possibilities.

His train of thought was interrupted by the sudden ring of his phone. It was Brandy. Her voice, usually a comforting melody, now sounded hesitant over the line.

"Hey, Bobby, when are you coming home?" she asked, a trace of worry lacing her words.

"I was just wrapping up some things with my mother," he replied, the fatigue evident in his tone. "I'll be home in about an hour."

The simplicity of the conversation belied the weight of the news he carried, a looming shadow over his thoughts. As he ended the call, a knot of apprehension tightened in his stomach. He realized that the hardest task awaited him—not the endless hours of crafting stories, but the moment he would have to break unsettling news to Brandy. The drive home seemed longer than usual as Bobby rehearsed the words he would say, each iteration heavier than the last.

Closing his laptop with a sense of satisfaction, Bobby glanced around his office, feeling a sense of pride swell within him. This was only the beginning of his journey, but already, he could feel the promise of something extraordinary on the horizon. He arrived home, and Brandy had already fallen asleep, and he lay down as well. As he drifted off to sleep, visions of his characters danced in his mind, eager to continue their tale in the light of a new day.

"The Weight of Unknown Risks"

Present Day: **The sun** was bright as Brandy stepped out of the pharmacy. As she fumbled around in her Gucci bag for her matching sunglasses, two women approached her, their faces lit up with excitement.

"Hey, aren't you Brandy Pope? Oh my God!" one of them exclaimed. "You are so amazing, Ms. Pope, and girl, you can straight-up sing."

The other woman chimed in, "We attended one of your shows last week, and once we saw it, we brought a few friends with us the next night and saw it again."

Brandy smiled warmly, shaking their hands. "Thank you so much. That really means a lot to me," she said graciously. "Are you okay?" one of the women asked. "Yes, I am fine. It was just one of those days, but the two of you coming up to me with such joy really helped bring me back. Well, girl, you are such a magical woman, and we really are some of your biggest fans," the woman replied. "Again, thanks, ladies," Brandy said with a big smile.

"Can we get an autograph and take some pictures with

you?" one of the women asked, holding out a pen and a small notebook.

"Of course," Brandy replied, her smile widening. She signed the notebook and then posed for several pictures, each snap of the camera capturing her radiant joy and the genuine connection she had with her fans.

As the women walked away, still giddy from their encounter, Brandy finished her search and found her glasses.

Once she found them and put them on, she looked at the prescription bags she had just picked up. She was still having trouble wrapping her mind around the news that her doctor delivered to her that morning. Dr. Thomas had wanted to discuss the results of her blood work with her...in person. That was not a good sign. Brandy was half-expecting news like maybe her husband, Bobby, had given her an STD or something. She was already rehearsing what she was going to say to that cheating bastard. Deep in her heart, though, she knew that Bobby would probably never cheat. He just wasn't built that way. He had a lot of self-respect and was very accommodating when it came to her. That is, until recently.

Brandy's train of thought led her down another path that made her even angrier than the thought of Bobby cheating on her. Up until a few months ago, Bobby Pope was the up-and-coming investment broker that everyone wanted to work with. Reflecting on their past, Brandy couldn't help but marvel at the trajectory of Bobby's career. Fresh out of college, he had been heavily recruited by the biggest investment firm in Chicago. His brilliance, exceptional grades, and unmatched confidence garnered him national recognition during his college years. The investment firm not only hired him but also covered all his back tuition and expenses, enabling the couple to move into their new house and later acquire a new high-rise condo in downtown Chicago.

Bobby's unstoppable drive to succeed had always set him

apart. His mother's words echoed in Brandy's mind: "Nothing can stop Bobby but Bobby." It seemed his unstoppable momentum was propelling them toward a bright future, yet recent developments in their relationship left Brandy questioning the shifts she had observed in her once unwaveringly devoted husband. He was very good at what he did, making money for everyone, especially for themselves. He was rubbing elbows with some seriously wealthy people in Chicago, and Brandy loved going to all the dinner parties as Bobby paraded her around on his arm.

She was no slouch, either. Faced with the financial strain of attending the Juilliard School of Music and the slow progress in her career, Brandy found herself under immense stress. The expensive costs were taking a toll, especially since she couldn't secure a full scholarship like some of her peers. Her partial scholarship didn't quite cover the expenses, and the burden was becoming overwhelming.

In the midst of these challenges, Brandy made a pivotal decision to transition to Southern University. This historically Black college and university (HBCU) held a special appeal for her. Not only did it offer a more affordable option, but culturally, it resonated with her on a deeper level. The sense of belonging and familiarity among her peers made the decision to switch schools a more comfortable choice.

Little did Brandy know that this shift to Southern University would not only alleviate her financial stress but also mark a significant turning point in her life. It was at Southern University that she would ultimately meet Bobby, and this change of environment and new connections would become the catalyst for her career's upward trajectory. Southern University would prove to be the place where her career would flourish, making it the pivotal moment that set her on the path to success. As part of one of the more popular theater groups in the city, Brandy was a minor celebrity herself. Her talent for singing was unquestionable, and as it turned out, acting was a strong suit, too. She had been a regular lead in her college productions. Because of her involvement with the theater group, she was often invited to many functions and events, which translated into "PARTAY!"

It just so happened that this is how she met Bobby... at a frat party. Yeah, he was a Kappa Man, one of those pretty brothers who carried themselves like they were the shit. She spotted him on the porch of the frat house at Southern University. He held a drink in his hand, but after observing him for a while, Brandy realized he wasn't drinking it at all. She hadn't met one guy who didn't drink while she'd been in college. This intrigued her even more. He was very handsome and had the whitest smile. His laugh was deep but not boisterous. He wasn't "clownin'" like the other boys were. Bobby defied the athletic stereotype yet commanded attention with a different kind of strength. Though he was built, his physique wasn't indicative of the stereotypical jock. Three times a week, he dedicated himself to workouts, balancing the demands of physical well-being with the responsibilities of his fraternity.

Away from the fraternity scene, Bobby was a different breed. He immersed himself in studies, carving out time to focus on his academic pursuits. There were no jokes or lightheartedness when it came to his vision for the future—he was a corporate-minded brother with a clear drive to pursue his goals.

Bobby's ambition and unwavering sense of self-set him apart. He was a man with a plan, solid in his identity, and unapologetically chasing success. On campus, the term "GQ with an IQ" wasn't just a catchy phrase; it was a mantra that perfectly encapsulated Bobby's image. The campus girls recognized it, and believe me. They couldn't help but be drawn to the magnetic combination of sophistication, intelligence, and ambition that he effortlessly exuded.

"Ummm, he's got some nice hair, too," Brandy thought to herself. He was dressed nicely enough for a college kid. But the real test was the shoes. Many boys try to front like they've got their shit together, you know, nice shirts, nice jeans, all pressed and in place. But then you look at their shoes, and they're wearing some raggedy-ass Chuck Taylors, or worse... no-name, generic brand kicks. Oh, hell no! That just ain't right!

Brandy slowly made her way to the porch, talking to people in passing, completely focused on this unusual man. And yes, he was a "man." She kept her eyes on him, waiting to get close enough to see his shoes, hoping to get close enough for him to notice her because he WILL notice her; of this, she had no doubt. Brandy was not only talented, but she was beautiful, and she knew it. She knew how to work it. Her skin was porcelain smooth and the color of coffee with a touch of cream. Not too light and not too dark. Her eyes were a light brown, but with perfect lighting, flecks of gold would shimmer in them. Her hair was the color of mahogany, long and wavy. And yes... it was hers... all hers. No weave on this girl! She loved her hair, and so did the brothers. She wielded it like a weapon, flipping it here and there. The bangs that framed her face fell seductively into her eyes at times. Yeah, she had it, and she worked it.

It took her a good twenty minutes to finally make it to the porch, but he hadn't moved from his perch on the porch railing in the corner. She adjusted the belt that circled her small waist, making sure her top was tucked in so as not to obstruct his view of her small, round, tight ass. Without even realizing it, because it was so ingrained in her, she checked the neckline of her button-up V-neck blouse to make sure just enough cleavage was showing. These, too, were perfect. Not too big, but enough to fill a man's hand.

She inched closer to his spot on the porch and waited. She waited for him to come to her, to introduce himself, to make his move. She waited some more. Finally, she realized that he wasn't coming at all. "What the hell is going on? This never happens to her. Brandy was not used to being overlooked or ignored; she made sure of it. So now what?"

What she didn't know at the time was that Bobby had noticed her and thought she was too beautiful for her own good. He knew what she was up to, waiting to see if he would push up on her like all these other fools. That wasn't his style. He didn't share the same frat boy mentality that his friends had. You know... get as much ass as you can while you can. That's not what he was in college for. Sure, he liked to have female company. He went out on dates, but when he didn't jump all over them at the end of the night, a lot of them actually acted offended. They acted like something was wrong with him! He didn't have time for all the games. He would tell himself, "Don't be afraid to be yourself. Don't worry about what everyone else is doing or thinking."

Now, here is the drop-dead gorgeous girl, and he couldn't stop the stirrings of physical attraction. She looked familiar, but he couldn't figure out where he'd seen her before. He wouldn't mind getting to know her and finding out what she was all about, but he decided he would just play it cool and see what happened. He found out early on in his college career that once girls found out what you're majoring in (translation: Is this dude gonna be making lots of cheese after graduating?), they try to pin you down like a tail on a donkey. The lady he ends up with is going to be someone who brings her own to the table—someone who will be his partner, work towards the same goal, and support each other in whatever endeavor or desire the other wants to pursue.

Right now, his goal was to be financially secure, but with time, that could change. He had always had a dream, one that he had never shared with anyone, but one that he was not ready to pursue at this point in his life. His overriding desire to not have to struggle financially wouldn't let him entertain anything else. He wasn't dirt poor growing up, but his family had struggled a lot, living paycheck to paycheck. This meant a lot of hand-me-downs, Goodwill stores, and buying generic brand items. But never once did his parents get on welfare. His father wouldn't stand for that. That just meant that both his parents had to bust their asses working to take care of him and his two brothers. Because of this, he wanted to make enough money to get the finer things in life and help his parents out now that they were at retirement age. He had always known he wanted to go to college, and he knew that he would have to get himself there. His parents had sacrificed so much and worked so hard all their lives that the least he could do was bust his own ass to guarantee a full academic scholarship. And he did.

He had a plan, and no chicken head was going to get him to deviate from it. But damn, if this girl was fine as hell! She was slowly making her way toward him, but he refused to acknowledge her, at least for now. When she was finally about seven feet away from him, he continued talking to the couple that was standing with him. But he wasn't really paying attention to what was being said. It seemed like forever before she made her move, and when she did, it wasn't directed at him.

Brandy had to play it cool and act like she wasn't interested in him. It pissed her off that he wouldn't come to her, but then again, the challenge he presented turned her on! She laughed to herself. "OK, so how was she going to pull this off?"

She seized her friend and homegirl Meeka, pre-law and destined to be a defense or even district attorney. Meeka was no slouch either—fine, bright, and loyal to the end. Brandy took her by the arm and said, "Hey, girl. Just walk and talk with me, okay? Act like we're discussing something funny and laugh." Meeka frowned in puzzlement, quickly glanced around the porch, and spotted Bobby. She knew what was up. Immediately, she started talking about something that happened during rehearsal that day, then threw her head back and laughed.

Brandy joined in and walked right into the girl who was talking with Bobby.

"Oh, my gosh! I'm so sorry! I wasn't watching where I was going," she sputtered.

"Oh, that's okay! Don't worry about it," the girl replied. She smiled and looked at Brandy. "Hey, aren't you Brandy Townsend?" the girl asked, wide-eyed. Brandy didn't expect that and looked at the girl in surprise. "Why, yes, I am. Have we met?"

"Oh, no, no! I saw you last week performing at the campus theater. You were great! Oh my gosh, girl, you can sing! It was a terrific show! My name is Angela, and this is my boyfriend, Malcolm."

Brandy extended her hand to both of them. She turned toward Bobby expectantly.

"Oh, my gosh, I'm sorry... this is Bobby Pope," Angela continued. Brandy flashed her beautiful smile at him.

"A singer, huh?" Bobby said to her. "Sounds like you're pretty good." He smiled back at her.

"Yeah, well, I can hold my own," she purred at him. Meeka was still standing there, completely unnoticed by any of them. She cleared her throat once, twice, and then coughed a little louder.

Without looking away from Bobby, Brandy said, "Oh, and this is my friend Meeka." "Oh, hello, I'm Meeka Pre-Law," Meeka replied, but as Meeka was about to extend her hand to him, Brandy pushed her away, saying, "But she's meeting someone, so she can't stay."

Meeka stumbled and caught herself before she fell to the floor, muttering under her breath, "Damn, girl, you know you're wrong for that!" But she took the hint and walked away. "I will see you in class tomorrow."

Bobby wanted to laugh! This girl had some nerve and sass. He liked that shit! He chuckled softly. Angela and Malcolm picked up on their vibe and slowly faded into the rest of the crowd on the porch.

"So, Mr. Pope, how are you liking college life so far?"

"It's alright... a lot of distractions, though," he replied with a smile on his face.

"Well, that's not bad if it's the right kind," Brandy replied coyly.

"Oh, really? And what is the right kind?"

"Well, you know...someone who can take your mind off your work for a few hours, relieve you of your stress when you need it, give you a shoulder to lean on. You know, stuff like that?" She flipped her hair over her shoulder. His eyes followed her hand as she buttoned her shirt and played with the button at her cleavage.

"Yeah, well, that's all good and all, but I'm here to get things done. I don't have time to be messing around, you know?"

"Well, you do know what they say about all work and no play?" Brandy's eyes were alight with mischief.

"Yeah, yeah... I have heard that. I certainly don't want to be labeled as a dull boy! Do you think you can help me with that?"

"Most certainly!" Brandy smiled, knowing she got this one hooked, or so she thought.

Bobby and Brandy became pretty tight quickly once Bobby realized how ambitious she was with her acting and singing. Man, that girl didn't play when it came to that! He loved her passion for her art. He loved her fearlessness, her boldness. She wasn't afraid to go after what she wanted. He tried to make it to all her performances, but being a finance major meant a lot of work and little free time. More often than not, he would make it to the first couple of acts in the play but then would have to leave to finish his homework or go to his part-time job,

It was customary for the theater group to throw a wrap party at the end of one of their production runs. Brandy often attended these alone because of Bobby's workload. She didn't seem to mind, and since she didn't make him feel guilty for missing them, Bobby was happy until he started noticing something different in Brandy.

She was getting moody. One minute she was happy and laughing, and then he would say something that would send her flying off the handle. They started arguing more and more. He noticed she was losing weight, too. She was tiny to begin with, so losing six or eight pounds was easily noticeable. At times, her eyes appeared glassy, but she waved it off as tiredness. Her nose was always running, so Bobby assumed her immune system was low due to weight loss and lack of sleep. He figured her body was trying to stave off a cold. Anytime he showed concern over her physical well-being, she would get upset, and they would argue.

Bobby wasn't sure what was going on with Brandy, but he had a gut feeling she was hiding something from him. They were spending less and less time together. He started to wonder if this relationship had run its course. The thought of it bothered him more than he cared to admit. He really cared about Brandy; he might even be falling in love with her. But she had been acting so crazy lately!

He thought maybe he should do something nice for her, surprise her. The group had just finished their two-week production. The wrap party would be starting at the theater house right after the last performance, which would end around 10 p.m. Bobby decided to put his schoolwork off for the night, pick up some flowers for Brandy, and show up at the party to surprise her.

As he got ready, he became more and more excited as he visualized the surprise on Brandy's face when he walked in. She would be so happy that he made time to be with her, to be part of the world that is so special to her. He smiled as he put on his Versace cologne. A man always has to smell his best, no matter how broke he may be. Brandy is always telling him how much she loves the way he smells.

Tonight was going to be all about her. He would bring her flowers, hang out with her and her friends, and then treat her to a special dinner at the best restaurant in town. Bobby didn't squander his money, and he had a pretty penny saved up for a college kid. He was going to go all out for his baby tonight!

Bobby could hear someone playing the piano when he opened the theater door. It sounded like the players were taking turns singing in an impromptu jam session. The song ended, but then he heard Brandy's voice telling the piano player to play "The Man I Love" by Billie Holiday. He entered the theater room and saw the kids sitting on the stage floor in various positions, with wine glasses and beer bottles set next to them. There was Brandy, standing at the piano, and her eyes closed as the notes from the piano washed over her.

Brandy swayed slowly from side to side. She loved Billie Holiday, and this song made her think of Bobby. "Damn, I think I'm falling in love with that man." She was scared. She had never cared about anyone so much outside of her family. She had many boyfriends, but none compared to Bobby. He was stable and dedicated. He knew what he wanted out of life and wasn't afraid to work for it. He was kind and considerate but was also no-nonsense. He didn't put up with any bullshit, especially from her. She was used to guys just giving her what she wanted, but Bobby didn't. He expected the best from her and believed in her art and talent. He made her better, made her feel better about herself—the person she was inside, not the pretty face everyone else couldn't get past. This scared the shit out of Brandy! She didn't know how to handle it.

Unknowingly, or maybe not so unknowingly, she was pushing him away. She picked fights with him, hoping that he would just give up on her. But he stood his ground when he disagreed with her about

Things, and eventually, she would give in and apologize. She couldn't stay away for more than a day or two. Once, she was able to hold out for three days but couldn't stand to be apart from him. She knew she was acting crazy. She knew a lot of it had to do with what she was doing at these parties. She was trying to escape the fear of losing Bobby, but at the same time, the things she was doing were probably going to cost her the man she was falling in love with. She opened her mouth, and the first few lines filtered out, full of melancholy.

"Someday, he'll come along, the man I love."

And he'll be big and strong, the man I love.

And when he comes my way, I'll do my best to make him stay.

Brandy's voice cracked with emotion at that last sentence, and a tear escaped her closed eyes. Bobby caught his breath, and his heart moved with the emotion Brandy was emitting from the stage.

He'll look at me and smile; I'll understand.

Then, in a little while, he'll take my hand.

And though it seems absurd,

I know we both won't say a word. Maybe I shall meet him on Sunday, maybe Monday, maybe not.

Still, I'm sure I'll meet him one day.

"Maybe Tuesday will be my good news day. He'll build a little home that's meant for two."

"From which I'll never roam. Who would? Would you?"

"I'm dreaming of the man I love."

As the piano's notes faded at the end of the song, everyone sat in silence in awe of Brandy's rendition and the pure heartache that seemed to be pouring out of her. Slowly, one person began clapping, then another, until soon, everyone on stage was clapping, hooting, and howling in appreciation. Bobby began to clap awkwardly because of the flowers he was holding, realizing that his eyes were threatening to spill over. He was about to let out a loud whistle of appreciation when he saw

Brandy pull something toward herself from atop the piano. She picked something off what looked like a plate. He stopped clapping as a gut-wrenching realization of what she was about to do washed over him.

Suddenly, it was as if everything went into slow motion. He started walking toward the stage as Brandy picked up the straw off the plate. She wiped away the tears that had fallen as she sang. She hesitated for a moment, her eyes never leaving the plate. Bobby continued to walk toward the stage, wanting to yell out to her to get her attention. But he just couldn't. Part of him wanted to see if she was actually going to do what he thought she was going to do. It was like not being able to tear your eyes away from a horrible accident. You don't want to look, but morbid curiosity takes control.

Brandy bent over the plate and lifted the straw to her nostril as she held the other closed with her finger. She quickly snorted one line, stood up, and rubbed her nose as she sniffled. She bent over the plate again and moved the straw to her other nostril, and snorted a second line. She stood up with her eyes closed, pinching her nose closed, and then released it, sniffing a few times. When she finally opened her eyes and focused, she saw Bobby standing at the edge of the stage, still on the main floor, looking up at her with so much hurt in his eyes. They stared at each other for what seemed like an eternity. A surge of emotions flooded through Bobby as he recalled the painful echoes of his brother Michael's demise. The vibrant memories of Michael, once full of life, are now intertwined with the haunting image of Brandy succumbing to the same temptations. The lines between past and present blurred as Bobby grappled with the harsh reality unfolding before him. He finally broke his gaze as he looked down at the forgotten flowers in his hand. He smirked as he shook his head. He looked back up at her and noticed that everyone on stage was looking at him.

He threw the bouquet on the stage, and in a quiet, steady voice, he said, "I'm done."

He turned and walked away, never once looking back. Brandy did not call out to him. She watched him leave, almost justifying to herself that sooner or later, he would have left anyway because that's the way it had always been. Anyone she loved and cared about eventually left, except for her sister, Christina, who was the one constant in her life besides her parents.

"Echoes and Shadows"

In the deepest corners of Brandy's memory, there lay a chapter she had long locked away, concealed from the world and even from herself. It was a chapter that spoke of her childhood, a time when shadows cast by the sins of her mother's past loomed large over her young life. Christina, her adopted sister, through hers and now Christina's adopted parents, had always sensed that there was something buried beneath Brandy's seemingly perfect façade, something rooted in the murky soil of their shared history.

Brandy was but a fragile bud in a garden of neglect, a garden tended to by her mother, Sylvia, who had a penchant for attracting the wrong kind of men. One of these unfortunate companions was Carl, a man who bore the title of father to Brandy, whose eyes sparkled with mischief and whose veins coursed with the poison of addiction. A "dopefeind," as he was often called, Carl had a voracious appetite for a multitude of illegal substances.

Carl was not merely a specter from her childhood; he was a wicked force that forever altered her perspective on men. The trauma inflicted by his actions cast a long, dark shadow over her life, one that would haunt her well into adulthood.

As Brandy grew older, her memories of Carl and the horrors he brought into their home became a tangled web of pain and confusion. She had witnessed a man who was supposed to be a protector, a provider, and a guide succumb to the abyss of addiction. In her impressionable young mind, he represented not just a single individual but a looming archetype of masculine failure.

Her relationship with her father, already strained, suffered irreparable damage as a result. Brandy's ability to trust men, to let her guard down, and to allow herself to be vulnerable had been forever compromised. It was as if the sins of Carl had tainted an entire gender for her.

The distrust ran deep, and any budding romance she engaged in was overshadowed by her fear of repeating her mother's mistakes. Brandy was innocently exploring her mother Sylvia's room when she was caught red-handed. "Brandy baby, what are you doing in my room?" Sylvia exclaimed with a tone of exasperation. "I'm just playing, Mama," replied Brandy innocently. Sylvia, however, was not in the mood for games. "Look, girl, if you don't come out of my room, I will beat your little ass," she warned.

Despite her mother's warning, Brandy's curiosity had been piqued by a small package that had caught her eye. It was a little plastic baggie, and to her young mind, it looked like it contained sugar. But the contents were far from innocent. Just as Brandy was about to taste what was inside, Sylvia stormed in and snatched it away.

The intensity of Sylvia's reaction was frightening. She pushed Brandy against the wall, her hand tightening around her little neck. "Don't you ever again come into this room without my permission," Sylvia seethed, her eyes blazing with anger. "I will hurt you, little girl. Do you understand me?" Brandy nodded, tears streaming down her cheeks as she mumbled, "Yes, Mama, I'm sorry."

Sylvia took the bag, tucked it into her bra, and hurried to the bathroom, locking the door behind her. Brandy, left alone, didn't fully understand what had just happened. However, this unsettling incident marked the first of many times she would see her mother with a mysterious little bag. It was a harbinger of trouble, signaling the beginning of a series of challenges that would impact both her and her mother profoundly. All this from her father and her mother's provider of what he called the "Good, Good." She later found out it was heroin and that it often pumped through her mother's blood like sugar from a candy bar.

Brandy's struggle with intimacy was deeply rooted in the emotional scars left by Carl. The trauma of their past relationship lingered, casting long shadows over her interactions with other men. In every new face, she saw echoes of Carl—a haunting reminder of the potential for darkness that had once engulfed her. This persistent fear acted as a barrier, making it difficult for her to open up and trust again. Each attempt at connection became a mental battleground, where she fought against the paralysis of her own fears, desperately trying to separate past experiences from present possibilities.

This dark legacy of Carl's actions was an anchor, a weight she carried with her into adulthood. It took years of self-discovery, therapy, trauma medication, and trust-building to begin to break free from the stranglehold of his memory and to allow herself to truly open up to a man.

But the mark he left on Brandy was indelible, a stark reminder that the actions of one person could have far-reaching and devastating consequences on the lives they touched. Carl's transgressions were not just a brief, traumatic event in Brandy's childhood; they were a shadow that eclipsed her view of men and love for a significant portion of her life.

Brandy, a mere child with innocence still etched on her face, bore witness to the nightly rituals of her mother and Carl as they danced on the precipice of oblivion. It was a deathly stroll, a performance that played out in the shadows of a dimly lit room. Sylvia, once a radiant woman, had become a hollow shell, her beauty tarnished by her own addiction.

The stench of cigarettes, alcohol, and despair clung to the wallpaper, seeping into the very fabric of Brandy's existence. Her childhood was a masterclass in survival as she navigated the risky landscape of a home ravaged by addiction. Carl's presence was a constant menace, a living example of the darkness that had ensnared Sylvia.

It was on one fateful night, as Brandy clung to her tattered stuffed bunny in the corner of her room, that the demon named Carl crossed a line that would scare her soul forever. The chilling touch of his hand, tainted by drugs and desire, sent shivers down her spine. She was too young to understand the depths of depravity that gripped him, but the terror that washed over her was a cruel teacher.

Sylvia, her eyes glazed and empty, knew the horrors that unfolded in her home, yet she was a prisoner herself, ensnared by her own addiction. The torment etched into Brandy's young heart was something she carried into adulthood, a heavy burden that shaped her choices, her fears, and her unspoken demons.

Years passed, and the scars of her childhood wounds were camouflaged by the mask of success and happiness that Brandy had carefully crafted. But deep within her, the traumatic experience remained—an indelible mark on her psyche.

The wounds Carl inflicted upon her tender soul were not mere scars but rather festering wounds, open and raw, like an unhealed gash that continued to throb with every beat of her heart. Each memory, a relentless echo, resonated in the depths of her being—an ache that transcended time and defied the soothing balm of passing years. These wounds were not silent reminders; they were a harshness of pain, a haunting symphony that played incessantly in the recesses of her mind, a relentless melody that refused to be drowned out by the passage of time. Each twinge of agony carried with it the weight of shattered trust, broken promises, and the echoes of an agitated past that lingered as a constant reminder of the profound scars etched upon her soul.

A month passed when Brandy finally swallowed her pride and built up her courage enough to call Bobby. She was miserable without him, missed him terribly, and finally came to her senses and admitted that he was the best thing that had come into her life in a long time. She pulled herself together; as hard as it was, she resisted the temptation to fall back into the partying that came with her social circle. What kept her strong was the memory of Bobby standing on that porch, holding that drink but not drinking it. She also knew that if she had any chance of getting Bobby back, she had to straighten up.

She was finally at a point where she could go to parties for a while, stay long enough to meet and greet folks, have a drink or two, and then excuse herself and go home. Yeah, this meant a lot of lonely nights for a while, but it was okay. She was learning to like this "alone" time. She got to know herself and really focused on what she wanted out of life. In the end, she knew she wanted Bobby. Not because he was handsome as hell or because he was going to make good money later on in his career, but because he loved her for her. He saw the ugly, insecure side of her and still loved her. He was an exceptional person with a big heart, and she loved the way he made her feel. She'd witnessed several girls throw themselves at him, even knowing that he had a girlfriend. You know, some "bitches" just don't care. She would watch from across the way, and each and every time, Bobby would discourage their advances. Eventually, he would look around until he caught her eyes. He would motion for her to come over and then introduce her. Usually, that would be enough to dissuade the come-ons. But there were always those few who just saw it as a challenge and tried to push up on him in front of Brandy.

Once, and just once, Brandy got pissed off and told the girl in no uncertain terms that Bobby was her man and she best step off. Bobby grabbed her hand, pulled her into his arms, kissed her lightly on the lips, looked at the other woman, and said, "Excuse us, but I'm taking my lady home."

Brandy had been all blazing with pride in the fact that he told that girl he was taking her home. He said it in such a way that it implied that they would be spending the night together, which was just fine with Brandy! But as soon as they were alone, he dropped her hand, turned towards her and said gently but firmly, "Please, don't ever act like that again. You are a classy lady. Don't ever fight with another woman over a man, especially me, because when you're with me, and we're with each other, that's something you'll never have to worry about." Brandy looked at him, shocked, and was about to go off on him, "What the fu...?" He placed his finger over her mouth to silence her.

"You will never, ever have to fight over me because I would never, ever disrespect you by flirting or cheating with another woman. You are so much better than that, and you deserve better than that. I'll tell you what. Just like tonight, whenever anything like this happens, and a woman is coming at me like that, I will look around for you until I find you. I will either come to you, or you come to me, and I will have no problem letting any woman know we are together and that I only have eyes for you."

Brandy shyly smiled at him and nodded her head in under-standing. She said to herself, "Well, damn, Mufasa—Mufasa—Mufasa, damn, that was sexy." Then her man took her home, and it was the best night of her life.

That's right; that was why Brandy had to get Bobby back. Why she risked losing him was a question she really could not answer.

But no matter; she was going to get him back no matter how long it would take. In the beginning, he wouldn't take her phone calls. Eventually, he did and accepted her apology for what happened. He still wouldn't see her, though. They spent many hours talking on the phone, which made Brandy fall in love with him even more if that was at all possible. Randomly throughout the day, she would send him texts—some funny, some just letting him know she was thinking of him. She did not hide the fact that she wanted to see him, to spend time with him. But until he gave her a definite indication that he wanted to see her, she went out of her way to avoid him on campus, which was pretty easy since the campus was so big.

After six weeks or so had gone by, she received a text right as she was walking out of class. "Meet me for lunch????" it said. She smiled as a gaggle of butterflies fluttered excitedly in her stomach. Brandy and Bobby have been together ever since.

After their initial meeting, a couple of months later, she found herself falling even deeper in love with Bobby during their first Valentine's Day celebration at a hotel she had chosen. The time had come for her to explore the depths of Bobby's character. She sat in the corner of the dimly lit hotel room, eagerly awaiting his arrival. Arriving an hour early, she meticulously arranged candles and Valentine window decorations, adorning the mirror above the dresser.

Cloaked in a blend of excitement and uncertainty, she donned a seductive satin bra and panties concealed beneath a long skirt, complemented by knee-high boots. Doubt crept in as she glimpsed herself in the mirror, feeling self-conscious about her attire and the entire plan. It was uncharted territory for her, making her feel like a stranger within herself. It took Bobby to unveil her true self from the shadows.

Having discreetly placed the hotel key card in a public area, she called Bobby, guiding him to its location without revealing the surprise she had in the store. Though it was not their first time together, it marked the first instance of her taking the lead and going all out for him. The intensity of her desire to be near him had reached almost compulsive levels.

As she anxiously waited for him, she replayed her plan on how to greet him and what she intended to do with him. Yet, each attempt to think further led to embarrassment, leaving her feeling nervous and anxious. The contemplation of a last-minute cancellation crossed her mind, but then she heard someone at the door—Bobby had arrived.

At that moment, her nervousness dissipated, replaced by an overwhelming desire to touch every part of him. She calmly observed as he walked into the room, unaware of her presence, until she stood up and approached him. Bobby's handsome and sensual presence ignited a clear understanding of what she wanted.

She playfully touched his chest, instructing him to undress as she circled around him. Bobby's initial surprise turned into a smile, and he complied, shedding his suit coat and untying his tie. Standing behind him, she ran her hands over his back, overwhelmed by her affection for that part of him. The anticipation heightened as she explored his body, revealing the genuine and unfiltered nature of their physical connection.

As the relationship unfolded, she discovered a newfound freedom, unburdened by the self-imposed restraints of her past. The acceptance and eagerness to explore each other's bodies and fantasies made their connection different, exciting, beautiful, and joyful.

In the quiet intimacy of their shared moments, where nuances and subtleties spoke louder than explicit details, they forged a treasury of cherished memories. These instances, delicately woven into the fabric of their collective experiences, held a timeless allure that lingered in her thoughts. Each stolen moment, marked by shared glances, tender gestures, and unspoken understanding, became an indelible part of the intricate tapestry woven by their connection.

These memories weren't just fleeting glimpses but rather enduring imprints on the canvas of their relationship. In the absence of those cherished moments when they made love, these instants took on a deeper resonance, transcending the physical to encapsulate the essence of their emotional connection. It wasn't the explicit actions or words that defined these memories but the intangible emotions and unspoken bonds that permeated each shared heartbeat.

As she carried these memories with her, they became more than mere recollections; they were a living testament to the profound connection they shared. The tapestry of their experiences, threaded with shared laughter, silent understanding, and unspoken promises, formed the foundation of a love that transcended the boundaries of time. These moments held a magical quality, forever etching the beauty of their shared journey into the very fabric of her soul.

"The Commencement and Vows"

The morning sun bathed the campus in a warm glow, casting long shadows on the towering oak trees that lined the pathways of Louisiana State University. The excitement in the air was palpable as students, adorned in their caps and gowns, made their way to the commencement ceremony. Among them were Bobby, Brandy, and Meeka, walking together, their hearts pounding with anticipation and pride.

Bobby had been chosen as the commencement speaker, an honor that both humbled and exhilarated him. As they reached the grand stage set up on the main quad, Bobby turned to his friends, his eyes sparkling with gratitude and love. "We made it," he said softly, a smile spreading across his face. Brandy squeezed his hand, and Meeka gave him a reassuring nod.

The ceremony began, and soon, it was Bobby's turn to address the crowd. He took a deep breath, stepped up to the podium, and looked out at the sea of eager faces, knowing that each one carried a story of struggle, triumph, and dreams yet to be fulfilled.

"Good morning, graduates, faculty, and esteemed guests," Bobby began, his voice steady and warm. "Today, we stand on the precipice of a new journey, one that will be filled with challenges, opportunities, and the unyielding pursuit of our dreams. As we leave this place that has been our home, our community, I want to share a few thoughts with you."

He paused, letting his words sink in. "We've all faced our share of challenges to get here. For some, it was financial hardship; for others, it was balancing work, studies, and family. Yet, despite these obstacles, we've persevered. Our bonds have strengthened us, and our hopes have guided us."

Bobby's eyes scanned the audience, connecting with the graduates. "The pursuit of dreams requires courage, resilience, and a willingness to take risks. It means stepping out of our comfort zones and facing the unknown. There will be times when the path ahead seems daunting, and the weight of the world feels heavy on our shoulders. But remember, it's in these moments that we find our true strength."

He leaned forward slightly, his tone becoming more personal. "We are not just individuals; we are a community. The friendships and connections we've made here will carry us through the tough times. Meeka, Brandy, and I have shared our joys and sorrows, our victories and defeats. And it's this support system that has made all the difference."

"As members of society, we have a responsibility to use our education and experiences to make a positive impact. We must be advocates for justice, equality, and compassion. Our actions can inspire others and create a ripple effect of change. It's not just about achieving personal success; it's about lifting others as we rise."

Bobby's voice grew stronger, filled with conviction. "As we embark on this next chapter, let's vow to support one another, to be there in times of need, and to celebrate each other's successes. The strength of our union, forged in the halls of this university, will transcend any distractions or challenges we face."

He concluded with a heartfelt message: "Let's chase our

dreams with relentless passion, knowing that we are capable of greatness. Let's face the consequences of our actions with integrity and courage. And let's never forget the power of our bonds, our hopes, and our shared journey. Congratulations, Class of 2010. The future is ours."

The crowd erupted in applause, and Bobby stepped down, his heart full. Brandy and Meeka were waiting for him, their eyes shining with pride. They embraced tightly, a moment of pure joy and unity.

After the ceremony, the trio headed to a local restaurant in downtown Baton Rouge. The atmosphere was lively, filled with laughter and the clinking of glasses. They found a cozy corner booth and settled in, the reality of their achievement sinking in.

Meeka raised her glass, a proud smile on her face. "To us," she said, her voice brimming with emotion. "I am so proud of you both. We've come a long way, and we've done it together."

Brandy and Bobby clinked their glasses with hers. "We couldn't have done it without you, Meeka," Brandy said, her voice thick with gratitude. "You've been our rock, our inspiration."

Bobby nodded in agreement. "You've fought battles and paved the way for so many, including us. We are equally proud of you, Meeka."

They vowed in that moment to always be there for each other, to support and uplift one another no matter what life threw at them. The strength of their bond, nurtured during their college years, would carry them through any challenge.

As the night wore on, Brandy and Bobby exchanged glances, their hearts full of love and excitement. They had made it through the journey together, and their love had never been stronger. They knew that whatever the future held, they would face it side by side, their bond unbreakable.

The night ended with laughter and promises of future adventures, their spirits high and their hearts full. They left the restaurant, ready to embrace the world with open arms, their dreams and hopes guiding their way.

Top of Form

Bottom of Form

Years later, a triumphant culmination awaited Bobby, Brandy, and Meeka as they stood on the precipice of their collective achievements, having successfully graduated from college. Their journey forward promised greatness, each paving a distinct path toward their aspirations.

In the aftermath of their college years, Bobby and Brandy, having transcended academic milestones, found themselves engaged and, with time, enveloped in the enchantment of matrimony through a breathtaking wedding ceremony. Meeka, a steadfast figure in Brandy's life, assumed the esteemed role of "maid of honor," symbolizing the enduring foundation of their profound connection. Meanwhile, orchestrating the symphony of love and celebration was none other than Christina, serving as the meticulous coordinator of the joyous occasion.

The ceremony unfolded like a scene from a fairytale, with Brandy radiating unmatched beauty in her ethereal Sara Burton dress. The air was thick with the palpable energy of love, sealing their union and propelling them toward a future defined by the promise of a splendid life together. Every attendee bore witness to the spectacle, a testament to the harmonious confluence of their individual stories into a shared narrative of love, accomplishment, and boundless possibilities.

"A Leap of Faith"

Bobby paced the living room, his mind racing with the words he needed to say. The sun had set, casting long shadows across the room, and the only light came from a dim lamp in the corner. He heard the front door open and close, followed by Brandy's footsteps.

"Bobby, I'm home," she called out, her voice tired from the day's events. She stepped into the living room and saw him standing there, a mixture of determination and anxiety on his face.

"Hey, Brandy, we need to talk," Bobby said, motioning for her to sit down.

Brandy raised an eyebrow, sensing the seriousness in his tone. She sat down on the couch, placing her bag beside her. "What's going on, Bobby? You look like you've seen a ghost."

He took a deep breath and sat opposite her, leaning forward with his elbows on his knees. "I resigned from my job about a week ago," he said, watching her reaction carefully.

Brandy's eyes widened in shock. "You did what?" she exclaimed. "Why on earth would you do that?"

"I've decided to pursue my dream of becoming an author

and a producer," Bobby explained, trying to keep his voice steady. "I know it sounds crazy, but this is something I've wanted for a long time. I've been thinking about it for months, and I finally took the leap."

Brandy stared at him, her face a mix of disbelief and anger. "Bobby, how are we supposed to make ends meet? You just up and quit a high-paying job to chase a pipe dream? We have bills to pay and a life to live! This isn't some fairy tale where everything just works out." Do you seek this beautiful high-rise condo we live in and the view over the city of Chicago? Do you feel the smoothness of the marble floors, man. We worked hard for this baby. You worked hard for this, and now you want to put all that in jeopardy.

Bobby sighed, running a hand through his hair. A pipe dream... damn, Bobby shook his head. "I know it's a big risk, Brandy, but I believe in this. I've always done the right thing according to what everyone else thought I should do. I've been committed to the process that's labeled as the route to success. I've dotted every 'I' and crossed every 'T' to be that guy. But now, it's time to do something for me."

Brandy shook her head, her voice rising. "You're a damn fool, Bobby. You need to get on the phone right now and call Dave. Tell him you made a mistake and that you'll be at work tomorrow. We can't afford for you to chase some fantasy."

Brandy stared at Bobby, her mind racing as she tried to process his resignation. The shock of it all felt overwhelming, and she could feel herself beginning to panic. Before she allowed herself to fully absorb the gravity of what Bobby had just shared, she decided to divert the conversation.

"So, baby, what do you want for dinner?" Brandy asked, her voice forcefully cheerful. "Oh, and I bought some new sexy lingerie from Vickie's. I can't wait to show you. You're really going to like it."

Bobby looked at her, surprised by the sudden change in topic. "Brandy, this is important. We need to talk about this."

But Brandy continued, ignoring his interjection. "Look, I had a long day. I'm gonna go take a hot shower, slip into something sexy, and then I'm gonna cook dinner while wearing it. And by the way, do you know our friend Meeka has announced that she is running for district attorney? I told her you were going to be so proud of her, just like I am. She is so excited. You really should call her and Fleet and congratulate them. Oh, and I told her we would contribute a healthy sum toward her campaign."

Bobby, frustrated by her blatant diversion, interrupted her. "Have you even been listening to me, babe?"

Brandy paused, her forced smile fading as she met his gaze. She could see the frustration and hurt in his eyes. She sighed, realizing that she couldn't avoid the conversation any longer.

"Bobby, I just... I don't know how to handle this," she admitted, her voice trembling. "This is a huge change, and I don't know if we can afford to take such a risk right now."

Bobby softened, reaching out to take her hand. "I know it's scary, Brandy. But I need you to trust me, just like I've always trusted you with your dreams."

She pulled her hand back, standing up and pacing the room. "You don't understand, Bobby. We have responsibilities: bills and medical expenses, and now you're telling me you quit your job? How are we supposed to manage all this?"

"Brandy, listen to me," Bobby said firmly. "I've always done what everyone else thought I should do. I've been committed to the so-called route to success, but it's not fulfilling. I need to do this for myself. And I need you to support me, just like I've supported you."

Bobby looked at her, his eyes filled with hurt and determination. "You know what's funny about this? You've always pursued your dreams. You're a performer at the theater, doing your acting and singing. And let's be real, that only happened because I supported you in every way possible to achieve that dream you're now living." And I'm so proud of that; every day in the office, I would brag about how you were living the dream and how wonderful a singer and actress you are. It was wonderful watching you perform and witnessing how you seemed to feel while you were doing your thing. That is what motivated me to believe that I wanted some of what you were feeling for myself.

Brandy paused, the truth of his words sinking in. She had always counted on Bobby's unwavering support, and now he was asking for hers. She softened slightly but still looked uncertain.

"Bobby, it's different. I had a steady income from the theater. I wasn't risking everything. What if this doesn't work out? What if you fail?"

He reached out, taking her hands in his. "I won't fail, Brandy. I have to believe that. And I need you to believe in me, too. I've always been there for you, and now I need you to be here for me. We can make this work together. We've faced challenges before, and we've come out stronger. This is just another challenge."

She pulled her hands back, standing up and pacing the room. "I don't know, Bobby. This is a huge gamble. How do you expect me to just go along with this?"

Bobby stood up, too, his voice calm but firm. "Because you love me and because we're a team. I've always supported your dreams, and now it's my turn. I've thought this through. I'm not asking you to blindly follow me, but I am asking you to trust me. Just like I've always trusted you."

Brandy stopped pacing, her eyes locking onto him. She saw the sincerity in his eyes, the passion that burned within him. She knew this wasn't a whim; this was something he truly believed in.

"Okay, Bobby," she said quietly. "I'll give you my support. But you have to promise me that we'll be smart about this. We need a plan, and we need to stick to it. No more impulsive decisions."

Bobby nodded, relief washing over him. "I promise, Brandy. We'll do this together, one step at a time. Thank you for believing in me."

She walked over to him, wrapping her arms around his waist. "I'm scared, Bobby. But I trust you. You better make this work."

They stood there in the dimly lit room, holding each other tightly, ready to face the uncertain future together. For better or worse, they were a team, and nothing could break their bond.

"Virtual Sessions"

Brandy settled into her usual spot in the corner of her softly lit living room, her laptop open in front of her. The familiar face of her therapist, Dr. Jensen, appeared on the screen, her expression warm yet professionally detached.

"Hello, Brandy," Dr. Jensen greeted her, adjusting her glasses. "How have you been managing this week? Any more episodes?"

Brandy sighed, a bit of tension releasing as she prepared to dive into her challenges. "It's been rough," she admitted. "The spells are about the same, but they haven't gotten worse, which I guess is something."

Dr. Jensen nodded, jotting down notes. "And your temper? Are you finding the techniques we discussed helpful in controlling it?"

"Yeah, the breathing exercises help a lot," Brandy replied, a flicker of pride in her voice. "I haven't lost it, even with everything going on."

"That's excellent, Brandy. Staying calm and composed is key. And how are things with Bobby? Last time, you mentioned he stopped working to focus on his writing."

Brandy's face softened. "He's really trying, which is great. But it's a big change, and with him being home more, we're adjusting. It's stressful, but we're talking more and trying to support each other."

"I'm glad to hear you're communicating. It's important, especially with such significant changes at home," Dr. Jensen responded, her tone encouraging. "Given all that's happening, and based on your feedback today, I think it might be prudent to adjust your medication slightly, just to help keep you balanced during these stressful times."

Brandy nodded, her expression one of reluctant acceptance. "I trust you, Dr. Jensen. If you think it's best."

"Stress is a significant factor, Brandy. It's the number one killer in this country, and we don't want it leading you back to old habits," Dr. Jensen continued, her voice firm yet caring. "Speaking of which, have you had any thoughts about using drugs again? I know it's a common escape for many."

Brandy shook her head quickly. "No, I haven't gone down that path. I don't plan to."

"Good," Dr. Jensen said, relief evident in her tone. "Remember, Brandy, these life changes—especially those out of your control—can be overwhelming. If you feel you need an extra session before our next scheduled one, please don't hesitate to reach out."

"Thank you, Dr. Jensen. I feel okay, really. It's just a lot sometimes, but I'm handling it," Brandy reassured her, managing a small smile.

"That's all I can ask for," Dr. Jensen replied with a smile of her own. "You're doing fine, Brandy, and I'm really pleased with your progress. Keep up the great work, and I'll see you next week."

"See you next week," Brandy echoed, feeling a weight lift slightly off her shoulders as the call ended. She stared at the blank screen for a moment, taking a deep breath, ready to face another week.

Truthfully, the spells were haunting her more than she admitted to Dr. Jensen. Despite her efforts to project stability, the unease clawed at her insides, particularly when she ventured outside. Whether heading to work or just to the store, a gnawing suspicion that she was being watched crept over her. Recently, a particular anomaly had begun to exacerbate her anxiety—a strange car, ordinary yet oddly everywhere.

Each time, a shadowed figure sat behind the wheel. The face was indistinct, blurred by distance or perhaps by her own trepidation, but the presence of the vehicle in too many coincidental locations unnerved her deeply. The first time she saw it parked a block away from her workplace, she told herself it was nothing. Then, she spotted it again near the grocery store and later, idling across the street as she visited a friend.

Her rational mind battled her instincts. She tried dismissing it as mere coincidence or perhaps the overactive imagination of a stressed mind. Yet, the more she saw it, the harder it became to rationalize the car's appearance as mere chance.

She hadn't mentioned this to Bobby, fearing it would sound too far-fetched or that it would add unnecessary stress to his new career focus. Nor had she voiced this to Dr. Jensen; how could she explain that, alongside her internal battles, she might also be facing a very real external threat?

As she sat at her kitchen table, the quiet of the morning shattered by the weight of her thoughts, she realized that this could not go on. She needed to act, perhaps mention it in her next therapy session, or better yet, discuss it with Bobby when he returned. Ignoring the problem wouldn't make it disappear, and her safety—both mental and physical—was at stake.

The next morning, the house felt unusually quiet. Bobby had left early to spend the day at his mother's house, a place he found surprisingly conducive to his writing. The change of scenery, he claimed, sparked his creativity. He would return later that evening, leaving Brandy alone with her thoughts and the silent hum of daily routine.

Brandy wandered into the kitchen and made herself a cup of coffee. She held the warm mug in her hands, feeling the heat seep into her palms. The quiet was both comforting and unsettling—a space to breathe and yet a reminder of her own restless mind.

Sitting at the kitchen table, she thought about her session with Dr. Jensen. The adjustment in her medication, the discussion of stress and old demons—it all seemed to loom over her like a cloud ready to burst. But she also felt a renewed sense of resolve. She was handling things, wasn't she? Managing her spells, keeping her temper in check, and supporting Bobby in his new career venture.

The day stretched out before her, filled with small tasks and personal time. Perhaps she would read or maybe start a new series on TV. But first, she decided to write something down—a journal entry, a way to process her thoughts, a practice that Dr. Jensen had recommended.

As she started to write, she found herself detailing not just her thoughts and fears but also acknowledging her strengths and the positive changes she had made. It was a small act of self-affirmation, one that felt increasingly necessary.

Today, she decided, was going to be a good day. As she continued to write, she didn't notice the time slipping by, the words flowing freely as if they, too were finding their place in the world, much like Bobby with his novels at his mother's house.

"CHRISTINA CHANGE WITHOUT ANNOUNCEMENT," 1993

It was a beautiful, sunny day. Seven-year-old Christina Brown and her grandmother, Mama-Lella-May, attended Sunday service as usual. She loved going to church. She loved singing. Her mama loved it when Christina sang, too. She said the way she sang was a gift from God. She loved making her mama proud. On the ride home, Mama-Lella-May told her which dress she should change into and which shoes she should wear. Her mother's friends from church would be coming over shortly for coffee and cake, and Christina would be their entertainment.

Lella-May Brown, a woman of unwavering faith and a heart as vast as the heavens, stood as a beacon of love and strength in the turbulent journey of her family. Her story unfolded as one of both sorrow and redemption, woven together by the threads of maternal sacrifice and divine compassion.

Lella-May's steadfast devotion was most prominently displayed in her role as Christina's guardian. After the tragic passing of Christina's mother during childbirth, Lella-May embraced the responsibility of raising her granddaughter with a grace that surpassed the weight of grief. Christina's mother,

Lella-May's own daughter, had fallen victim to the torment inflicted by an unstable and violent partner. The shadows of abuse cast a long and sinister pall over her life.

It was a heart-wrenching tale that unfolded in the birthing room. Christina's mother, a young woman with dreams as fragile as the petals of a spring flower, endured unspeakable violence at the hands of her boyfriend, who also happened to be the father of her unborn child. The brutality inflicted upon her during pregnancy had dire consequences, leading to a moment of harrowing choice for the attending doctors.

Lella-May's daughter, lying on the cliff of life and death, made a selfless plea to her mother. In the throes of agony, she implored Lella-May to ensure the safety and well-being of her newborn daughter, Christina. It was a promise born out of unimaginable pain—a promise made with the awareness that only one life could be salvaged from the wreckage of violence.

Lella-May, fueled by a mother's love and a grandmother's devotion, held Christina close to her heart from that fateful day forward. With the resilience forged in the trial of sorrow, Lella-May became not only a caregiver but a nurturing force, determined to shield Christina from the shadows that had claimed her own daughter.

In the embrace of Lella-May's love, Christina found solace and stability. Lella-May, with her weathered hands and a heart that bore the scars of life's trials, became a guiding light for the young girl. She imparted not only the wisdom of the years but also the enduring strength that comes from overcoming adversity.

Lella-May's legacy is one of sacrificial love, an enduring testament to the power of a grandmother's promise and the resilience of the human spirit. In raising Christina, she not only fulfilled a daughter's dying wish but also ensured that a new chapter unfolded—one defined by love, stability, and the unwavering belief that, even in the face of darkness, light can prevail.

Her smile could ease any problems or worries away, and her kindness radiated from her warm, brown eyes. She was never boastful or an attention getter...except when it came to Christina. But it was never done with a self-deserving intention. She told Christina time and time again, "Your voice is a blessing from God. It would be a sin to let such a gift wither away, child. It's meant to bring joy to those around you!" Then she would wrap her arms around the little girl and pull her into her big comforting bosom, into the safety of what Christina knew to be her mother.

So, every Sunday after church, Mama's friends would arrange themselves around her living room in an array of mismatched chairs grabbed from various rooms of the house. Meanwhile, her mother would be primping and dressing Christina for the big show. Her excitement was infectious and would stir up the butterflies in Christina's stomach. The minutes before her grand entrance torture for Christina.

Waiting to hear her mother's introduction was like time standing still. She would wring her little hands in the folds of her skirt while she attempted to slow down her breathing and calm her fast-beating heart.

"And now, ladies, I am proud to present my baby girl, Christina Brown, who will entertain you with her beautiful voice!"

Christina would jump through the makeshift stage curtain, which was nothing more than a flowered sheet nailed across the doorway between the living room and the hallway that led to the bedrooms in the back of the house. The church ladies would applaud enthusiastically, but none more than her mother. All the butterflies would disappear the minute she stepped in front of the women. A calmness would enter her little body as she inhaled and got ready to sing. Singing brought joy and peace to Christina, although she was too young to understand this at the time. Seeing her mother sitting with her friends, with her beautiful smile on her face and both hands clasped together in front of her heart—that was what Christina lived for. Seeing the love in her mama's face made Christina sing with everything she had. Her mother believed in her. Her unconditional love was always there for the world to see. This is what gave Christina the ability to overcome her naturally born shyness and her insecurity. Little did Christina or any of them know that today would change the rest of their lives forever.

After they entered the house, Lella-May sat down on the sofa, grabbed her daughter with both her hands, and pulled her towards her.

"Oooh, child! Mama is tired for some reason. Now you go 'head and change into the dress I laid out for ya, okay? Mama's gonna lay down for a minute before the ladies get here. I'll be there in a minute to check on ya." That's when Christina noticed the perspiration on her mother's brow and her shallow breathing.

"Are you okay, Mama?" Christina looked at her mother with concern.

"I'm gonna be just fine, baby girl. You scoot and get ready, ya hear? I'll be in in a minute to check on ya. You're gonna look as beautiful as you sing!" Lella-May wrapped Christina in her comforting embrace and placed a kiss on her cheek. She then held Christina away from her, turned her around, and lightly swatted her on the butt to send her on her way.

Christina skipped to her bedroom and changed her clothes. She brushed her hair, put a bow in it, and then sat down and waited patiently for her mother to come in and give her the once-over. She waited and waited...and waited. It seemed like she waited forever, but her mother never came. But being the obedient child her mother had raised her to be, she still sat on the bed and kept waiting. She didn't know how long she had been sitting there before she heard knocking on the front door.

Oh, no! Mama's friends are here!

"Yoo-hoo! Lella-May! We're here," one of the ladies called through the screen door. She rattled the handle as if she was going to walk in, but the eye-hook lock was in place. The women behind her continued to chatter among themselves.

"Hey, Lella-May! I see you, girl. Open this door and quit playing!" Christina heard the woman chuckle as she kept knocking on the door. She didn't know what to do! Should she go find Mama or open the door for her friends? As she stood there, unsure of what was going on, the woman at the door started knocking harder, and the tone of her voice changed from playfulness to what... concern, fear??? "May... May... May... May, wake up, baby. We've got to get this door open. Call 911; something is really wrong."

Something was wrong. Christina could feel it in her bones. She slowly ventured out of her room, down the hallway, past the makeshift stage curtain, and walked toward her mother. She was still lying on the couch. "Mama fell asleep!" But the lady at the door just kept knocking harder, more insistently.

Vaguely, Christina noticed that the other women had stopped talking. It seemed as if all the noise had fallen away from the world, except for the knocking at the door.

"Hey, Mama! Wake up!" She reached out and grabbed her mother's hand, which was dangling over the side of the couch. She shook it vigorously to no avail. She bent over her mother's still form and spoke directly into her ear, "Mama, the ladies are here. Do you want me to let them in?"

When the woman at the door saw Christina, she started talking directly to her with urgency in her voice, "Christina, come here, sweetie. Let your 'Aunt Martha' in. Just open the door for us, honey!"

But Christina was fascinated by how still Mama was. She touched her cheek with her little hand and rubbed it around and around. "Mama, Mama. Wake up, Mama! I've got to sing for you." When she didn't get a response from her mother, she repeated herself again, but louder. But there was still no response. The woman at the door raised her voice, too, trying to get Christina's attention. The ladies standing behind Martha started clucking like chickens, trying to peek around her and into the house.

"Baby, baby... open the door! Let us in so we can help you, sweetie!" She pulled on the door harder. The panic and urgency in the woman's voice began to surround Christina and then permeated her spirit. Why is the lady shouting at her? Why isn't Mama waking up? She shook her mom harder and started yelling at her to wake up. Tears welled up in her eyes, but she didn't know why! What is wrong with her mama? She won't wake up!

"Noooo, Mama! Wake up... wake up! I have to sing for you... Maaamaaaa!!!" Panic swept through.

Christina's little body shook as she sobbed over her mother; her tears rained down on her sweet face. The woman at the door finally pulled the door free and rushed into the house. She tried to gently move Christina aside, but she would not let her mother's hand go.

She motioned for one of the other women to come and take hold of Christina. "Sweetie, go with Ms. Roberta. She's going to take you to your room. Just go lie down and try to calm down, OK? We're gonna do everything we can to help yo' mama, OK?" But she wouldn't budge...she clung to her mother's hand, screaming for her to wake up. Finally, Ms. Roberta picked her up, and pried her hand away from her mom's, and started to carry her back to her bedroom. Christina could hear one of the women weeping quietly while "Aunty Martha" sternly instructed one of them to call the ambulance.

The last memory she had of her mother was of her lying on the couch while Aunty Martha put her ear over Mama's face. Then she put two fingers on her mother's neck, and all the women closed in around her still form. Someone started praying, and in the distance, the sound of the ambulance's siren was getting closer and closer. Christina couldn't stop screaming for her Mama, arms outstretched trying to reach her, legs flailing as she tried desperately to escape Ms. Roberta's firm grasp on her.

"NOOOOO.... MAMA.... PLEASE, WAKE UP! I HAVE TO SING FOR YOU... I HAVE TO SING FOR YOU!!! PLEEEEEEEZ GIVE ME MY MAMA! MAAAMAAA!!! WAKE UP!!"

Christina spent a couple of months in the foster center before she was placed into a foster home. The family she went to had a mommy, a daddy, and a daughter. Mrs. Caroline Townsend and her husband, James, were kind people. Mrs. Townsend paid a lot of attention to Christina. Her heart just couldn't help but go out to the withdrawn, sad child. She couldn't even imagine what it would feel like to lose your mother at such a young age and then be put into a house full of strangers to boot!

The caseworker said no one came forth to claim any kinship to Christina. They couldn't find her biological father, and it looked like he had been out of the picture for a long time. Questioning Christina didn't get them anywhere either; she completely closed up and wouldn't talk to anyone.

Townsend hoped that her own daughter, Brandy, would be able to help Christina break out of her self-imposed prison. Brandy was almost seven years older than Christina, who was now six years old but was mature for her age. Mrs. Townsend suspected it was the constant turnaround of foster children that went through their home. A few were sent back to the center due to emotional issues. Others, like Brandy, were adopted after being in their home long enough to become attached. Mrs. Townsend felt bad for all the "brothers" and "sisters" that Brandy kept losing, but she really believed that as long as she and her husband were there for her, provided for her, and loved her unconditionally, Brandy would be okay.

What they didn't realize was that all the comings and goings were affecting Brandy. It hurt her so much when another child was removed from their home. After a while, she developed a coping mechanism, and she would not allow herself to get too close to any of the children anymore. If anything, she pushed them away by being mean to them. She also felt that she had to fight for her parents' love and attention. She did everything she could think of to have all eyes on her, for someone to notice her and treat her special.

She wasn't prepared for Christina's arrival. Brandy thought this girl would be gone in a couple of months, but she was so wrong. One evening, she snuck out of bed after hearing her parents talking rather earnestly in their bedroom. She listened at the door, not feeling a lick of guilt for doing so.

"Baby, we can give her a stable home with two parents! She's been through so much! Don't you feel anything for that child?" Brandy's mom said to her husband.

"What kind of question is that? Of course, I feel bad for her, but this is a big step, girl! Adopting her??? That's a lifetime decision, Caroline! I'm not sure if I'm ready for that," James replied.

"Listen, baby, I promise I will deal with her. I will take care of her emotional needs and be the closest thing to a mama I can be for her. I know in time, you will think of her as one of your own. You're a good man, and I know your heart. Whatever doubts and fears we may have aren't important right now. We need to do this for Christina and for ourselves. This is bigger than you and you, James!"

Let's be clear, James, our status has remained constant. The inability to have children has always weighed heavily on me. But when we welcomed Brandy into our lives through adoption, my world experienced a positive shift. Imagining two lovely girls running around our home, growing up together, is nothing short of a blessing from God. I really want this to happen, James. I want this to happen, and I need you to share with me what I'm feeling. This will be our complete family, encompassing everything we've ever yearned for as if we had created it ourselves.

Brandy heard her father take a deep breath and was shocked and a little hurt when he replied, "I know you're right, Caroline. That little girl's welfare is more important than any worries I have about taking her in. It's the right thing to do. God brought her into our lives for a reason. If you're sure, then I'm in. But... you're gonna have to break it to Brandy!"

Brandy quickly and quietly returned to her room. "What is going on? Why are her parents deciding to keep this kid? Don't they like her as their daughter? Is she that terrible that they want to replace her? She'll show them how good she can be! She can be a hundred percent better than that stinky Christina."

She's a big crybaby, anyway. All she does is cry into her pillow every night. And she doesn't even talk to anyone, even when they ask her a question! Her mama has always told Brandy that she should speak when she's spoken to, but she never says anything to that big baby!

Brandy was angry, although she didn't fully understand why. She just knew that she had to be better than Christina. Her mama was always talking to her in a soft voice, hugging her, and singing to her. It just wasn't fair! That was "her" mama, not Christina's!

After the adoption was finalized, the Townsends made the courageous choice to completely transform the room, now christened "Christina's Sanctuary." The space, once a practical sanctuary for both boys and girls, bore witness to the boring and neutral décor of the past. However, the present life of the room echoes with a captivating transformation. The walls, once adorned with generic colors, now showcase a vibrant tapestry of colors, reflecting Christina's unique personality. Elegant furnishings and personalized touches have replaced the former simplicity, creating an atmosphere that exudes warmth, comfort, and a sense of belonging—transforming the room into a haven that mirrors Christina's newfound place in the Townsend family. Christina still wasn't talking, and trying to get her opinion on what she wanted for her room was impossible, so Caroline asked Brandy for help in decorating the room. It was fun picking stuff out until it all went into Christina's room. In all honesty, it looked a lot like Brandy's room, but all of Christina's stuff was brand new. That did not sit well with Brandy.

One day, Caroline was cooking in the kitchen, and as usual, that big baby was coloring and coloring at the kitchen table. Brandy walked in and sat down at the table opposite Christina. As usual, her mama was trying to get her to talk, just rambling about something from when she was a kid. She would ask Christina a few questions here and there, but the child never answered; she just kept coloring without even looking up.

The anger was building in Brandy. Why doesn't her mama talk to her like that, telling her stories about when she was a little girl? She wanted her mother's attention and not the bad attention she normally gets when she is mean to Christina or disobeyed her parents. She wanted praise and affection, not discipline and punishment.

Slowly, Christina pushed herself away from the table, and she stood up and walked to the middle of the kitchen. She wasn't sure what she was going to do, but she closed her eyes, took a deep breath, and let whatever filled her come out with all the feeling she had pent up inside her. She opened her mouth....and started to sing very softly at first.

One of these mornings won't.

Be very long. You will look for.

"Me, and I'll be gone."

"I'm going to a place where I'll have nothing."

Nothing to do but walk around.

walk around heaven all day

Brandy's eyes shot up, and she put her crayons down. Her mouth opened, and she started to silently mouth the words to the song. By the second verse, Christina was singing from deep inside when she suddenly heard a second voice join in, very timidly at first. For a second, she wasn't sure if she was actually hearing that second voice, which blended so well with her own. She opened her eyes and saw Christina at the table, singing with her and tears rolling down her face. Caroline turned away from the stove and dropped the big spoon she was using to stir whatever was in the pot. She gasped as her hand flew to her mouth.

When I get to heaven, I'm going to
"Sing and shout. Nobody will be able
to put me out
My mother
I will be waiting.
And my father, too.
And we'll just walk around.
Walk around heaven all day

Christina slowly stood up, eyes locked with Brandy's. They both continued to sing as Christina's voice started to match Brandy's in emotion and volume.

"Dear Lord above, don't you hear?
I praying, "Walk right by my side."
Hold my hand when my way gets a
"Little Cloudy, I need you; I need you."
"to be my guide."
"Every day will be Sunday, my dear."
"Lord Sabbath will have no end."
And we'll do nothing but sing and
"Praise him. Then he'll say, 'Well done.'"
And my race, my race, will be won.
And I'll walk around, walk around heaven.
"All day. Walk around heaven."
"I'll just walk around heaven all day."

By the time they were done, both were breathless; both were crying. Brandy didn't understand why the tears streamed down her own face, but suddenly, she felt connected to her new sister. Caroline ran over to Brandy and hugged her with all the love a mother could give her child. Then, she. Then, she walked over to where Christina was still standing, her silent tears turning to heart-wrenching sobs. Caroline knelt down before them, embraced both her girls, and cried with them.

After the emotional display in the kitchen, Caroline sent the girls to their rooms to rest before dinner. This would give her a chance to tell James of the miracle she witnessed that day and that their daughter had a hand in it. Meanwhile, the girls went to their respective rooms to lie down. After a few minutes, Brandy went to Christina's door and politely knocked. No answer. She knocked again, and when there was still no answer, she turned the knob, opened the door, and peeked her head in. Christina was lying on her side, clutching a stuffed animal facing the door.

"Can I come in?" Christina nodded. Brandy entered and closed the door behind her. She didn't know why she had gone to her room, and she started to feel a bit awkward. She slowly walked around the perimeter of the room, touching and looking at things absentmindedly.

"You, o.k.?"

Again, Christina nodded.

"I didn't know you could sing. You're pretty good. Almost as good as me." Brandy stood at the foot of the bed, rocking her body to and fro, not really looking at the girl.

Christina smiled.

"Where did you learn to sing, anyway?"

Brandy didn't really think she would get an answer but was surprised when Christina replied, "Church." "Oh! Me, too," and after a brief pause, she asked, "Why'd you start crying?"

Christina slowly sat up, clutching the stuffed animal to her stomach. After what seemed like an eternity, she answered, "That song made me think of my mama." Her eyes started to well up.

"No... no... don't cry! My mom's going to get mad at me if she thinks I made you cry!"

Christina swallowed the sob that was threatening to escape. She looked down and wiped her eyes, sniffling. She really wanted Brandy to like her.

Brandy walked over to the side of the bed, unsure of what to do. She felt bad for the girl, but there was still some residual resentment she just couldn't shake. However, she didn't want her crying, either. She sat down on the edge of the bed.

"Wanna play a game or something?" she asked in an attempt to distract Christina from her sadness. Christina shrugged her shoulders. "Sure, all right."

Brandy walked over to the shelves that held a bunch of board games that hadn't been opened yet. She picked the easiest game she could find. She still wasn't sure how to play "UNO," and the instructions were a little too hard to understand. So, they made up their own version. By dinnertime, they were both rolling around on the bed and giggling like crazy.

James and Caroline stood outside Christina's door and looked at each other in amazement and joy. Brandy finally had a sister, and Christina had a family again. They hugged each other, for they knew deep in their hearts that this was meant to be.

Caroline and James, Christina and Brandy's adoptive parents, were hosting a family gathering. They had invited James's brother, Uncle Willy, and his wife, Vee-anna. Uncle Willy was known for his humor and thick Southern accent, hailing from the heart of Alabama. As soon as the doorbell rang, James called out to Caroline.

"Hey, babe, my brother and Aunt Vee-anna are at the door. Can you let them in?"

"Sure, baby," Caroline replied, making her way to the door. As soon as she opened it, Uncle Willy wasted no time starting with his usual observations and jokes.

Brandy and Christina ran into the living room, their faces lit up with excitement as they greeted their beloved relatives.

"Well, hello, Brandy babe! You look so pretty today," Aunt Vee-anna exclaimed warmly.

"Thank you, Auntie," Brandy replied with a smile.

"And who is this?" Aunt Vee-anna asked, her gaze shifting to the younger girl.

"This is my little sister," Brandy said proudly, introducing Christina.

"Your little sister? Oh, and she's pretty as well. Hello, it's nice to meet you," Aunt Vee-anna said affectionately.

"Nice to meet you, too," Christina responded softly.

"Aww... you can call me Aunt Vee-anna, like the sausage," Aunt Vee-anna added with a chuckle.

"Yeah, and if you forget that, baby, just look at her head. It looks just like a Vee-anna sausage!" Uncle Willy teased, causing the room to erupt in laughter. "Oh, drop dead, you old coon," said Vee-anna.

Brandy, especially close to her uncle and aunt, found Uncle Willy's humor irresistible. The girls settled in, basking in the warmth and love of their family.

"Boy, James, these two girls look just alike! They look like family. They've got similar creatures," Uncle Willy said with a wide grin.

"You mean features, Willy," Aunt Vee-anna corrected, rolling her eyes. "I swear, the older you get, the crazier you get."

"And I swear... the older 'you' get... the uglier you get, but you don't hear me trying to correct that, right?" Uncle Willy shot back, causing everyone to laugh.

"Oh, shut up with your limp-leg ass," Aunt Vee-anna retorted, playfully swatting at him.

James and Caroline laughed along with them. "Hey, Willy, be careful with your language. These girls are young and don't need to hear that," James said, trying to keep a straight face.

"Oh hell, here we go with the suckideyness," Uncle Willy said, mispronouncing "Siddity." "It's 'Siddityness,' Uncle Willy," Christina corrected, giggling.

"Hell, I know what it is. All I'm saying is I have that anointment about these things, and these girls look related," Uncle Willy insisted, his accent thickening with each word.

"Well, they are both from the same area in Chicago, so anything's possible," Caroline said, trying to pacify him.

"I'm telling you, these churrin are connected. I know 'cause I got that spiritual gift. I can sense when people are done walking down the same pathway. That's all I'm saying," Uncle Willy proclaimed, nodding sagely.

"Well, we appreciate your insight, Willy," James said, patting his brother on the back. "Let's get some food and enjoy the evening."

As they moved into the dining room, the atmosphere was filled with warmth and laughter. Uncle Willy continued his comedic commentary, pointing out various quirks and features of the house; each comment met with laughter from the family.

"James, you ever thought about fixing that squeaky step? Every time I step on it, it sounds like a cat in a blender!" Uncle Willy exclaimed.

"Only you, Willy, only you," James replied, shaking his head with a smile.

Aunt Vee-anna, not to be outdone, joined in. "And James, what's with that ugly painting in the hallway? Did y'all lose a bet or something?"

"That's called modern art, Vee-anna," Caroline said, laughing. "We thought it added a touch of sophistication."

"Sophistication? Looks like a toddler went wild with a crayon," Uncle Willy quipped, causing another round of laughter.

The evening continued with stories and jokes, the family bonding over shared memories and new experiences. Brandy felt a sense of belonging and warmth, the earlier troubles of the day fading away in the presence of her loved ones.

As the night wore on, Brandy found herself sitting next to Uncle Willy, who was in the middle of another animated story about his youth in Alabama.

"And then, I told that gator, 'You ain't scaring me none!' And sure enough, it turned tail and ran," Uncle Willy said, his eyes twinkling with mischief.

"Did that really happen, Uncle Willy?" Brandy asked, laughing.

"Well, parts of it did," he admitted with a grin. "But it makes for a better story this way, doesn'tdoesn't it?"

Brandy nodded, feeling grateful for the laughter and love that filled the room. Despite the day's setbacks, moments like these reminded her of what truly mattered: family, love, and the shared joy of being together.

As the gathering wound down, Uncle Willy made a final observation. "You know, these family get-togethers are good for the soul. We need to do this more often."

"I agree, Willy," James said, raising his glass. "To the family and to many more nights like this."

"To family!" everyone echoed, clinking their glasses together.

And with that, the night ended on a high note, leaving everyone looking forward to the next time they could all be together again, laughing and sharing stories in the warmth of each other's company.

From that point on, the girls were almost inseparable. From the beginning, Brandy was the more outgoing of the two, and Christina remained quiet and timid. Brandy tended to boss Christina around a lot. Christina really didn't mind; she just wanted Brandy to keep liking her, so she usually went along with whatever Brandy had in mind. But there was one thing that Christina would not share with Brandy.

She had a box of keepsakes that reminded her of her mother.

There was a photograph of them together that was taken at the last church social they attended. There was also the silk flower her mother would put behind Christina's ear when she was getting ready to perform for her friends in their living room. A brooch Mama always wore to church was also among the items in her private box. No matter how much Brandy begged, pleaded, badgered, or threatened Christina, she would not back down from Brandy. Those were personal memories of her life before becoming Brandy's sister, and she wanted to keep that little bit of "her" to herself.

There was another place in which they were equals, more or less, and that was the church choir. They each had their respective strengths and took turns singing solos. The difference between them, though, was that Brandy's strong personality would come out. She wasn't afraid to strut back and forth in front of the choir as she sang. She put on a show and would whip the congregation into a frenzy. Christina, on the other hand, loved the slow, soulful gospel songs. She could drive people to tears with her emotional, heartfelt renditions.

What each girl didn't know is that what they envied in each other was something they wished for themselves. While Brandy wished her singing could move people's spirits so much that they cried, Christina wished she had the spirit and confidence Brandy had to just get out there and do her thing! The only time she felt like she could conquer the world was when Mama was alive.

The girls were as close as could be all through elementary school and middle school. But when they started high school, things changed. With Brandy being so outgoing and confident, she soon fell in with the more popular crowd. Christina tried to hang around her as much as she could, but it soon became apparent that Brandy didn't have time for her anymore. She was caught up in the social whirlwind of high school, and Christina was cramping her style.

Christina eventually made her own friends and adjusted well

enough, but she missed her sister. They were no longer as close as they once had been, and sadly, this wasn't going to change for a long time. Right now, though, Brandy's energy and spirit overshadowed Christina. But she was content to let it remain that way... for now.

Once both Brandy and Christina left the security of their adopted parents, Caroline and James, their lives underwent a dramatic transformation. The emotional support and comfort provided by their loving parents were abruptly taken away when James and Caroline were involved in a tragic car accident that claimed both their lives.

This devastating loss left both sisters deeply broken, forcing them to rely on each other to stay stable. However, the impact of the loss was particularly profound for Brandy. Having already experienced so much turmoil in her life, this event chipped away at her resilience, leaving her struggling to cope with the overwhelming grief and absence of the only true family she had ever known.

Brandy's reaction to the loss highlighted her deep connection to their adopted parents and the sense of security they provided. While both sisters faced the grief together, it became clear that Brandy bore the weight of this tragedy more heavily, leading her down a path where the pain of loss would shape her future decisions and relationships in profound ways.

"New News, Troubled Intention"

The sound of a voice at her side brought Brandy out of her recollection. She was still holding the prescription bags in her hands and was standing still in the middle of the sidewalk as people walked around her. She shook her head to clear the memories as she began walking toward the corner of the street where her car was parked. She never noticed the man who was watching her from across the street. As she turned the corner, she let out a gasp, then began shouting and running toward her car.

"Hey… wait one damn minute. What are you doing with my car? Get away from it!"

The tow truck driver looked at her, unmoved by her anger. "Hey, lady, you gotta pay for it in order to keep it, ya know? You can pick it up at the impound if you can make your payment." He handed her a business card.

"What the hell do you mean, 'I gotta pay for it'? That car is being paid for, and it's up to date! Get my car off that damn tow bar right damn now."

"Lady, I just follow orders, and this paper here says you're behind five months on this car. I'm just doing my job." He shrugged his shoulders and continued to pull the car up onto the bed of the tow truck. People were looking at them; some were snickering and pointing.

"What about my stuff that's in the car?" she snapped at him.

He poked his finger at the business card she had pinched between her fingers. "Call that place and make arrangements to pick up your personnel." She stood there watching him with her mouth wide open. She couldn't believe this shit! It was all Bobby's fault! Now she didn't have a damn car, and it wasn't just any car. She loved that car. The vibrant red Jaguar F-Type S series with a convertible top stood gleaming in the sunlight as the tow guy continued his final steps before pulling out, its sleek lines and powerful engine commanding attention wherever it went. Brandy, having recently acquired the car, couldn't help but revel in the admiring glances it attracted. The purr of the engine echoed the promise of exhilarating drives and newfound freedom.

No matter where she went, the Jaguar seemed to effortlessly draw eyes, turning heads as it navigated through the city streets. The convertible top, when down, exposed the interior, inviting the world to catch a glimpse of luxury and sophistication. It was a statement to people who saw her in it, signaling that she was not just anybody but a confident and empowered black female —or simply "badass."

As Brandy cruised down the boulevard, the wind tousling her hair, she felt a surge of pride and confidence. The attention the Jaguar garnered was more than just admiration for a beautiful car; it reflected her journey from a tumultuous past to a future filled with possibilities.

Stopping at a traffic light, Brandy couldn't help but notice the envious glances from neighboring cars. The distinctive roar of the engine hinted at the power within, mirroring the strength she had discovered within herself. The Jaguar, with its impeccable design and attention-grabbing allure, became a symbol of her resilience and success.

At a café, as she parked the Jaguar, passersby couldn't resist stealing glances at the striking vehicle. Brandy reveled in the attention, her confidence boosted by the knowledge that she had overcome hardships and earned the right to enjoy life's luxuries.

The convertible top is lowered with a button, revealing the carefully crafted interior. Brandy settled into the plush leather seats, a smile playing on her lips as she savored the feeling of accomplishment. The Jaguar wasn't just a car; it was a statement, a declaration that she had triumphed over her past and embraced a future filled with beauty and elegance.

However, the tide turned abruptly. Here she is now, parked conspicuously in front of the Walgreens in downtown Chicago on the corner of State Street and Randolph Street. Brandy's beloved Jaguar became the center of an unexpected event. A tow truck pulled up, drawing the attention of pedestrians and onlookers. The shock on Brandy's face mirrored the disbelief of those witnessing the scene.

The once proud symbol of Brandy's triumphs was now being towed away, repossessed in broad daylight for everyone to see. The sight was devastating, a harsh reminder that even the most beautiful moments could be fleeting. As the Jaguar disappeared around the corner, Brandy stood there, a mixture of embarrassment and sadness overwhelming her.

Passersby exchanged curious glances, and whispers of speculation filled the air. Brandy, left alone on the sidewalk, took a deep breath, steeling herself against the sudden turn of events. It was a humbling experience, a reminder that material possessions, no matter how glamorous, were not immune to the challenges of life.

In the face of this unexpected setback, Brandy found strength in her resilience. As she stepped away from the scene, the echoes of her past challenges and triumphs remained with her. The Jaguar might have been taken away, but the journey of overcoming adversity and embracing a brighter future was still very much hers to navigate.

What the hell was she going to do now? How the hell was she going to get home?

She pulled her cell phone out of her bag and dialed Bobby's number. "Hey, baby, what's up?" he answered.

"Don't you 'baby' me, Bobby Pope! My fucking car just got reposed, Bobby! I'm downtown with no way to get home! Why did they take my car, Bobby? Why????"

"Brandy... Brandy, I'm sorry, baby! I just couldn't keep up with the car payment! I've been paying as much as I can. It's gonna be okay! As soon as I sell my novel, we'll have the money to get you another car. We'll figure this out, okay? Together, we're gonna get through this!"

"BOBBY!!!" she yelled into the phone. "You better figure something out...FAST!!! This isn't what I signed up for, BOBBY! YOU HEAR ME!!!! THIS IS BULLSHIT!!" She hung up on him. She didn't think she could take this anymore. First, the doctor's visit, and now this??? Why is everything falling apart?

Oh, she knew why! Because Bobby suddenly decided that he wanted to be a writer! He walked away from a six-figure career to be a broke-ass writer! They went from going to every high-society event to this? How were they going to survive? She didn't make a chump change, but because of this new health issue, she had stepped down from the theater. How the hell was she going to cover her medical expenses now? It took everything in her not to break down and cry right there.

"Damn, it breaks my heart to see such a beautiful woman look so sad," a man said into her ear.

She jumped back, startled. She looked at the man with a look that could kill him. "Excuse me, sir, but I would appreciate it if you would back the hell up. This is not the time."

"I'm sorry, I'm sorry," the man said, holding up his hands and backing away. "I just hate to see a beautiful woman in distress; that's all."

Brandy rolled her eyes at him and turned back to her phone, trying to decide who she could call to come pick her up. The only person she could count on was her sister, Christina. When she wasn't working or at church, that girl would be stuck in her house by herself. Brandy never understood why because her sister was pretty enough. .She is not sexy or gorgeous like herself, but pretty in her own simple way. She was just so painfully shy. That's how Brandy knew she would be available to come pick her up. She didn't notice that the man hadn't moved away. He stood back, watching her with an intense look on his face. It was obvious he had something on his mind.

"Hello? Hello? Christina, this is Brandy. I need you to come pick me up. Don't worry about where my car is; come get me! What do you mean you can't? Why, what are you doing? Christina...Christina???" Brandy pulled the phone away from her ear. Oh, hell naw, that little girl didn't just hang up on her! She recalled the number, but her sister was not answering her phone. What the hell is going on? And she was whispering too like she didn't want to be overheard by anyone. The world is going fucking crazy. That's the only thing Brandy could come up with.

She looked up and saw that man still standing there, watching her. She finally took a moment to take him in. Oh, okay! He was dressed in a very nice, expensive suit. Shoes...check. Watch...yep, nice. Hair cut close to the scalp and lined up nicely. Clean-shaven, and the most interesting eyes with thick lashes. Hmmm, not bad, Brandy thought to herself. He took her appraisal as a sign of acceptance, so he stepped a bit closer.

"I couldn't help but overhear that you need a ride. I would be happy to drive you anywhere you need to go." She looked at him like he was crazy.

He chuckled, "I'm sorry, let me introduce myself," he held out his hand. She looked at it reluctantly but then shook his hand. "My name is Timmoreia Branklin." He held her hand a few seconds longer than necessary. That's an interesting name. It's Greek, he replied. How do you pronounce it again? I tell my friends it's like saying "Tie- it - tighter," Ti- Mori-a. Well, ok, Mister Ty-Mori-a Branklin.

Timmoreia Branklin had a commanding presence with a stature that towered above most, his tall and bald figure cutting an imposing silhouette. Despite the lack of hair, his rugged charm emanated from every pore, a paradoxical combination of striking handsomeness and a somewhat unpolished wardrobe. His clothing choices, though not refined, carried an undeniable rugged allure that added an intriguing edge to his persona.

There's an enigmatic quality about Timmoreia; his appearance doesn't conform to any particular stereotype, but that's precisely what makes him stand out. The incongruity between his polished charm and the rough-hewn garments creates an arresting contrast that captures attention. It's as if he deliberately defies expectations—a deliberate choice to keep people guessing.

One might notice something peculiar about Timmoreia's hands—they are notably small, an unexpected feature that adds an element of quirkiness to his otherwise imposing figure. His hands, though diminutive, possess an exceptional persuasiveness that defies their size. There's an art to his gestures, a subtlety that amplifies his innate charm.

A peculiar divergence from his otherwise well-groomed appearance is found in his shoes. Unlike the meticulous care he seems to take in presenting himself, Timmoreia's footwear tells a different story. They lack the polish and sheen one might expect, hinting at a casualness that might give pause to the discerning eye.

Yet, despite these subtle contradictions, Timmoreia Branklin possesses a charm that transcends the boundaries of superficial judgments. His most captivating feature is his eyes—a mesmerizing shade of light gray that draws you in with an almost magnetic force. They exude warmth and sincerity, creating an inviting aura that is hard to resist. It's these eyes that hold the power to dissolve any skepticism, making Timmoreia's charisma all the more potent.

Brandy, encountering this intriguing figure, feels a sense of hesitation, torn between the unease in his appearance. However, as she locks eyes with Timmoreia, the captivating light gray orbs dispel any reservations. There's an undeniable charm, an authenticity that transcends the external contradictions, leaving a lasting impression of Timmoreia Branklin—a man whose allure lies in the intriguing harmony of his contradictions.

"Mr. Branklin, I appreciate the offer, but I'm a married woman, and I don't know you. So, I think..."

"Well, maybe we can get to know each other over a cup of coffee," he interrupted her.

"Ummm, I don't think so. I'm sure my husband wouldn't appreciate it either." Usually, her cold rejection would send a man packing, but this guy was persistent.

"Why? We aren't going to be doing anything but drinking coffee and conversing. What's the harm in that? Besides, what he doesn't know won't hurt him. I betcha I can put a smile back on that pretty face too, make you forget about all your troubles... for a little while, anyway." Brandy looked at him, surprised at herself that she kind of wanted to talk to this strange, beautiful man.

"I mean, we're just gonna talk and drink coffee, right?" she told herself. "Besides, Bobby is all wrapped up in trying to finish the last chapter of his book and find a publisher for it. He hasn't noticed Brandy in weeks—hell, months, even!"

Timmoreia could see the mental and moral struggle she was in, so he poured on the charm even more. "I'll tell you what... let's go have some coffee and talk, and when we're done, I'll pay for your cab ride home. That way, you know you're safe, and your husband won't see a strange man bringing his wife home. How's that?"

Brandy contemplated it a few seconds longer. She really wasn't in the mood to see Bobby right now. She might just punch him in the throat; she was that mad about her car. But he did deserve to know that she found a way home and that she would be there shortly. She looked up at Timmoreia, smiled, and said, "OK, why not?"

She sent the text to Bobby, put her phone in her purse, and they walked to the nearest coffee house on the corner of Michigan St. The next two hours flew by as she spilled her frustrations about Bobby and talked about her love of singing and performing. He made her laugh and made her feel pretty. The attention he was giving her filled a void she had been feeling for a few months now, ever since Bobby started with his nonsense about his book. As promised, Timmoreia hailed a cab for her. She gave the cabby her address, and Timmoreia asked how much it would cost. "Holy cow," it was going to cost a pretty penny to drive her to the other side of town! Brandy started to protest, but Timmoreia pulled some bills out of his wallet and handed them to the driver.

He leaned into Brandy's open window. "It's been a real pleasure getting to know you, Brandy. I wish you all the luck in the world with that husband of yours. Maybe someday I'll be able to catch one of your performances." He laid his hand over hers and gently rubbed the back of it with his thumb.

"I would like that," she replied a little breathlessly. He patted the side of the car door, alerting the driver that he was free to go. Brandy sat back in her seat with a smile on her face as they drove away.

As Brandy departed from the presence of Timmoreia Branklin, a lingering suspicion nestled itself in the recesses of her mind. It was a subtle whisper, a nagging feeling that urged her to delve deeper into the enigma that was Timmoreia. His charismatic conversation had been so impeccably timed, so engaging, that she found herself willingly dismissing the pressing need to unravel the mysteries that played in the backdrop of her thoughts.

The conversation had been a dance of words, a choreography that seemed to sweep away any doubts or hesitations. Timmoreia's timing was impeccable. His and his words were a symphony that resonated with charm and persuasion. The artful finesse with which he navigated the dialogue left little room for Brandy to scrutinize the underlying currents of her instincts.

In the wake of their interaction, as she navigated the space outside his magnetic aura, there was a latent realization that her instincts harbored questions left unexplored. A part of her consciousness hinted at the need to peer beyond the captivating façade to decipher the subtext that danced beneath the surface of their exchange.

However, the allure of the moment, the captivating presence of Timmoreia, had momentarily eclipsed her innate instincts. It was as if time had conspired with charm to create a bubble, shielding her from the scrutiny that her own intuition demanded. The suspicion lingered, an unspoken undercurrent, yet Brandy chose to let it drift away in the wake of the perfectly orchestrated conversation.

Sometimes, the allure of a well-timed discourse can act as a veil, obscuring the need for deeper introspection. As Brandy walked away, the suspicion still lingered a faint echo in the corridors of her consciousness, waiting for the right moment to resurface and demand the attention it rightfully deserved.

Timmoreia Branklin watched the car pull away with his own smile. Damn, that was easier than he had planned. He didn't expect her to be so damn thirsty! The man at home must have been dropping the ball when it came to her because she had literally come to life with just a little bit of attention. Some compliments, a few discreet touches to her arms and her knees—she was eating it up!

As Brandy walked away, her departure did not mark the end of Timmoreia's contemplations; rather, it ignited a spark of intrigue within him. His eyes lingered on her retreating figure, and a sly smile curved his lips, a smile that held a hint of mischief and calculation. To Timmoreia, Brandy was not just a beautiful woman; she was a revelation, surpassing even his imagination.

In the quiet aftermath of their encounter, a plot unfolded in Timmoreia's mind. There was a deliberate pacing to his thoughts, a meticulous consideration of the steps that lay ahead. The wheels of a plan began to turn, driven by an undercurrent of cunning intent. His gaze remained fixed on the corner where Brandy's car disappeared, a moment pregnant with the promise of intrigue.

With a deceptive smile playing on his lips, Timmoreia whispered to himself, "So, it begins." The words held a certain satisfaction, a recognition of the game that was set in motion. The humor in his smile betrayed a sense of amusement as if he relished the complexity of the scheme that brewed in the recesses of his mind.

In that fleeting moment, as the plot unfolded and the first move was made, Timmoreia's eyes sparkled with a glint of mischief. The smile lingered, a cunning expression that hinted at the layers of deception yet to be revealed. The stage was set, and with a calculated step, Timmoreia embarked on a journey where charm and strategy entwined, creating a narrative that promised to be as intriguing as the enigmatic smile that marked its inception.

"The Impacts of Change"

Oh, no! She knew Brandy was going to be really mad for hanging up on her, but Christina had just been called to the stage for her audition. She felt terrible for leaving her sister hanging like that, but she had no choice. This was her chance, and if she thought about it too much, she knew she would chicken out and run out of the building! Besides, Brandy has some explaining of her own to do. Christina was quite surprised when she showed up for an open call for the theatrical group to which Brandy belongs, only to learn that the part being auditioned was Brandy's part!! Apparently, she resigned from production and from the whole group, citing personal issues as the reason. The only problem that Christina was aware of was Brandy's discontent with Bobby's decision to quit his high-salary career. If truth be told, she wasn't merely unhappy with Bobby's decision, she was downright PISSED!! And Brandy, being Brandy, was not shy about letting everyone know about it, too.

But that still wasn't a good enough reason to quit her job. Heck, if anything, it meant she needed to keep it now more than ever. Christina wondered if this was Brandy's way of forcing

Bobby to go back to his firm. She had a knack for being manipulative, but Christina wasn't aware of that tactic ever working on Bobby. Besides, she knew Brandy really did love her husband. Why wouldn't she? Bobby was dependable, faithful, intelligent, talented, and fearless, not to mention handsome as all-get-out. He was always kind to Christina, going out of his way to make her feel welcome in his home and listening to anything she had to say, which was hard to do with Brandy around.

However, this wasn't the time to worry about Brandy, Bobby, or their income. It was time for her to go after her own dream, the one that she had tried to repress for years. The one her mother had for her since the day Christina sang her first note. She really didn't think she had a chance of winning the part, but she just had to give it a try. She owed it to her mother's memory, to herself. There would be no more playing small for Christina.

After the medical scare, she had a few weeks ago, she wasn't going to let life pass her by anymore. Her doctor had called her a week after her exam to tell her that one of the tests came back abnormal. They scheduled another appointment with a gynecologist to have him perform a colposcopy to rule out the possibility of cervical dysplasia or cancer. The actual procedure only took about 15 minutes and was pretty painless. Waiting for the results, however, turned out to be the longest week of her life! Her active imagination carried her to the worst-case scenario. But the test results came back normal. The whole incident made Christina realize that she couldn't take life for granted. She had to stop being afraid to go after her dreams.

This was her chance, truth be told. In the intricate duet of life, Christina and Brandy, two sisters bound by blood and rivalry in many aspects, staged a dramatic performance fuelled by their singing talents and individual journeys. The spotlight often fixated on their vocal prowess since childhood, cast shadows that extended far beyond the musical stage.

Christina, possessing the undeniable crown of the better singer, found herself in the shadows of Brandy's unyielding self-assurance. Brandy's performances were a testament to her confidence, transcending the musical notes and resonating in the grand symphony of life's accomplishments. While Brandy was undoubtedly a talented singer and performer, she harbored a silent acknowledgment that Christina, when embracing her true self, held the power to outshine the most dazzling performances.

Since childhood, the seeds of competition had been sown by Brandy's relentless drive. The stage wasn't limited to the concert hall; it expanded into the realm of life's achievements. Brandy's competitive spirit sought not only vocal triumph but also the attention and recognition that life's grandeur could offer. In this saga, Brandy consistently emerged as the victor, with Christina often cast in the shadows despite her exceptional vocal gifts.

As the real-life drama unfolds, the narrative begs the question: Can Christina break free from the overshadowing effects of Brandy's confidence, not just in singing but in the broader tapestry of their shared existence? The spotlight now rests on the intricate choreography of their life stories, challenging preconceived notions and perhaps paving the way for a harmonious resolution to their sibling rivalry. This was her risk to take, no matter the consequences.

If she was completely honest with herself, she would have to admit that Bobby Pope was the initial catalyst for her epiphany. The way he just got up and quit his job because he wanted to become a novelist was not only shocking but inspiring. To be that fearless, to truly believe that he could break into a difficult trade and be successful, was crazy, to say the least. But it was also rousing! It made her sit up and take notice. It made her wonder if she could do something so life-changing, too.

There was only one way to find out. No one could do it for her; she had to step out of her comfort zone and be courageous. She had to be daring! She had to believe in herself, and an open-door opportunity was knocking! There was no turning back now. She had the stage...literally.

She walked to the tape marking her spot and turned to face the auditorium. The lights were bright, and she could only make out the first five or six rows of seats. Anything after that was cloaked in darkness.

"State your name, please," came the disembodied male voice from the darkened seats. "Hello, my name is..." "We can't hear you, miss. Please speak up. I hope you sing louder than you speak," the voice said exasperatedly.

Christina cleared her throat, her hands wringing in the folds of her full skirt. "My name is Christina..." The voice cut her off.

"Well, Christina, this is how this is going to work. First, you will sing the song you were assigned this morning. I hope you're familiar with it."

Christina started to nod her head that she was, but she wasn't sure if the person was even looking at her because he continued talking before she could complete a full nod.

"Then you will read the lines that you were given. One of the other actors will come on stage to read the other parts. You are allowed to use the copy, but please use it minimally. What we're looking for is your emotion... your reaction to what is going on in the story, but you still must be able to memorize your lines. Understand?"

Again, Christina began to nod her head, but the voice continued on as if she weren't even there.

"Then you will be given the opportunity to sing a song of your choice. It does not need to be relevant to the story but should be able to showcase your singing ability. Understand?"

This time, Christina spoke clearly and firmly, "Yes, I do."

Christina offered up a quick prayer to God to help her remember her lines and then another quick prayer to her mother, asking for strength and confidence. As the lights dimmed even lower and a single spotlight shone on her, the piano keys softly began to play the introduction to the song. Christina closed her eyes and immediately felt that inner peace she always felt when she sang. Her eyes fluttered open in surprise when she thought she felt the pressure of a hand on her right shoulder. She softly smiled, closed her eyes again, opened her mouth and let out the beautiful sound her mother loved so much.

When all was said and done, Christina was so relieved, but she also had a gut feeling that whoever was in the audience really liked how she performed. Of course, she couldn't tell by the response, "Thank you. Someone will be in touch with you within a week."

No applause, nothing, but she still had a feeling that she nailed it. She was on cloud nine as she left the theater. She was so proud of herself for taking the chance, for throwing caution to the wind and going for it. She couldn't wait to tell Brandy about...

"Oh, no," Christina stopped in her tracks. "Brandy! I forgot all about Brandy," she said aloud to herself.

Christina started chewing on her thumbnail in worry. Well, she'll have to deal with Brandy sooner or later, preferably later. And she wasn't going to mention her audition to her, either. If she doesn't get the part, then no one has to know she even tried out for it, right? And if, by some miracle, she does get it, well, she'll just cross that bridge when she comes to it.

Christina ran to catch the bus that was just about to pull away from the studio to take her to the parking lot where her car was. She allowed herself to stop worrying about Brandy and instead ran through her audition once again in her mind. She was happy with how she had performed. She did pretty well with the reading, too—better than she had expected. Now comes the really hard part: waiting for the phone call.

"Trusted Conversations"

Fleet, Bobby's enduring friend since their college days and Meeka's man. Despite leading starkly different lifestyles, their bond remained unbroken. Fleet, however, seemed to have a knack for attracting trouble, a relentless pursuer that he could never quite outrun. His spontaneous nature led him down unpredictable paths, often landing him on the wrong side of the law and in the company of friends who cared little about morality and believed they were beyond reproach.

In stark contrast, Bobby was the voice of reason, always quick to criticize Fleet for the seemingly senseless escapades. He tirelessly attempted to convince Fleet that he was capable of more, urging him to rise above the chaos. Bobby, with his strong moral compass, believed in doing what was right.

Beneath the camaraderie, Fleet held conflicting emotions. While he admired Bobby and considered him a brother, a subtle undercurrent of envy lingered. Witnessing Bobby's progress in life, Fleet harbored a deep-seated desire for similar success. Yet, Fleet's approach was fundamentally different; he sought the path of least resistance, taking risks at every turn, believing he could achieve success swiftly and with minimal effort.

Their friendship, a complex dance between loyalty and diverging paths, painted a vivid picture of two individuals navigating life's challenges in vastly different ways. Despite the clashes in values, Bobby's unwavering belief in Fleet's potential remained a constant undercurrent in their turbulent friendship. Fleet sat at the kitchen table, going through the mail. Honestly, it was more bills than anything else. Letter after letter, it was someone or another letting him know he was behind on something, and they wanted their money. He threw the pile on the table and put his head in his hands. Ever since he got out a few years ago, anxiety had been growing inside him. He has faith that God will see him through, and he knows that we all must bear our own burdens from time to time, but he was getting to the end of his "hope" rope. Something had to give...... like soon.. He remembered someone once saying, "To every season, there is an end." He was ready for his ending that was for damn sho!

He started sorting through the envelopes again. "Bills, bills, and more bills." He looked at the envelope from Publisher's Clearing House. He smirked at it while he contemplated whether he should send it in. After he finished filling out the form and putting it in the return envelope, he said to himself, "Maybe I should pray over it." He held the envelope sandwiched between his two hands, closed his eyes, and bowed his head.

"Lord, I'm only asking for a small break. Now I know I've done wrong, but I'm trying to live my life as best as I can... this might give me some new hope." "I don't hurt anybody, well, anymore, if I'm being honest; I just look out for others, like I did when I was in prison." "Now, Lord, "You know I had to knock a couple of them busters on their backs." "...but it was only in the protection of my guys." "I'm willing to bear this burden for as long as you see fit." "Lord." "But please bestow some favor on me." "I don't ask for much." "...but I would love to be able to take care of Meeka now." "You know." "Give her something back for all she has done for me." "She's been holding us down for a while." "...and I'm doing everything I can to stay on the right side of things this time." "I'd like my turn to do right by her." "In Jesus' name." "I pray." He felt selfish asking for favor. "But what could it hurt, right?" He put the envelope down and looked at it for a minute.

"I probably won't win anyway since I didn't order any magazines. Everybody knows that black folks don't ever win because they don't buy any magazines." He shook his head at himself and chuckled.

He eyed the Publisher's Clearing House envelope with a smirk, contemplating whether he should take a chance. After filling out the form and sealing it in the return envelope, he decided to add a touch of faith to the mix.

He continued, acknowledging the seeming absurdity of pinning hopes on a sweepstakes entry. "I know this might seem really stupid, but something like this could be the shift I need to bring my life into balance. It might keep me from veering down some dangerous paths and empower me to choose what's right over what's easy."

As Fleet voiced these thoughts, there was an underlying urgency, a realization that his current trajectory held perilous consequences. "I've been entertaining some risky ideas lately, and maybe winning something, even as unlikely as this, could be the sign I need to change my ways. It's time to break free from this cycle of deceitful thinking and do right by Meeka and me. I can't keep forcing myself down the wrong path." The sincerity in his voice suggested a genuine desire for transformation, a plea for a chance to redirect his life toward a more positive and fulfilling course.

"Man, you're crazy, Fleet! And why are you sitting here talking to yourself like a damn fool?" his conscience said.

He pushed himself away from the table and walked into the

living room. He looked around, trying to find anything that needed his attention. But the room was nice and tidy. He'd already washed the breakfast dishes, and he had taken a roast out of the freezer for dinner. He went to the upstairs bathroom to see if there were any clothes in the hamper that needed washing, but there were only a couple of things in the basket.

He walked back downstairs and sat on the couch. He hated not having anything to do. He hated not having a job and holding his own. It made him feel less of a man. He didn't know what he would do without the love and support of his baby, Meeka. She was a force to be reckoned with. She was smart as hell and strong—strong in conviction and spirit. And she believed in Mr. Fleet. She had so much faith in him and what he was capable of. Fleet had no doubt that the good Lord blessed him when He put Meeka in his life. She came in during one of the darkest periods he had ever been through.

Ten years ago, Fleet was incarcerated for something he said he didn't do but was simply in the wrong place at the wrong time with the wrong crowd. His court-appointed lawyer was worthless and didn't spend the time, nor did he have the desire, to fight for Fleet's freedom. Fleet felt a hopelessness that almost engulfed him. After acclimating to his surroundings and learning the unwritten rules required to survive in prison, Fleet focused all his attention on taking as many classes as possible that the prison offered. He had a background in construction and dreamed of starting his own company one day. The trade classes the prison offered taught a lot of things he already knew, but he needed the class as a prerequisite to taking other classes, and he was determined to get into the business management class. He knew that would get him a step closer to owning his own business once he got out of the joint. He had a couple of friends who came to visit him occasionally, and one had told Fleet about a local organization that worked with prisoners claiming to be wrongly convicted. They reviewed their cases and evidence and would fight to get their convictions overturned. Of course, this meant a lengthy interview process to determine if the outlook was promising and worthy of all the volunteered man hours the members of the organization would dedicate to the cause.

Fleet placed a call to "Unity for Freedom" and answered a long list of questions regarding his case and background information about his life prior to his arrest. He was told someone would be contacting him once everything had been reviewed. And that was it—he didn't hear a damn thing for months. Then, he started calling every few weeks and was told his case was still being researched. After a year, he figured nothing was going to come of it and just let it go.

Then, one fateful day, he was summoned to one of the private visitation rooms. He wasn't aware of having anyone scheduled to visit, and he sure wasn't prepared to see a stranger sitting at the sole table in the dingy, gray room. The young woman stood up and held out her hand to him. Fleet quickly took her in, from her shoes to her face, which was framed with shoulder-length, black curly cues. She was dressed in a nice gray skirt, which she filled out nicely. Her waist was small, which accentuated her hourglass figure. She had full breasts that were currently straining against the top buttons of her silk blouse. She pushed her glasses to the top of her head with her other hand. What caught Fleet off guard was that she unabashedly scrutinized him right back from head to toe. She didn't smile as she waited for him to shake her hand. He finally snapped out of it and took her hand. To this day, he cannot explain the jolt that ran through him when their hands touched. Was it excitement, joy, or lust? Hell, it was probably all three, Fleet thought to himself.

"Hello, I'm Meeka Johnson. You're Mr. Fleet Wood, is that correct?" She sat back down and opened a file on the table.

"Uh, yeah, that's me. What's this about?" Fleet sat down across from her and clasped his hands together on the table.

"Well, Mr. Wood, I'm with Unity for Freedom. I am a defense attorney. After extensive research into your case and the evidence presented at your trial, we have concluded that you are an ideal candidate for our services. We will begin the appeal process and have lawyers working pro bono to see this through every step of the way. My job is to get your side of the story while also determining your character."

"Wait, what? Determining my character?" Fleet didn't mean to sound ungrateful and defensive. Meeka's eyes shot up to look at him with raised eyebrows.

"Yes, that's what I said. Do you need me to explain further, sir?" she snapped.

"Hey, lady, I know what you mean. But you have all the information you need in the trial transcripts, and there is a lack of evidence."

Meeka took her glasses off and leaned in ever so slightly. Then she said in a dead-serious voice, "Mr. Wood, I am here on my own time to interview you and make sure you're not full of shit. So, I'm going to ask you questions, and you will answer them honestly. So please, let's not waste any more of my fucking time, and let's get to work. I'm not one to be played with."

She leaned back in her chair, crossed her arms and her legs, and waited for Fleet's agreement. "Holy shit," she was something wonderfully unexpected—and challenging! He didn't know how long they sat there looking at each other, but he finally broke the moment when he smiled and held up his hands in surrender.

"Okay, okay, Mrs. Johnson. My bad!" he chuckled.

"It's Miss Johnson, Mr. Wood," she replied while she leaned forward again and started rifling through the papers in the folder.

"Well, you can call me Fleet."

"You can call me Miss Johnson," she said without missing a beat. That made Fleet smile even more.

That's how it all began. After numerous visits, Meeka finally started to warm up to Fleet. He loved the contradiction that was all Meeka. Yes, she was a professional and could handle her own in any business situation. But damn if she didn't hesitate to cuss you out when she felt like it. She called you out, too, with no hesitation.

The appeal process was long, and it took years before he was finally given a court date. All the hard work that the folks at Unity for Freedom finally paid off, and Fleet would forever be grateful to each and every one of them, especially Meeka.

"Allies in Chains—On Hold"

In the shadowed corridors of power and peril, Fleet and JT Will found themselves ensnared in a dangerous web of obligations and threats. The crux of their predicament was a colossal debt owed to a formidable Russian organization—an affiliation marked by ruthlessness and an ironclad demand for loyalty. Originally, the agreement seemed straightforward: carry out a high-stakes assignment within the confines of a maximum-security prison—eliminate a key figure who posed a threat to their creditor's interests.

In exchange for this perilous task, they were promised not only protection within the prison walls but also a substantial sum of money. This payment was crucial, intended to erase a slew of other debts accrued through a series of ill-fated gambles and disastrous financial decisions. Desperation had driven them to this pact, sealing a deal that promised to wipe their slate clean at a steep and dangerous price, along with a risk that carried with it inevitable consequences.

However, their failure to execute the assignment effectively spiralled into a nightmare. The task was botched, leaving the target alive and the organization furious. The repercussions were immediate and severe. The promised sum of money turned into an additional debt of $200,000—an exorbitant price for their failure, with the ominous stipulation of certain death should they fail to repay.

This misstep was not merely a setback; it was a damning testament to a harsher truth they had long ignored: the choices one makes irrevocably shape the course of one's life. For them, this was not merely a philosophical musing but a concrete reality —a reality that sealed their fate, binding them to a path from which there was no return, underscored by the relentless shadow of their debt and the ever-looming threat of retribution.

In the dismal confines of the state penitentiary, JT Will and Fleet Wood—known inside these walls—shared more than just a cell; they shared a desperate urge for freedom. Time, unyielding and slow, dragged on. JT Will was counting down the days, with just a month left of his five-year sentence for a triad of crimes: fraud, robbery, and attempted murder. Meanwhile, Wood was tangled in a thicker web of legal woes, a seemingly endless ten-year stint as he awaited an appeal that dangled like a mirage on the horizon.

Woods' newfound hope rested in the hands of Meeka Johnson, a brilliant and fiercely dedicated attorney. Over the past year, as she pored over his case, their professional relationship had taken an unexpected turn. Meeka, moved by Fleet's stories and unwavering declarations of innocence, had found herself drawn to the man behind the inmate number. Their conversations, once strictly legal, now whispered of a future on the outside. In a moment of vulnerability, Fleet had asked Meeka to marry him upon his release—a proposal that surprised them both. But for Meeka, who believed in his innocence as if it were her own, the idea was increasingly intriguing.

JT Will, on the other hand, was not romantic. His mind was occupied with more immediate concerns. He and Fleet were under the crushing weight of debts accumulated from gambling and other costly favors within prison walls, along with old debts from their life before bars that refused to be forgotten. The men they owed were not known for their patience or mercy.

As JT Will's release approached, the pressure mounted. Each tick of the clock was a reminder of the debts calling his name and the danger that awaited them both outside. Despite Fleet facing a longer path to freedom, he shared JT Will's urgency. They needed a plan, and they needed it fast.

With a renewed sense of purpose, they returned to their cell. The plans they crafted now had higher stakes—not just freedom, but a life worth living on the outside. Wood's resolve hardened; he would walk out of these gates a free man, bound for a new beginning. As for JT Will, with just a few weeks left, the game was on to clear his path, pay his debts, and avoid the shadows that awaited him beyond the prison walls.

Their alliance, formed in the unlikeliest of places, had grown into a bond that neither the cold steel of the prison nor the looming threats of the outside world could easily break.

In the dim light of their cell, under the constant hum of surveillance cameras, JT, Will, and Wood sat back against the cold, unyielding walls, the weight of their predicament pressing down upon them. The "get-paid" scheme, a desperate gamble they had once thought clever and sure, had spiralled out of their control, entangling them in consequences far graver than had anticipated.

"It's like a nightmare that won't end," JT Will murmured, his voice barely above a whisper as he ran his hands through his hair, a gesture of frustration and despair. "Even if we get out, this mess follows us. It's not just the prison; it's the shit that waits for us outside."

Fleet, his expression set in grim lines, nodded slowly. The stakes of their ill-conceived plan were now painfully clear. Their actions had not only jeopardized their safety within the confines of the prison but had also sown seeds of danger in the outside world. They were marked men, and the shadows of their deeds extended beyond the bars and barbed wire.

"The street doesn't forget, and neither do the guys who got burned by our scam," Fleet added, his tone laden with regret. "Getting out of here is just the first step. We need a plan for after, a way to make things right, or at least protect ourselves from the backlash."

JT Will looked over, his blue eyes meeting Wood's. "Do you think Meek can help with that, too? Maybe she can find some protection and talk to the right people?"

"It's worth asking," Wood replied. He knew Meeka Johnson was their best shot, a beacon of hope in their dark situation. "I'll mention it next time I speak to her. She's connected and knows people who can help us navigate the waters once we're out."

The conversation hung between them, a mix of hope and daunting reality. The prison, with its stark routines and looming threats, was but one aspect of their ordeal. The true challenge would come once the gates opened—navigating a world where their scheme had left a trail of bitterness and revenge.

As the days slowly ticked down, the atmosphere around them grew tenser. Each glance from a fellow inmate carried potential threats; each whispered word was a possible harbinger of violence. Yet, amid this, JT, Will, and Wood continued to meticulously plan, not just for their hoped-for release but for the uncertain and possibly even more dangerous days that would follow.

Amidst this chaos, an unexpected visit from Meeka brought a brief respite. Her presence in the visiting room, always a stark contrast to the drab surroundings, reminded Fleet of the life that awaited him—a life he dared to hope for.

"Everything is moving along with the appeal," Meeka assured him, her hand briefly touching his across the cold metal table. "And about... our conversation last time. I've been thinking about it... Fleet, I'm in—all the way. When you're out, I'm yours—if you'll still have me."

Fleet's heart thudded heavily. Her commitment was a lifeline thrown across the dark waters of his current existence. "Nothing would make me happier," he responded, his voice thick with emotion.

"That's great, baby. I know you got this," said Fleet. "Meeka, we've been thinking. Getting out is one thing, but my cellmate and I have stirred up a lot of bad blood. We took some risks because we wanted to survive here...and something went wrong. "Well, tell me what happened, Fleet, said Meeka. It's best that this stay in here and not get to you. I guess you're right, said Meeka. We need some sort of plan for now and when we're outside, Fleet Spoke. Any help, any advice you can give would really mean a lot."

Meeka's response was thoughtful measured against the reality of their situation. "I understand," she said. "Let me see what I can arrange. There are some people who owe me a favor. But listen, you two need to stay low and avoid making any more waves. I'll work on setting up a safety net for when you get out." "Thank you, baby. I knew I could depend on you."

Relief, tinged with residual fear, washed over Wood as he relayed the conversation to JT Will. They both understood that their road to redemption—or at least to safety—was fraught with obstacles. But with Meeka Johnson on their side, perhaps there was a chance to escape the long shadow of their past actions.

In the prison's relentless cycle of day and night, amidst the echoes of doors clanging and distant shouts, JT, Will, and Fleet clung to the sliver of hope that Meeka's efforts outside would forge them a path to not just freedom but a chance to start anew, away from the mistakes that had so deeply defined their current plight.

"A Girls' Luncheon in Downtown Chicago"

Meeka and Brandy met at their favorite café in downtown Chicago for a much-needed girls' luncheon. The café, nestled between towering skyscrapers, exuded a cozy charm with its exposed brick walls, rustic wooden furniture, and the aroma of freshly brewed coffee. They settled into a corner table by the window, where they could watch the bustling city life outside while enjoying their lunch.

"Life has been so crazy lately," Meeka sighed, stirring her latte absentmindedly.

"Tell me about it," Brandy replied, her eyes scanning the menu. "What's been going on with you?"

Meeka hesitated for a moment before diving in. "Well, I've started seeing someone new. His name is Fleet. He's... currently in prison." Fleet that sounds familiar. Bobby has an old friend named Fleet who went to Jail years ago for killing someone, said Brandy. "Is his name Fleet Wood, asked Meeka. I am not sure; I never really knew him. He and Bobby were close back when Bobby was in college, but he never went to college. Instead, he got caught up and went to jail. Wow, well, I will have to talk to

Bobby about him the next time I see him. Yes, you really should, girl," said Brandy.

Brandy's eyes widened in shock. "Prison? Meeka, are you serious? How did this happen?"

Meeka took a deep breath. "I don't know, Brandy. It just happened. I took his case pro bono for a charity group I work with on the side. As we worked on his case, I found myself falling for him. I know it sounds crazy, but there's something about him."

Brandy put down her menu, her expression turning serious. "Meeka, you really need to be careful. This is not just a bad boy phase. He is in prison. What happens when he gets out? What kind of life can you have with him?"

Meeka shrugged, looking down at her drink. "I don't know. I just... I feel a connection with him, like he understands me."

Brandy sighed. "Just promise me you'll be cautious. I don't want to see you get hurt."

The conversation shifted as they ordered their lunch, the tension lingering but momentarily set aside. They talked about Bobby and his newfound drive to author his novel and eventually produce a movie.

"He's so focused on this project," Brandy said, a mixture of pride and frustration in her voice. "I love that he's enthusiastic, but it's causing some problems."

Meeka raised an eyebrow. "Problems? Like what?"

Brandy hesitated, then lowered her voice. "Our sex life is... struggling. And with all his focus on the novel, our financial situation is starting to become an issue. It's like everything else is taking a backseat."

Meeka nodded sympathetically. "I get that. It's tough when your partner is so engrossed in something. But you guys will figure it out. You always do."

Brandy took a sip of her iced tea. "I hope so. By the way, there's something I need to tell you: I met someone."

Meeka's eyes narrowed, and her posture stiffened. "What? Brandy, you can't be serious. What about Bobby?"

"It's not like that," Brandy said quickly. "We just talked. He's interesting, but I haven't done anything."

"Girl, don't be stupid," Meeka snapped. "Don't put yourself in a compromising position with some smooth-talking guy. Think about what you have with Bobby."

Brandy bristled at Meeka's tone. "And what about you? You are seeing a prisoner, Meeka. How is that any better?"

Their conversation escalated into an argument, voices rising above the café's ambient noise.

"Look," Brandy said finally, her voice softening. "You're my best friend. We will work through this shit, and it will not come between you and me. I love you, girl."

Meeka's expression softened, and she nodded. "I love you too. But you need to be careful, Brandy. I just want what's best for you."

Meeka sighed, leaning back in her chair. "How are you doing with your medications and therapy sessions?" "Why do you always have to go to that every time something new is exposed to you about my life?" said Brandy. "Look, I am stable and feeling good.

Brandy smiled slightly. "It's going fine." "Okay," said Meeka, "but sometimes I feel like there's more going on with you that you're not telling me."

Meeka looked at her friend, a mixture of concern and suspicion in her eyes. "Girl, I've got to go. I have a meeting with a group of people who are asking me to consider running for district attorney next year."

Brandy's eyes widened in surprise. "District Attorney? That is huge, Meeka!" Question? If that is the case and you do decide to run, won't this guy you're dating be a problem? I mean, with his being in prison and all. Brandy..., Fleet is innocent, and that is why I am representing him, Meeka said. It will not be a problem. Ok, girl, I am just asking, Brandy said. I am proud of you, though, girl. And it could not come at a better time cause me and you boy Bobby might need some of that District Attorney's money, Brandy said as she smiled. Well, you know I got you girl. You and Bobby are my heart, and we go back deep.

Meeka smiled, her earlier tension melting away. "Yeah, it is. But it's a big decision. I'll let you know how it goes."

They hugged tightly before parting ways, their bond as strong as ever despite the challenges and disagreements. As Meeka walked away, she could not shake the feeling that Brandy was hiding something. But for now, she had her own path to focus on, one that could change the course of her future.

"Love and a Deceptive Plan"

Fleet sat on the couch, smiling as he reminisced. Just then, the lady herself walked in the front door. She put her briefcase on the bench in the foyer and kicked off her sexy pumps. She threw her jacket over the back of the bench and padded into the living room to sit next to Fleet.

"Hey, baby. I can't tell you how happy I am to be home!" She leaned in and gave Fleet a big, juicy kiss before laying her head on his broad shoulder.

"I'm glad you're home, too. How was work?"

"Oh my gosh, the same shit as always. I get tired of dealing with folks who have no damn business sense. It makes me wanna throat-punch a bitch."

Fleet cracked up and wrapped his arm around her. She leaned her head back to look up at him.

"What'cha been doing all day, baby? Did you look for more jobs? Anything promising?"

"Girl, you know I look online every day for a job. There aren't any construction foreman jobs open right now, at least not any willing to hire a felon, even if I was vindicated and cleared of all charges. I mean, I'm at the point where I'm contemplating entering that Publisher's Clearing House Sweepstakes."

Meeka looked at him sideways with a smirk on her face. "You serious?"

"Then a heart attack," said Fleet as he looked at her with exaggerated, wide eyes.

"Boy, you are crazy," she laughed.

"You know, black folks don't ever win that thing—especially if you don't buy any magazines!"

He laughed with her. "Yeah, but what's the harm in trying? My luck's got to change someday, right? I already filled it out and sealed it up. Can you drop it in the mail tomorrow?"

She pushed herself off the couch and started to go upstairs to change out of her work clothes.

"Yeah, I can do that. I'll put it in my bag, so I don't forget. But there is one thing you can do for me." She stopped at the foot of the stairs and turned to look at him.

Fleet stands up and walks toward her with a hungry look in his eyes. "Baby, you know I've got what you want," he said as he licked his lips and eyed her up and down.

"Sir, I don't need any of that," Meeka said, laughing and putting a hand on his chest in a weak attempt to keep him away. "Well, not right now, anyway." She leaned forward and kissed him teasingly on the lips.

"I was thinking that maybe we could go out to dinner on the pier in downtown Chicago." She placed her other hand on his chest and looked up at him through her thick lashes. She took his breath away when she looked at him like that, all sexy and shit. He put his hands on her hips.

"You know, just the two of us. Have a wonderful meal and maybe a glass of wine." She ran her long fingernails down his chest towards his waist and then along his strong forearms.

"Then maybe... well, you know... maybe you can pop the question and ask me to marry you." She snuck a look up at him, waiting for his reaction, holding her breath and slightly trembling with hope and possibility.

Fleet's chin dropped to his chest while he tried to come up with a response that wouldn't hurt her feelings but would also convey how much he loved her.

"Now you know we've talked about this before, right?" he said somberly.

"Talk about what?" Meeka asked innocently.

A half-smile appeared on Fleet's face. He slightly shook his head as he replied, "About getting married."

Meeka let out a quiet sigh. "Baby, all I'm asking from you is a little reassurance that this thing we have is going somewhere."

"Meeka, I've been with you for five years now." She cut him off.

"And that's five reasons why we need to do something different. What are we waiting for?"

He pulled her close and wrapped his arms around her. He loved the feel of her full figure against his body. She was all soft curves.

"Listen to me. There's no other woman in the world for me—well, except maybe Halle Berry." He smiled down at her.

Meeka playfully slapped his chest. "Why are you playing with me?"

He threw his head back and laughed. But when he looked at her face again, the smile disappeared, and his gaze was intense and serious.

"There's no other woman in the world I'd rather be with than you. No one I want to spend my life with other than you. Have you ever wondered why I love you?"

"Why do you love me?" she asked softly.

"I love you because of the simplicity of who you are. I love you because I find no fault in the things that make you imperfect. To me, what's imperfect in you brings perfection to who we are together. I love you because you believe so much in an imperfect me. I love you because in your presence, I can walk through failure. I look to my side and see you right there telling me, 'This too shall come to pass.' I love you because as long as I dream with the passion and belief that I can make it happen, instead of you telling me that I'm crazy, I can look into your eyes, and without you saying a word, I hear your spirit say to me, 'No matter what it is, I got your back.'

"I love you because you're the mate of my soul, the joy in my laughter, and the hope in my tomorrow. I love you because you encourage my fight and push me through the struggles that sometimes make me want to quit. I love you because you place a great demand on me to maintain my strength as a man, but at the same time, you understand my weakness. Everything you are to me. To me, you're my everything."

She leaned against him and laid her cheek on his chest. "You always know what to say," she said.

She pulled away and started walking up the stairs. She looked back at him and paused.

"What's wrong, baby?" Fleet asked with concern.

"You said all those pretty words, but..." She hesitated, a worried look on her face.

"But what?" Fleet started walking toward her.

"Yo, ass still didn't answer my question about why we're waiting to get married." Then, a huge smile spread across her face.

"Girl! I'm about to get your ass," he said as he ran towards her. Meeka shrieked in surprise as she turned to run up the stairs, laughing. Fleet reached out and managed to slap her on her backside. Meeka shrieked again, with Fleet hot on her trail. When she reached the bedroom, she flung herself across the bed and turned on her back. Fleet was right there, smiling from ear to ear.

"I like the way you look on that bed, girl!" He put a knee

between her slightly sprawled legs and bent over her, placing his hands on either side of her head.

"You know I'm going to make an honest woman out of you, right? There's nothing I want more. I just need to get on my feet financially. Once I do that, I'll give you the world," he said as he looked earnestly into her eyes.

"Baby, I don't need the world. I just need you in my world… and maybe some of this, too," she said as she reached out to caress his manhood through his jeans. Oh, he was ready for her. She smiled up at him as he leaned down to kiss her. It was one of the best afternoons Meeka had had in a long time.

Christina knocked on their door the next morning just as they finished breakfast. Meeka let her in and gave her a sincere hug. "Hey, girl, what'cha doing here so early?"

"Oh, I'm sorry! I should have called first. Did I interrupt something?" Christina said, embarrassed.

"Naw, girl, you're fine," Fleet said as he stood up from the table. He picked up his plate and glass and put them in the sink.

"Baby, I gotta go. I'm meeting with some buddies of mine to talk about a project we want to start. If it comes together like we think it will, I might be my own boss… sort of." He leaned down to give her a peck on the cheek.

He strode out the door with keys in hand. "Baby, don't forget to mail that thing out for me," he called over his shoulder.

"I got you, don't worry," Meeka responded before he closed the door behind him.

"Do you want some coffee?" she asked Christina.

"Oh, yes, please," Christina said. Meeka took a closer look at her.

"Girl, what's going on?"

"Oh, nothing. I just had trouble sleeping last night. My mind was all over the place. You know how you think about one thing, and then you think, 'But if this happens, then that will happen, and then what do I do now?' Now I'm not sure I did the right thing."

Meeka placed a cup of coffee in front of Christina, along with a spoon for her sugar and cream. She turned, poured herself a cup, and sat down across from her.

"What did you do?" Meeka asked with concern. This didn't sound good.

"It's nothing bad, really. I just don't know how to tell the family about it."

"Girl, are you going to tell me what you did? You got my stomach in knots," Meeka said, exasperated.

Christina laughed, "Okay, okay!" She spread her arms out across the table in front of her, with her shoulders hitched up to her ears, rocking back and forth.

"Girl, you better get on with it," Meeka said.

"Alright! Geez!" Christina clasped her hands together in front of her and tried to relax her shoulders. She took a deep breath and looked at Meeka.

"I auditioned for an off-Broadway play last week," she squeezed her eyes shut, waiting for Meeka's reaction. None came. She peeked through one eye, and Meeka sat there looking at her like, "Yeah, and what?"

She opened her other eye. "Did you hear what I just said?" she asked Meeka, who was looking at her sideways with wide eyes.

Meeka fanned her hand back and forth at Christina. "...AND? What, did you go down on the director or something? What?"

"Oh my gosh, Meeka! No! I did not... do what you just said!" She could feel her face getting hot.

"SOOO, what's the big deal, then?"

"Well, that in and of itself is not the issue. But after I auditioned, someone from the production mentioned that they recently lost the actress who had the part I auditioned for. Then he told me that it was Brandy! She backed out at the last minute, saying it was due to personal reasons!"

"Wait, what? Has she said anything about that to you or Bobby?" Meeka asked.

"She hasn't said a word to me about it. I haven't really talked to Bobby much with all the drama between him and Brandy lately, so I don't know if he knows."

"So, what the hell is going on between them, anyway?"

"You don't know? Girl, Brandy is beside herself because Bobby walked away from his job so he can work on his novel and get it published. You know Brandy; she likes the finer things in life. She doesn't understand why he would do something like that."

"Ooh, girl, I know she must be pissed!" Meeka said.

"That's an understatement! I mean, I can kind of see her point, though." "You get accustomed to a certain lifestyle." "I mean, Bobby made it very comfortable for her while she pursued her acting career." "But then, to see how important writing this book is to Bobby, it gives you pause for thought." "He is so determined to make this happen." "Honestly, "He's kind of the reason I decided to audition for this play." "To believe in something so much and have that burning desire—how beautiful and inspirational that is!" It made me realize how much I miss singing in front of others. When my grandmother died, my passion for singing died, too. But seeing Bobby fearlessly chase his dream and take the risk of leaving everything behind to do it sparked something in me. I want that in my life. "When I saw they were holding open auditions, I went down there before I could change my mind. I think it went pretty well, but I haven't heard anything back from them."

"Girl, that's great! You know nothing will change until you decide to do something different. I'm sure they'll be calling you back. But I don't get why you're worried, though."

"It's dumb, really," Christina paused to gather her thoughts.

"I just don't want Brandy to be mad at me for trying out for her part. It's like I'm infringing on her territory, you know?"

Meeka looked at her like she was crazy before she pointed a finger at her, saying, "Now you know Bandy is my best friend and all, but she is the one who walked away from that part." "Brandy is the one who is keeping all that a secret." "And even if she had told her, so what?" "Just because she held the part before, does that mean it's off-limits to you forever?" "Hell naw!" "You do you because I'll betcha she wouldn't hesitate if the shoe was on the other foot!" "Don't you feel bad about that at all!" Hell, secretly, Brandy really admires you and loves you. You're her sister, and I think, ,at some point, she'll be really happy for you. Meek's mind escaped to the time when Brandy told her about Christina and how she felt. The cozy living room was filled with laughter and the sweet aroma of freshly brewed coffee. Brandy, with her infectious energy, was animatedly recounting stories from her latest performance to Meeka. The two had been inseparable since their college days, sharing the highs and lows of life. No one knew Brandy better than Meeka did.

As they sipped their coffee, the conversation shifted to family, and Brandy couldn't help but bring up her sister, Christina. She reminisced about the day she introduced Christina to Meeka, a day that marked the beginning of another significant bond.

Meeka, with a warm smile, interjected, "I remember that day like it was yesterday, Brand. You were so excited for us to meet, and it didn't take long for Christina and me to hit it off. Little did we know we'd become good friends, too."

The room echoed with laughter and shared memories as they delved into stories about Christina's quirks, Brandy's competitive streak, and the dynamic between the two sisters. Meeka, having witnessed their ups and downs, understood the underlying currents in their relationship.

"You know, Meek," Brandy confessed, her tone slightly more serious, "Christina and I have had our fair share of competitiveness. But it's not about who's better; it's about something deeper. It's rooted in insecurities and past experiences that I've been carrying."

Meeka nodded understandingly, having glimpsed the complexity of their sisterly bond. "Brandy, you've got to let those insecurities go. Christina is family, and I've seen the genuine love you both share underneath it all. Embrace her as your sister, not just a competitor. It's time to support each other rather than compete."

Brandy's gaze softened as she absorbed Meeka's words. "You're right, Meek. I want the best for Christina, and I appreciate you embracing her as a sister. I need to do the same."

As they continued their heart-to-heart conversation, the bond between Brandy, Meeka, and Christina grew stronger. In that moment, surrounded by friendship and understanding, they found a path toward fostering a healthier, more supportive relationship as sisters.

"Yes, you're right, I know. But Brandy has always been the one at the forefront when it comes to us. It feels a little wrong to try and step out of her shadow."

"Uh-uh, nope!" Meeka was vigorously shaking her head, her hoop earrings swinging back and forth. "You stop that right now. You deserve happiness and success just as much as she does. Don't apologize for creating your own happiness, Christina. Let Brandy do Brandy. You just do you!"

Christina smiled at her friend. She loved Meeka. They hit it off the minute her sister introduced her to the family.

"Yeah, okay. I'm letting that stress go—for now. But I still wonder why Brandy just walked away. I mean, I know she and Bobby are going through some changes, but why quit now? Especially after Bobby left his job. It doesn't make any sense."

"Your sister is crazy, that's why!" Meeka laughed as she stood up.

"Are you hungry? I can make you some eggs and toast if you like."

"No, I'm good. But I would like more coffee if you have any," Christina replied.

Meeka poured her another cup, and they sat, talked, and laughed for a couple more hours. It was exactly what Christina needed.

"Family Matters"

Christina was enjoying a quiet Friday evening at home. She still hadn't heard back from the production regarding her audition. She tried to keep herself busy so as not to dwell on what their decision might be. Music was streaming from the Bluetooth speaker she had connected to her cell phone while she swept the floors of her two-bedroom home. It was quite relaxing to sing along while she cleaned. The music engulfed her and caressed her soul with rhythm and emotion. Occasionally, she would stop what she was doing to close her eyes and sing along to the song. She always felt silly when she realized she had done that; she laughed at herself.

Suddenly, the music stopped when her cell phone rang. She walked over to the phone and turned off the Bluetooth connection before answering.

"Hello," she said as she sat on the edge of the sofa.

"Hey, Christina, this is Bobby. How are you doing?"

Christina was surprised to hear Bobby's voice, and it took her a few seconds to gather her thoughts and respond.

"Oh, hey, Bobby! This is a surprise. I am doing good," her voice trailed off, not knowing what else to say.

"Uh, well, I was calling to see if you had some time to meet with me. I'm in a bind and was hoping you would be willing to help me... ... me and Brandy."

"Oh, sure, y'all can come over; I don't have anything going on today." Christina looked around her house to make sure it was acceptable for a visitor. It's not close to being as fancy as Bobby and Brandy's house, but it was nice, comfy, and clean.

"Well, Brandy isn't coming with me. As a matter of fact, she doesn't know I'm calling you. I want to talk to you first before I say anything to her."

Christina hesitated, worried about how Brandy would react to her husband coming to her house by himself, but also about how she was going to react to whatever Bobby planned to tell her. She started to get an uneasy feeling in her stomach.

"Hello? Are you still there, Christina?"

"Yes—yes, I'm here. Sorry, I got lost in thought. Sure, you can stop by. What time were you thinking?"

"Oh, that's great! I can be there in 20 minutes! See you soon!" Bobby hung up before Christina could respond.

"Twenty minutes!" She turned and looked at herself in the mirror hanging over her fireplace. She pulled the scarf off her head. Christina was a portrait of internal beauty, carrying herself with an understated grace that often went unnoticed. Internally radiant, her allure was eclipsed by a tendency to downplay her own appearance and grapple with self-insecurities. Yet, beneath the veil of modesty, she was a stunning young woman.

Her long, naturally curly hair cascaded down her shoulders, a testament to her mixed heritage—her mother being half Native American. Her skin, nearly flawlessly toned and smooth, revealed the unique blend of her ancestry. Christina possessed a naturally sexy shape and body, though it often remained concealed by her choice of attire. She had a penchant for dressing as if she were in the comfort of her own home, a deliberate effort to deflect attention.

However, when Christina allowed herself even the slightest attention, a transformative beauty emerged. With a touch of self-care, she became an astonishingly beautiful girl, radiating a captivating charm that drew admiration. Her internal beauty and external allure, when unveiled, created a harmonious blend that showcased the depth and richness of Christina's true essence.

"Oh my gosh! I look crazy," she said to herself. She ran toward the back of her one-story house, where the bedrooms and the bathroom were. She grabbed a pair of clean jeans and an oversized T-shirt to change into. She went to the bathroom,quickly brushed her wavy brown hair, and then washed her face. She contemplated putting on some makeup but decided against it. She walked out of the bathroom but changed her mind and went back to the bathroom. Maybe just a little mascara. She scrambled through her makeup basket, which didn't hold very much makeup. She used just enough to accentuate her features. After she put on the mascara, she turned to walk away but decided that maybe she needed some lipstick. She applied a light layer of a brown-bronze color to her lips. She decided a little bit of powder probably wouldn't hurt either.

As she walked to the living room, she asked herself why she felt the need to look nice for Bobby. He's her brother-in-law. Brandy loves him; he loves her. What ,was this weird feeling she was getting in the pit of her stomach? Was it... excitement fluttering around in there? If she were completely honest with herself, she would admit that a tiny part of her was a bit happy that Brandy wasn't coming with him. If she allowed her mind to go down that path, she would also have to admit that being around Bobby stirred something inside her. But she didn't allow herself to look too closely at what was running through her mind; she buried that deep inside.

A few minutes later, Bobby knocked on her door. She ran her hands over her clothes nervously and then over her hair. She took a deep breath and opened the door. Bobby was standing there, looking so handsome in his short-sleeve button-up shirt and jeans. He flashed a smile at her and then leaned in to give her a hug.

"Hey, Christina. I'm so thankful you had time to talk to me today," he said by her ear as he gave her a quick squeeze. She pulled away from him and invited him to have a seat.

"Do you want some coffee or some water?" she asked.

"No, no, thank you," Bobby said. He sat in the armchair while Christina sat on the sofa.

"So, what's this about, Bobby? And where is Brandy?"

Bobby sighed heavily as he rested his elbows on his knees, his eyes on the floor. After what seemed like an eternity, he finally looked up at Christina.

"Honestly, I don't know where Brandy went off to. She's been in and out of the house a lot lately. It must have something to do with the theater. She's not really talking to me right now."

"She hasn't said much to me, either. I haven't talked to her for a few days," Christina said.

"You know I'm trying to get my novel published," he said.

"Yes, I think it's great! I'm sure it will be a big success," she replied sincerely.

"Yeah, that makes just two of us feel that way. Brandy is very angry with me right now, and I can't say that I blame her. But deep in my heart, I feel that this is what I'm supposed to be doing right now. I have to see this through, ya know?"

Bobby's eyes were bright with passion and excitement. She could feel the determination, the certainty, radiating from him. It was contagious. She couldn't help but smile at him.

"Bobby, I hope you know how inspiring you are. To be so sure about something and pursue a dream regardless of the obstacles you face—well, that right there is simply amazing!"

Bobby reached out and grasped her wrist.

"You don't know what it means to me. I wish everyone felt the same way," he said sadly.

"Brandy will come around, I'm sure of it," Christina replied.

She really believed what she was saying. She understood Brandy's current attitude. The change to Bobby and Brandy's lifestyle was huge. Of course, it took her by surprise. But she must see how important this is to Bobby. She must see how his whole face lights up when he talks about his book. How can she not be excited for him...for both of them? Yes, change can be very scary, but you either roll with it or let it steal your happiness. It may take Brandy a minute to work through her feelings, but Christina believed she would stand by Bobby and support him in his dream.

"Well, the reason I'm here is to ask you a huge favor. It might just make Brandy madder than she already is." Worry creased his brow as he looked at Christina.

"You know I'll help any way I can, Bobby. We're family!"

"Did you hear about Brandy's car being repossessed?"

"Who hasn't heard about it?" Christina said, shaking her head from side to side with displeasure.

"Yeah, well, it's about to get worse," he hesitated. Bobby, despite amassing a considerable fortune and making strategic investments, faced an underlying issue: Brandy's desire to live beyond their actual means. While Bobby never vocalized his concerns, he went along with Brandy's aspirations for a lifestyle that outpaced their true wealth. The financial faucet, primarily fueled by Bobby's job, once flowed abundantly. However, when that source of income ceased, the inflow no longer matched the extravagant outflow.

Their expenditures, fueled by a desire to live lavishly, proved unsustainable over an extended period. The racial disparity between incoming funds and outgoing expenses became stark. Although Bobby dipped into the profits from his investments to maintain their lifestyle, it soon became apparent that it was not enough to bridge the growing gap.

As the financial strain intensified, Bobby found himself

caught in a delicate balance, juggling the expectations of the life-style they had embraced with the harsh reality of diminishing resources. The investments that once seemed like a safety net were now being tapped into more urgently. The looming question was whether they could recalibrate their spending habits to align with their actual financial standing or if the discrepancy between their aspirations and their true wealth would lead to deeper challenges ahead.

"I got a call this morning from our mortgage company. We've lost the condo. We have sixty days to get out. I have not told Brandy yet. But I'm hoping that maybe—if you're willing—the shock won't be so bad if she knew we had somewhere to go, temporarily, of course," he looked at Christina expectantly.

It took a minute for it to register what he was saying. Christina's eyes grew wide with surprise.

"Are you asking me if y'all can stay here?"

Bobby started talking fast. "It will not be for a long time. Just until I can get my book published, and my agent said that she's received some positive responses from a few publishers. I still have some money saved, and we will probably have to sell some furniture and some of the art we've collected over the years so I can pay you rent while we're here. We'll stay out of your way as much as possible and help around the house, I promise!"

He sat there looking at her with so much hope that she would say yes. How could she say no to this man? And it would be to help her sister; at least, that's what she wanted to believe.

"I suppose you can stay in the extra bedroom. It's not very bi...." Bobby cut her off before she could finish. He jumped up and pulled her to her feet, and tightly wrapped his arms around her.

"Oh, my gosh," he said to the side of her head. "You don't know how much this means to me. I think it will help Brandy a lot, knowing she has her sister's support. It's not going to be easy breaking the news to her, but I've got to believe we'll be all right." He sounded like he was on the verge of crying with relief.

Christina was filled with the warmth of happiness, knowing that she was able to relieve some of the stress he was feeling. She squeezed him back and noticed how good he smelled. That brought her back to her senses, and for a quick second, she was filled with guilt. She pulled away from Bobby. She couldn't look him in the eye for fear he might see something there that he didn't need to see.

What is happening here? Why is she getting these feelings for her sister's husband? First, she auditions for Brandy's vacated position in the play, and now she is catching feelings for her husband. What kind of person is she? All these questions raced through her mind so quickly that they almost didn't register.

The quietness caught her attention. She looked up at Bobby, wondering why he had suddenly become so quiet. She found him looking intently at her. He slightly took her breath away. Being this close to Christina, Bobby was able to see a light sprinkling of freckles scattered across the apples of her cheeks and across the bridge of her nose. They were so light they were barely noticeable. But now that he saw them, he thought they were cute. That realization made him want to look at her even more closely.

While they were no longer embracing, they were close enough to each other to realize they were in each other's personal space. They made eye contact, and some unspoken emotion passed between them. The longer they stood there, the more inappropriate it felt. Yet they both knew that the other didn't want to move away. A quiet wave of temptation wove its way through their minds and bodies. Christina was the first to break the spell that had come over them.

"Ummm, well..." she stammered awkwardly, her eyes darting everywhere but at Bobby. "Would you like some coffee or something?"

"No, no, I'm good. I better get back to the condo and wait for Brandy. I better think about how I'm going to break the news to her. I'm not gonna lie, Christina; I'm a little scared about how she's going to react."

Instinctively, she reached out and laid a hand on his arm. "It's all going to work out, Bobby. I just know it will, and I will do whatever I can to help you guys."

There it was again. That electric feeling between them. Bobby put his hand over Christina's hand.

"You don't know how much that means to me." He rubbed his thumb lightly over her hand before turning away toward the door. Before walking out, he paused and turned to look at her. He gave her a smile laced with what seemed like a tiny bit of sadness.

"Shadows of Revelation"

Downtown Chicago sprawled around Bobby, its skyscrapers reaching toward the heavens like modern-day monoliths. Within this urban jungle, Bobby found himself nestled in the comforting ambiance of a local coffee shop, a sanctuary he and Brandy frequented, where the aroma of freshly brewed coffee intertwined with the hum of conversations.

As he sat alone at their usual spot, Bobby's mind danced between the lines of his novel outline and the recent rift between him and Brandy. He couldn't shake the image of her upset face, the memory of their last conversation lingering like a stubborn shadow. The familiarity of the coffee shop only intensified his longing for her presence, for the ease of their conversations and shared moments of people-watching.

Bobby's gaze drifted to the window, where the city's pulse thrummed outside. He watched the rhythm of pedestrians navigating the streets, their movements a silent ballet of everyday life. Each passerby held a story, a fragment of existence waiting to be unraveled, and Bobby, ever the observer, absorbed it all, his writer's mind turning over possibilities.

As he observed the ebb and flow of people on the street, Bobby's imagination kicked into gear. A woman hurried by, her coat billowing behind her in the brisk wind, her expression tense with worry. Who was she? What was her story? Perhaps she was a protagonist fleeing from something ominous in his novel.

Next, a group of teenagers laughed and chatted as they passed by, their backpacks slung over their shoulders. Bobby pondered whether they could be side characters, adding depth and flavor to his fictional world.

A street performer caught Bobby's attention with his lively guitar playing, drawing a crowd with his infectious energy. Could this musician inspire a subplot, a tale of dreams pursued against all odds?

Lost in contemplation, Bobby was jolted back to reality by the shrill ring of his phone, a sudden intrusion on his thoughts. His heart quickened with hope, a silent prayer that it might be Brandy reaching out to mend their fractured bond. But as he glanced at the caller ID, disappointment washed over him like a cold wave. It wasn't Brandy; it was Fleet, his friend, sounding agitated and desperate for conversation.

Reluctantly, Bobby answered the call, his mind still tethered to the thoughts of Brandy. Yet, as Fleet poured out his troubles, Bobby's empathy stirred within him, pushing aside his own concerns momentarily. He listened intently, offering words of comfort and solidarity, the bond of friendship weaving its threads through the airwaves.

Despite the interruption, Bobby's mind continued to churn with ideas, his surroundings providing a rich tapestry of inspiration. As he hung up the phone, a resolve ignited within him—a determination to mend not only his fractured friendship but also the narrative of his novel, one observation at a time.

"Listen, Fleet, I know things have been tough for you. I mean, you got home not too long ago from being incarcerated. But you are really in a good place with Meeka. That woman is something special, and if you do right by her, she will help you achieve the dreams you have, without question."

"Fleet, I really need to run something by you. I don't really believe there's anyone I want to share what's going on with me but you. Is it possible for you to come to the café and talk with me for a little bit? It is really important, and I think we can have a conversation that will help each other with whatever we are dealing with. Can you meet me downtown on Michigan Street?"

"Yeah, man, are you okay?"

No, I really need to run something by you; it is really important.

Fleet arrives at the café where Bobby is waiting.

"Hey, my brother, what's going on with you?"

Look, I need to make some decisions about my life and my future.

"What kind of decision, Bobby?"

Decisions about my job and the pursuit of my real dreams.

"Look, Bobby, you have been one of the most solid brothers I have ever known. You're always on top of things, and you're always in control of most, if not everything, that you have had to deal with. But today, man, you look really shaken. What's really going on?"

"Listen, I left my job."

"What? Are you crazy, man?"

See, that's not what I need from you right now. I'm sorry, but I am a little bit shocked. You do very well at that job and make a lot of money. Hell, I only wish I was in a position like that.

"Look, man, you're the only one I trust to give me some solid advice and to help me navigate through this. I left my job for a lot of reasons, but mainly because I need to pursue my true dream."

"Okay, well, what is that?"

"Okay, hear me out before you judge me. I want to be a

writer. I have been writing for some time now, and I want to devote my time and energy to the fulfillment of that dream."

"Fleet, so help me with this. Are you willing to take the risks of losing everything to pursue something that you are not even sure will be able to put food on your table?"

"Yes, I am, and I believe that I have the talent to make this even more lucrative than what I have been doing. You have heard of Tyler Perry, right? Yeah, man, but that brother is an exception. Look, corporate America is not for me anymore. There is no winning in that. It's just a game that always leads you down a road to stress and disappointment."

"Fleet, bro, how is making over $250,000 a year a disappointment?"

"Bobby said, look, Fleet, I can't do this anymore. Let me tell you something else. A while ago, I did a push on behalf of the company. They were pressing me to push this stock. I really didn't want to do it because I knew it was going to just take my clients' money. Money that these people had worked hard for. However, the company was slated to get a large kickback for pushing the stock. So, against my better judgment, I went along with it. As a result of that, I had people take some very bad hits, and some lost everything, particularly this one brother I was dealing with."

Well, how much did he lose?

"About 1 million dollars—everything, I believe he had."

"Look, man, that's not your fault; people take risks every day, and the decision is their own."

"I know, I know. I tried to tell him and the others that, but they didn't listen. Anyway, they lost, and I was given some of the kickback under the table to the sum of about $1.5 million."

What? Did you say "1.5 million

"Yes, that's right. Okay, now I see what you mean. I knew it; you always have a plan. Hell, if that's the case, go ahead and do your writing. Since you know about investing, you can turn that into a whole lot of money."

No, you don't understand. I vowed that I would never use that money unless it were absolutely necessary, so I put it away in a safe spot so nobody could get to it.

"Look, man, I am trusting you to never tell anybody about this. The company made me sign a waiver to never divulge the fact that I got it. In fact, they sold it to me as a Christmas bonus. Again, Brandy, Christina, or Meeka can't know anything about this... you got that, Fleet...?"

"Yeah... man, I got it. So, what are you going to do next?"

"Look, Fleet, the guy who lost the money, his name was Jay something. I can't really remember. But what I do remember is that he had hazel eyes that were really wicked."

As Bobby recounts the events, a heavy atmosphere settles in the café, dimming the lights as if to reflect the weight of the secrets shared. The clatter of coffee cups and distant chatter form a haunting backdrop to Bobby's revelation, casting a pall over the once-lively atmosphere. Fleet, now leaning in, listens with a mix of disbelief and concern, his eyes reflecting the gravity of the situation. The room becomes a theater of emotions, each word echoing with the consequences of decisions made and the burdens carried.

As the weight of Bobby's revelation settled in the room, Fleet's reaction spoke volumes. It wasn't just a casual reception of information; there was a discernible intensity in the way Fleet absorbed the news. His eyes, normally steady, now flickered with a calculating and suspicious gleam as if the gravity of the moment transcended the words being spoken. It was as though he perceived a deeper layer to the situation, something far beyond the immediate events unfolding before him. The air thickened with tension, each second passing feeling like a carefully measured beat in a suspenseful symphony. Fleet's response seemed to suggest that this moment carried implications that reached into the shadows of something more profound than what was openly revealed.

Bobby's revelation of his hidden bonus from his previous company did something to Fleet. As they sat in the dimly lit café, Bobby casually mentioned the windfall he had kept secret, thinking it was just an interesting anecdote. But for Fleet, it was a trigger. Bobby didn't know it, but his words set Fleet's wheels turning once again.

Fleet tried to suppress it and focus on the positive path he was on with Meeka. She had been his rock, supporting him through thick and thin, helping him believe in a future that didn't involve the mistakes of his past. But that inner voice, the one that had guided him through his darker days, began to speak to him again. It whispered insidiously, reminding him of the quick wins and easy money that had once been his reality.

In the past, whenever that voice spoke, Fleet would follow its lead, and while he would initially prevail, he ultimately suffered the consequences. It was a vicious cycle that he had been trying so hard to break. He remembered the feeling of invincibility, the rush of adrenaline when things went his way, and the inevitable crash that followed. Each time, it cost him more than he could afford to lose.

Fleet's mind raced as Bobby continued to talk, oblivious to the turmoil he had sparked. The idea of easy money was tempting, especially with the financial pressures he and Meeka were facing. But he knew where that path led, and he didn't want to go back there—not now when things were finally starting to look up.

"Hey, you still with me?" Bobby's voice cut through his thoughts, bringing him back to the present.

Fleet forced a smile. "Yeah, just thinking about what you said. That's a nice chunk of change you've got there."

Bobby laughed, unaware of the internal battle Fleet was fighting. "Yeah, it was. It came at a good time, too."

Fleet nodded, trying to push the thoughts away. He had promised Meeka he would do better, be better. And he wanted to keep that promise more than anything. But the struggle was real, and he knew he couldn't face it alone.

As they finished their coffee and parted ways, Fleet made a decision. He needed to talk to someone, and there was only one person who understood him well enough to help him sort through this.

"The Impacts of Change"

Brandy arrived at the oncologist's office and signed in. She took a seat facing the low-volume TV set up in the waiting room. She looked around at the three other people waiting, then picked up a magazine and started quickly flicking through the pages. She still hadn't told anyone about her diagnosis. She wanted to find out what her options were for treatment before saying anything. But most of all, she was hoping that maybe they had misdiagnosed her or that the situation wasn't as severe as the doctor initially announced. Brandy hesitated for a moment, staring at the paper gown in her hands. The cool, sterile air of the examination room seemed to intensify the gravity of the situation. She could feel the weight of the unknown pressing down on her shoulders. Slowly, she began to undress, her mind a whirlwind of thoughts and fears.

As she carefully donned the flimsy gown with the opening in the front, the vulnerability of her situation enveloped her. The hospital-issue attire, usually a symbol of routine medical procedures, felt like an emblem of her newfound fragility. She removed her top and bra, exposing herself to the stark reality of the examination that awaited her.

The nurse's instructions echoed in her mind, urging her to leave her pants, underwear, and shoes on. It was a small act of defiance, an attempt to retain some semblance of control amidst the uncertainty. The cold, metallic table beneath her held a discomfort that mirrored the unease in her heart.

As Brandy settled onto the examining table, the silence in the room was deafening. The low hum of medical equipment served as an ominous backdrop to her racing thoughts. She couldn't escape the persistent question that lingered in the recesses of her mind—what if the doctor confirmed the worst?

A gentle knock on the door interrupted her contemplation, and the doctor entered, a mixture of empathy and profession-alism etched across their face. Brandy's gaze shifted to the white coat, a symbol of expertise and authority. The doctor began the examination, and their movements were deliberate and thorough.

The minutes felt like an eternity as Brandy's mind oscillated between hope and dread. She yearned for the doctor to say some-thing reassuring, to dispel the shadows of uncertainty that loomed over her. The room became a battleground of conflicting emotions, the sterile environment contrasting sharply with the emotional turbulence within her.

The doctor, after completing the examination, spoke in measured tones, detailing the next steps. Brandy listened intently, absorbing every word with a mix of apprehension and determination. As the doctor left the room, leaving her to ponder the impending revelations, Brandy found herself at the precipice of an overwhelming journey—one that demanded resilience, courage, and an unwavering pursuit of hope in the face of adversity.

Yet ,at this moment, internal and external battles converged, propelling Brandy toward a place she had vehemently vowed never to revisit—the haunting prison of her past. Echoes of Sylvia, her mother, resounded in the recesses of her mind, beckoning her toward a semblance of solace through familiar, destructive paths.

It was a tug-of-war within her soul, a struggle against the gravitational pull of coping mechanisms she had sworn off. Sylvia, in times of adversity, sought refuge in substances that would transport her mind to distant orbits, muffling the deafening storms surrounding her. The legacy of that painful heritage cast its shadow upon Brandy's present, testing her resilience against the allure of old vices.

The siren call of a familiar escape route echoed in her ears—a call to the wrong answer that carried the weight of risks far exceeding the challenges she currently faced. The taste of impending absorption lingered on the edge of her senses, the substance's allure tempting her like a forbidden fruit.

In the confines of a bathroom stall, Brandy grappled with the convincing whispers, the haunting sound of relief promising to be the antidote to her pain. The struggle played out in the seclusion of that small space, where the walls seemed to close in with each heartbeat.

"No, no, I won't do it, Mama. Not again," Brandy vehemently declared, her shouting an act of defiance against the ghostly echoes of her past. The internal battle raged on; Brandy's resolve was being tested as she sought refuge in the sanctuary of the bathroom, a symbolic battlefield where her strength clashed with the shadows threatening to engulf her.

Memories flooded back, vivid and haunting. As a little girl, she had watched Silvia and Carl prepping their drugs. The moment the substance was lit with the lighter, her small nostrils would fill with the eerie, acrid smell. It was a scent that had lingered in the corners of her mind, waiting to resurface in moments of weakness. Now, standing in the bathroom, she could almost smell it again, as if it were calling her name, whispering promises of escape and numbness.

The drugs tried to convince her conscience that they were

the only symbol of relief from the uncertainty of her diagnosis and the impending destruction of the perfect life she had built with Bobby. The weight of the recent news about her health pressed down on her, threatening to shatter the fragile balance she had worked so hard to maintain.

But Brandy was not the same helpless child she once was. She had fought too long and too hard to let the past dictate her future. The mirror reflected a woman torn between the seductive call of old habits and the fierce desire to forge a new path. She gripped the edge of the sink, knuckles white, grounding herself in the present.

Her mind flashed to Meeka, her unwavering friend, always there with tough love and endless support. Meeka had her own battles, yet she stood strong. Brandy knew she had to be strong, too, for herself and Bobby. They were facing their own challenges, but giving in now would only add to their burdens.

Brandy took a deep breath, forcing herself to focus on the positives and the reasons to fight: Bobby's determination to write his novel and produce a movie someday, their shared dreams, and their love. She couldn't let her past mistakes or the fear of the future destroy what they had.

"No, I won't," she whispered fiercely to her reflection. The bathroom, her battleground, became her sanctuary. She straightened up, wiping away a tear that had slipped down her cheek. With a final, resolute glance in the mirror, she turned and walked out, ready to face the world and her demons head-on.

As she rejoined Bobby in the living room, she felt a renewed sense of purpose. She would fight for their future, no matter how uncertain. And with Meeka by her side, she knew she could overcome the shadows of her past. She reached into her purse, grabbed her meds, and placed one of the pills in her mouth. She then, with her palm, placed it under the running water and grabbed enough to swallow the pill. This time would not be the one she gave in to the pull of the horrors of her past.

"Chase Me While I'm Down"

Brandy sat crying in one of the stalls at a small café not far from the doctor's office. She couldn't face Bobby right now, but she didn't want to be alone, either. She thought about calling Christina but decided against it. She just didn't want to face her family at all right now. It would make it all too real once she announced that she had cancer. She didn't want to deal with this; it was just too much!

She looked in her bag to pull out her makeup bag, which only held the essentials: face powder, lipstick, eyeliner, and the eyeshadow she used to outline her bottom lash line. She pulled herself together and walked out of the stall. She placed her items on the counter and looked at herself in the mirror. She looked perfectly healthy. No one would be able to tell that she had stage 2 breast cancer. The doctor sounded optimistic about the outcome, but even after all the treatment, she might still need to have a mastectomy. She could feel the tears welling up in her eyes.

"No, you stop that, girl," she said aloud to herself. "You are going to be all right. Do not let this dim your light!"

She wiped her eyes and blew her nose. She opened her

makeup bag and leaned into the mirror to reapply her eye makeup. Then she powdered her face and reapplied her lipstick. Though Brandy had been crying and was completely mentally off track, an older woman entered the bathroom and brushed against her as she was walking past. The woman looked at Brandy and said, "Wow, you are such a beautiful woman. Is everything okay with you?" Her voice was gentle yet filled with concern.

Brandy fought to make a smile and looked up at the woman, her eyes still wet with tears. "Yes, I am good," she managed to reply, though her voice betrayed the turmoil within her.

The woman smiled a knowing and comforting expression. "Strangely, everything that will happen to you in the coming weeks will be good as well."

Brandy looked at the woman and noticed her striking seawater blue eyes, surrounded by the purest white she had ever seen, which immediately brought her comfort. A profound peace washed over Brandy, and she felt much better at that moment as if the weight of her worries had been lifted, if only slightly.

Brandy turned back to the mirror to finish fixing her face. She took a deep breath, feeling the renewed sense of calm settle within her. When she turned around to thank the woman, she found that she was gone. The bathroom was empty, and it was as if the woman had never been there.

Brandy stood still for a moment, reflecting on the brief but impactful encounter. The woman's words and presence had brought her an unexpected sense of hope and peace. With a final look in the mirror, Brandy wiped away the last of her tears and straightened up, feeling stronger and more determined to face whatever lay ahead. "Okay, that was better." As she put her makeup back in her purse, she noticed her cell phone flashing. She had a voicemail from the theater and a text message.

"Hey, Brandy! This is Sonia. I wanted to let you know that

someone came by the theater looking for you. He said his name is Timmoreia Branklin or something like that. He wanted your phone number when I told him you weren't here. I did not tell him about your hiatus, either. But he left his phone number for you. I'll text it over to you. I hope you're doing fine, and we all miss you so much! Please keep in touch! Love ya!"

Brandy always liked Sonia. She was always so sweet and happy. So, Mr. Branklin wanted to talk to her. This is an interesting turn of events. She looked at her reflection in the mirror. She turned sideways to look at her breasts. Yes, they were one of her favorite features. Nothing made her feel more feminine. Who would she be without them? How would any man find her attractive if she lost them? The doctor had mentioned reconstructive surgery. But something about having artificial breasts slightly repulsed her. She thought they made women look cheap and trashy. The doctor said the option was there if she ever changed her mind.

An urgent need to cry hit her, but she fought it. She looked at the text message from Sonia. She touched the phone number in the text, and the phone feature opened. She looked at the call button for a minute before touching it. The phone rang three times.

"This is Timmoreia Branklin," a deep voice said at the end of the line. "I'm so glad you called back. Look," said Brandy, "you can't be following me around and going to my job to see if I was there. What kind of shit is that?"

"I'm sorry. I meant no harm by it. I was just curious and wanted to apologize for my actions and assure you that I only want to be your friend."

"Listen, if you're not busy, would you like to meet to talk and get some really good food?"

"Look, Timmoreia, I am a married woman. Or did you just conveniently forget that?"

"I completely respect and understand that, but I am just

trying to help you get through some of the challenges you might be having in your life right now. So, how about it? Dinner?"

"Damn," Brandy said reluctantly. "Yes, but you know I don't have a car."

"No worries. Take a cab, and I will pay for it once you arrive. I'll send you the address. See you soon."

Brandy sighed as she hung up the phone, feeling a mix of frustration and curiosity. She couldn't ignore the odd sense of familiarity and concern in Timmoreia's voice. Despite her reservations, she decided to give the meeting a chance, hoping it might bring some clarity or resolution to the strange situation.

She quickly got ready, hailed a cab, and set off to the address Timmoreia had sent. As the cab navigated through the bustling streets of Chicago, Brandy's mind raced with questions and doubts. What did Timmoreia really want? And why did she feel a peculiar sense of anticipation mingling with her skepticism?

Stepping into the hotel, Brandy navigated toward the reception desk, her purpose clear—she sought directions to the restaurant. However, before reaching her destination, a gentle hand landed on the small of her back, eliciting a startled spin. The initial mix of fear and anger swiftly transformed into recognition as she realized the familiar touch belonged to Timmoreia.

"There you are," Timmoreia smoothly uttered, his voice a silky blend of charm. "Looking as lovely as I remember." Leaning in for a light hug, Brandy's instinct was to pull away. Yet, he exuded such a captivating charm, and his fragrance—distinctively Bobby's OUD by Tom Ford—permeated the air. Overwhelmed by a momentary nostalgia, Brandy allowed herself to be drawn into his brief embrace. Sensing her hesitation, Timmoreia released her swiftly, offering his arm to escort her toward the restaurant.

"So, is this where you're staying?" Brandy inquired, her gaze sweeping across the hotel's interior. It emanated a subdued elegance, characterized by a minimalist décor that spoke of refined taste. The ambiance hinted at untold stories lingering within the walls, adding an air of mystery to the surroundings in the bustling heart of downtown Chicago. A little too modern for her taste, but the lines were clean, and the colors were bright and airy.

"Yes, for a few days until I head back home to Michigan," he replied. They reached the hostess podium and waited to be seated. Brandy started to feel awkward. What was she doing here with this handsome stranger? This had to be the dumbest thing she'd ever done. He could be a rapist or a serial killer! What the hell was she thinking?

As they approached their table, Timmoreia exhibited an unexpected touch of chivalry, pulling out Brandy's chair for her. It was a moment of civility in a world that had lately seemed anything but. However, as she settled into her seat, a sinister whisper echoed in her mind: "Would a serial killer have manners?" Her internal dialogue swirled in doubt, cautioning her against the façade of normalcy that could mask a lurking danger. "You are so dumb, Brandy," she murmured, the words escaping her lips almost involuntarily.

"I'm sorry, I didn't catch that," Timmoreia said, casually reaching for his glass of water, a benign action that took on an ominous undertone given Brandy's internal musings.

"Oh, nothing... just talking to myself. Bad habit," Brandy quickly responded, attempting to shake off the disconcerting thoughts. The urgency to finish her dinner and escape this unnerving situation propelled her to eat like someone who hadn't seen a meal in days. Raising her glass to her lips, she locked eyes with Timmoreia, a fleeting moment of defiance.

"I was afraid you wouldn't get my message, or worse...decide not to call," he remarked, adopting a relaxed posture, crossing his legs and clasping his hands across his knee.

"Honestly, I had second thoughts about calling you. Why did you go looking for me in the first place?"

Timmoreia drew a deep breath, his gaze shifting downward to his hands. "Honestly, Brandy, I just couldn't stop thinking about you. I know you're going through some difficult times with your husband." "It just bothered me to think that you're going through that alone, with no one to talk to." "I mean, I'm sure you have family and close friends, but they might be too invested in your life and your marriage." "Sometimes, you need someone that's separate from the day-to-day of your life to be able to express how you feel, what you're thinking without getting any judgment or unsolicited advice. You just seemed so... sad and hurt."

"You were worried about me?" Brandy found it hard to believe, yet a glimmer of validation stirred within her. To know that Timmoreia could perceive her pain, even in the midst of her chaotic life, left her feeling a little less alone.

"Yes, of course," Timmoreia leaned forward, his fingers reaching for Brandy's hand. The gentle motion of his thumb rubbing the back of her hand sent a shiver down her spine. Brandy couldn't help but notice the surprising softness of his hands, igniting an unexpected imagination of what it would feel like to have those hands caress her body. A flush of shame and embarrassment colored her face as she abruptly pulled her hand away. Timmoreia's brow furrowed, registering her reaction.

"I just want to be your friend, and friends are there for each other through thick and thin," he said in a serious tone, breaking the tension. Then, a broad smile appeared on his face. "But it sure is hard to just be a friend when you're so damn attractive!" He chuckled, his eyes looking down, almost embarrassed by his candid admission.

Caught off guard, Brandy chuckled in surprise. Her laughter ceased when she noticed the intensity in Timmoreia's gaze. His eyes traced a deliberate path from hers down to her lips, lingering, then slowly exploring the swell of her exposed breasts in the low-cut blouse. She should have felt offended, but instead, a different sensation stirred within her. His gaze, combined with the image of his broad shoulders and bulging biceps, unexpectedly aroused her. Panic set in.

In an attempt to distract herself, she picked up the menu, flipping its pages back and forth. Those mesmerizing eyes had to be avoided; they felt as if they were hypnotizing her. The lust that surged within her drove away any hunger she might have felt moments ago. Eating seemed impossible now.

Sensing her discomfort, Timmoreia picked up his menu, feigning interest in the choices. He needed to back off, not lay it on too thick, or risk her abruptly leaving and disrupting his plans. The waiter approached, asking about their drink choices.

"The lady will have..." Timmoreia looked at Brandy, a query in his eyes.

"Pink Moscato," Brandy replied, while Timmoreia requested a scotch and water.

"Very well," the waiter said with a polite bow. They sat in silence, Timmoreia watching her intently and Brandy avoiding his gaze.

"I sense you're feeling uncomfortable. If you would rather go, I'll understand," Timmoreia said quietly.

Brandy shifted in her chair, her hand absently patting her hair before resting on her neck. She met his eyes and confessed, "I don't know why I'm here, and quite honestly, I'm a little confused about how I'm feeling about being here." The air crackled with unspoken tension as uncertainty lingered between them, setting the stage for the unfolding drama of the evening.

Timmoreia exhibited a heightened awareness of Brandy's needs, surpassing that of a mere stranger. His attempts to court her appeared meticulously planned, aligning seamlessly with a broader agenda. His comprehension of Brandy's emotions and the nuances that brought her comfort resembled someone who had been carefully examined, perhaps with the intention of both seducing her and subtly influencing her mindset. While his charm took center stage, it became apparent that his ambitions were guided by a purpose that extended beyond the surface of mere attraction.

"Look," Timmoreia began, his tone gentle yet firm, "we're not doing anything wrong. We're just going to eat and talk. No hidden agenda, no obligation. I just couldn't stop thinking about you after our last conversation. I genuinely wanted to see how you're doing. I'm glad I reached out and that you called because you sound like you really need someone to talk to, more so than before. Is there something else going on?"

Brandy's breath caught in her throat, a tumult of emotions swirling within her. She averted her gaze, attempting to conceal the tears welling in her eyes. "Don't cry, don't cry," she silently urged herself, though the vulnerability threatened to spill over. Timmoreia was torn between the desire to comfort her and the need to maintain emotional distance. His plan, carefully crafted and non-negotiable, hung in the balance. Patiently, he sat as she struggled to regain composure, a palpable tension lingering between them.

In an attempt to divert her thoughts, he asked about her order. Brandy subtly wiped away a tear, her focus momentarily shifting to the randomness of her right eye tearing up first. A strange distraction, but it served its purpose, momentarily diverting her from the overwhelming emotions.

She picked up her menu again, determined to regain control. Opting for a simple chicken Caesar salad—a choice designed for a swift exit—she discovered an unforeseen obstacle: Timmoreia's order of steak clashed with her expedited departure plan.

"Are you going to tell me what's wrong?" Timmoreia inquired. "You sounded upset on the phone. Is there anything I can do to help?"

"It's nothing. Just one of those days," Brandy deflected, shaking her head. "I let things get to me, that's all. All part of being a theater diva, I suppose," she added with a soft laugh, masking the true weight of her tumultuous life.

"Hmmm. You don't come off as being a diva. You impress me as a strong, determined woman—one who doesn't back down from a challenge. Not someone who gets upset when things aren't going her way."

"Oh, really? You learned all that from the one time we had coffee weeks ago?" Brandy responded with a skeptical smile.

"Hey, I'm pretty good at reading people? What can I say?" Timmoreia flashed a brilliant white smile. While undeniably handsome, his eyes told a different story—they held the color of soft grey clouds just before light rain, adorned with the longest, curled lashes she had ever seen on a man. A peculiar musing crossed her mind: Why did most men have the best eyelashes? His gaze, seductive and secretive, added an extra layer of allure, especially as he stood before her, looking down with a magnetic intensity. The air around them crackled with unspoken tension, as if an invisible thread connected their fates, weaving a story that had only just begun.

"I just received some unexpected news, and it feels like I'm being bombarded with changes I didn't anticipate. I'm not sure if I can navigate through them," Brandy confessed, her voice trembling with a mix of overwhelm and fear. The weight of unforeseen circumstances pressed on her, leaving her grappling with an uncertain future. "I don't know what to do next, and I feel like I don't have time to sit and really think things through and plan."

The emotions stirred within her, and she continued, "Don't you ever feel like you're at the mercy of the universe, or God, or whatever it is that you believe in? Like no matter how much you plan or how much you believe someone's got your back, somehow you still end up with the short end of the stick?" As her frustration grew, Brandy's tone shifted from sadness to anger. She felt the weight of her situation pressing on her, resentment bubbling up toward Bobby, her doctor, and even Christina, her sister, for not reaching out amidst the chaos of Bobby's novel-writing endeavors. Brandy felt abandoned and confused, entangled in emotions she shouldn't be experiencing with another man while still married to Bobby.

Unaware of her rising intensity, Brandy's animated outburst drew sideways glances from other customers. As she realized the attention she had garnered, embarrassment washed over her. Abruptly standing up and grabbing her handbag, she apologized, "I'm sorry. I didn't mean to get carried away like that. I'm so embarrassed. I'm just going to go. Thank you for the invite, and please forgive me."

Timmoreia, understanding her turmoil, quickly threw bills on the table and chased after her. He caught up in front of the building as she waited for a taxi. "Hey, why don't you just walk with me for a bit? We don't need to talk about anything. Let's just enjoy this beautiful city and people-watch." Offering his arm, he stood closest to the street—a gesture not lost on Brandy. Hesitating for a moment, she looked up at him, captivated by his eyes, and accepted his arm. They embarked on a leisurely stroll, immersed in the vibrant city life. They paused to appreciate street performers, indulged in window shopping, and shared laughter about the eccentric characters they encountered.

Lost in the moment, Brandy was unaware of how much time had passed until her stomach reminded her of the passing hours.

"Girl, is that your stomach growling?" Timmoreia chuckled, breaking the tension of the emotional conversation.

Brandy blushed. "Oh my gosh, I'm so embarrassed. But yes, I'm starving!"

"Well, I guess we need to do something about that." Timmoreia scanned the street, spotting a hot dog vendor. Playfully, he warned, "Now, please don't tell me that you're too good for a street dog."

Brandy laughed, "Oh, heck no! I can eat two with all the toppings."

"Two? Damn... A woman after my own heart. Let's go, then!"

They grabbed hot dogs and found a pedestrian bridge. Timmoreia, with his hands full, effortlessly lifted Brandy onto the ledge. At that moment, carefree laughter and the city lights surrounded them. To Timmoreia's admiration, Brandy devoured both hot dogs. Afterwards, he discarded the containers, and Brandy kicked off her heels, rubbing her feet.

"Oooh, boy! My dogs are barking! We walked more than I realized," she confessed.

Timmoreia, seizing the opportunity, began to massage her foot. Surprised, Brandy pulled away, revealing her aversion to feet. Timmoreia found her distaste amusing, causing a bout of laughter. The conversation took a turn to pedicures, and Brandy insisted on the unpleasantness of all feet.

"I've never heard such nonsense," Timmoreia laughed.

"It's not nonsense...it's...it's...cleanliness!"

Amused, Timmoreia teased, "So, your husband doesn't touch your feet? Rub them down after a long day?"

The atmosphere shifted when Brandy admitted, "Bobby's too busy with his book to touch anything on me these days." Suddenly, the laughter faded, replaced by a poignant silence. Brandy, sliding off the ledge, realized Timmoreia's height without her heels. She began to put on her shoes, seeking stability by grabbing his arm. Timmoreia, looking down at her, remarked, "I can't imagine any man not wanting to touch you, Brandy."

His words left her breathless. As they locked eyes, a magnetic force drew them closer. Finally, their lips met, igniting a surge of desire. Brandy, torn between the forbidden and her own wants, reluctantly pulled away, sensing the wrongness of their actions.

"I really need to get home. I didn't realize how long we've been together... walking, um, you know."

"Oh, for sure! I understand. I'm sorry about, you know," Timmoreia gestured from his lips to hers. "I really should not have done that. My bad."

"Hey, don't worry about it. No big deal! We will just forget all that... happened."

Timmoreia, slightly flustered, suggested getting a taxi. Brandy agreed, avoiding direct eye contact. Once she was situated in the cab, Timmoreia leaned down and whispered, "Brandy, I am sorry if I overstepped. I just could not help myself, and damn it if I don't want to kiss you again right now."

She kissed his cheek, expressing gratitude, and the taxi carried her away. Alone, Timmoreia questioned his actions, realizing that his unexpected feelings for Brandy were not part of the plan.

"The Descent into Timmoreia's Abyss and Jay's Purpose for Revenge"

Timmoreia's departure from Brandy's company marked the end of a carefully choreographed act, a performance designed to manipulate her perceptions and lure her deeper into his web of deceit. The luxury car he had borrowed for the occasion was returned with haste, an expensive prop used to bolster the illusion of success. The façade had to be maintained at all costs, as Timmoreia's relentless pursuit of his ulterior motives demanded it.

Once the car was relinquished, Timmoreia found himself in the gritty reality of his own life. Opting for an Uber to navigate the urban maze, he wound his way through the treacherous streets of Chicago's South Side, his destination a one-bedroom apartment on the lower end of Monroe Street. A place forsaken by affluence, it was the only shelter he could afford despite its location in a perilous and impoverished neighborhood.

As he crossed the threshold into his abode, the stark contrast to the façade he had presented to Brandy became painfully evident. The apartment was a dilapidated relic, its walls crawling with pests and the unmistakable presence of a mouse scurrying away from the prying eyes that bore witness to its existence. The air hung heavy with the stench of neglect, the atmosphere oppressive and rife with the echoes of a once better life now shattered.

Timmoreia Branklin, once a man of means and family, now stood alone in the squalor of his own making. Stripping away the borrowed veneer of success, he exchanged it for the tattered remnants of his true identity. A beer, the cheapest solace available, was retrieved from the barely functional refrigerator, and he sank into a chair that had long lost its former glory.

The television, a mere seventeen inches of cathode-ray obscurity, crackled to life. An array of wires, a desperate attempt to boost its limited capabilities, dangled from the top like a technological life support. The absence of cable or antennas further accentuated the desolation of Timmoreia's surroundings. To call this place a dump was an understatement—it was a poignant testament to his fall from grace.

In the place he lived, surrounded by dilapidated buildings and everything falling apart, there was a closet he called his "bat closet." This small sanctuary was secured with multiple padlocks, each one a precautionary measure against the possibility of local robbers breaking in and stealing his most prized possessions. Additional security was essential in a neighborhood where theft was a common occurrence, and he couldn't afford to lose his carefully accumulated valuables to the local thugs.

Once the door was unlocked and released from its numerous padlocks, he stepped inside the closet and flicked on the light. The illumination revealed a space that shone like a bank vault. Among his treasures, he had a few pairs of Mezedanze shoes, each costing about $1,000. These high-end shoes were more than just footwear; they were a symbol of his hard-earned success and his personal taste for luxury in an otherwise harsh environment.

The closet was meticulously organized, a stark contrast to the chaos outside its doors. Shelves lined with designer clothes, expensive accessories, and neatly stacked boxes hinted at the life he aspired to live. Each item had been chosen with care and represented a step toward the future he envisioned for himself, away from the crumbling reality of his current surroundings.

Alongside the shoes were bottles of OUD Tom Ford cologne, the luxurious scent adding an air of sophistication to his persona. He also had a series of hazel contacts to heighten the attraction of his eyes, making them a striking feature that complemented his overall look. Watches, some real and others fake, adorned a velvet-lined shelf alongside necklaces of varying authenticity. It was the closet of a well-off gigolo in the home of a broken conman.

Each item in the closet was a relic of past hustles and gambling victories, even from his days when he attempted to be a pimp. His collection also included weapons: knives and a few small handguns hidden behind a false panel. Most of his possessions were funded by the accomplices from whom he took his marching orders, their criminal enterprises providing the means for his collection.

Once done meticulously placing his costume from his evening with Brandy back in its rightful place, he surveyed the contents of his "bat closet." This ritual of organizing and securing his valuables was more than just a habit; it was a way of affirming control over his life, a fleeting but necessary assertion of power in an otherwise powerless existence.

Like Batman, there was a life in the light and a life in the night. His metaphoric mask and cape allowed him to move among the shadowy opportunities of the night without revealing the true weaknesses he harbored in the light. In the daytime, he presented a façade of normalcy, but it was at night that he embraced his true self, navigating the underworld with a cunning that masked his vulnerabilities.

He closed the door, reattached the padlocks, and stepped back, feeling a sense of satisfaction and readiness for whatever the next day would bring. The "bat closet" was not just a storage space but a testament to his resilience, adaptability, and unyielding hope for a better future despite the relentless shadows of his past.

In the dim glow of the flickering screen, Timmoreia reached for the one possession of substantial value he still possessed—an Apple phone. A lifeline to his clandestine operations, it was time to check-in. The digits were dialed, anticipation hanging in the air, but the voice that answered belonged to his accomplice, absent and elusive.

"Hello, I can't come to the phone right now. Leave a message, and I'll get back to you," the recorded message echoed, its tone indifferent. "I can't answer your call right now, but leave a message, and I will get back to you."

The urgency in Timmoreia's voice cut through the silence as he left a message, the desperation evident. "Hey, you need to get back to me. I need additional funds to keep this shit going and push this plan forward. Call me back; let me know where we can meet. The clock is ticking."

As Timmoreia sank into the worn contours of his dilapidated chair, his gaze drifted toward the scant remnants of a life that once held promise. The walls bore witness to a collection of faded photographs, suspended memories that now hung in silent reproach. On a makeshift table, weathered by time and neglect, were images that told the story of a love that had crumbled like ancient ruins.

The pictures spoke of a time when happiness was a tangible reality. A radiant smile adorned the face of his once-beloved wife, Janet, a woman who had been the cornerstone of his world. Beside her, a cherubic figure—Castle, his daughter—radiated innocence and joy. Their images were frozen in time, a testament to the love that had once thrived within the walls of their family.

Timmoreia's eyes lingered on each photograph, a bittersweet dance with the ghosts of his past. The warmth that once emanated from these images had been replaced by the cold, harsh reality of his present. He had loved them with a fervor that consumed him, yet his relentless pursuit of misguided ambitions had severed the ties that bound them together.

The echoes of his former life reverberated in his mind. Once a formidable hustler, Timmoreia had traversed a path strewn with wrong turns and ill-fated decisions. The pinnacle of his undoing lay in a gamble that would forever alter the trajectory of his existence. In a moment of recklessness, he had staked his claim on the inheritance left by his distant father's passing—a sum that could have been a lifeline for him and his family.

The advice of his wife, a voice of reason drowned out by the clamor of his own ambitions, had fallen on deaf ears. Janet had pleaded with him to safeguard the windfall, to invest in education or a trade that could elevate their lives. The choice to break free from the shackles of a life marred by poor decisions lay before him, a chance to rewrite the narrative for his family's future.

Despite the temptation of quick riches and fleeting success, Jay T. Willabee, known by the Greek name "Timmoreia," meaning "revenge," couldn't resist the lure. The wedding photo, inscribed "Timmoreia and Janet Willabee together forever," now mocked him—a cruel reminder of a promise broken by his own choices.

As Timmoreia traced his daughter's face in the photo, a surge of regret overwhelmed him. The love that once drove him now seemed like a distant memory, a reminder of the price he paid for a misspent life. The worn chair creaked under the weight of a man burdened by lost love and the irreversible consequences of his actions.

In the dim light of his small apartment, memories and reflections wove a haunting tapestry of anger and misdirected revenge. The photographs on the walls, once symbols of love, now kindled a smoldering rage. These images, which should have brought comfort, fueled his burning desire for justice against the man who led him down a path of risk and ruin.

The warmth of love that once emanated from those pictures now metamorphosed into the fiery resolve that flickered in Timmoreia's eyes. His wife's pleas for prudence and his daughter's innocent laughter now echoed as ghostly whispers, stoking the flames of resentment within him. The illusion of success he had chased had led him to a precipice, and now he teetered on the edge, fueled by a relentless desire for retribution.

As it was each night, Timmoreia found himself unable to sleep, haunted by memories of his past days as a convict and a failed hustler. The constant need to watch his back in prison from the goons who, on occasion, used him as a night item for their sickened pleasure left deep scars. The trauma of those nights, filled with fear and humiliation, lingered long after his release, casting a shadow over his every waking moment.

Unable to find peace, Timmoreia sought rest in alcohol. This nightly ritual was the only way to close his eyes and prevent the demons of his past from invading his dreams. Each evening, as the sun set and the world around him quieted, he would retreat to his small, cluttered kitchen. There, he kept a stash of cheap whiskey and vodka, their presence a silent acknowledgment of his ongoing struggle.

Pouring a generous amount into a glass, he took a seat by the window, looking out at the flickering streetlights and the occasional passing car. The first sip burned his throat, a harsh reminder of the pain he was trying to escape. But with each subsequent drink, the edges of his reality blurred, the oppressive weight of his memories lifting just enough to allow for a temporary reprieve.

Timmoreia knew that this wasn't a solution. The alcohol only numbed the pain, pushing it to the edges of his consciousness until the morning light brought it all rushing back. But it was the only way he knew to cope, to survive another night without succumbing to the overwhelming darkness that threatened to consume him.

As he finished his drink, the familiar warmth spreading through his body, he felt the pull of sleep begins to take hold. He stumbled to his bed, the room spinning slightly, and collapsed onto the mattress. His last conscious thought was a fleeting hope that maybe, just maybe, tomorrow would be different.

But as sleep finally claimed him, the shadows of his past remained, lurking just beyond the veil of his dreams, waiting for the moment they could resurface. And so, each night, Timmoreia continued his ritual, seeking solace in the bottom of a glass and fighting a battle that seemed destined to repeat itself endlessly.

"Fractured Foundations"

Brandy was sitting at the breakfast nook with a hot cup of coffee, going over her schedule for the day. She was now more mentally stable but still grappling with the conflict of all that was going on. She remained as isolated as she could in order not to feel the pressure of succumbing to the need to tell everyone what was really going on. She had another doctor's appointment that morning to begin laying out her treatment plan. She knew she had to tell Bobby and Christina sooner rather than later. But she just did not have the energy to deal with their reactions. She had some business to wrap up at the theater after that, but her day was pretty open afterward. What could she do to keep herself busy and away from Bobby? Now that he did not have an office to go to, he was home a lot. He spent a lot of time in his home office, tweaking his novel or calling publishers at his editor's instruction. But he was still home, and she felt like he was infringing on her day simply by being in the same building as her. Although she had to give it to him—he was hustling his ass off for that book!

She did not hear Bobby enter the room until he bent down to give her a kiss. She quickly closed her planner and offered him her cheek. This slight was not lost on Bobby, and he hesitated for a split second before giving her a quick peck.

"What are you doing today, baby?" Bobby asked as he put a slice of bread in the toaster.

"Ummm, I have to go to the theater and run some errands," Brandy replied as she looked out the window. She felt an overwhelming sense of frustration and irritation. Part of her wondered if her reaction to Bobby had anything to do with her thoughts of Timmoreia and how much she enjoyed spending time with him. He made her feel attractive and special. Bobby made her feel like his roommate since all he was focused on was his writing. As soon as that thought popped into her head, she felt stupid. How can she feel jealous about his writing? But that question had not even fully formed in her mind when she felt anger wash over her because she didn't like feeling stupid, and that's how Bobby made her feel. Yes, she knew that he wasn't doing it intentionally, but right now, she dismissed that fact and focused on raw emotion.

Bobby sat his happy ass across from her with his freshly buttered toast and cup of coffee. He smiled at her.

"What are you smiling at?" she asked irritably.

"I'm just happy to be here with you. And I got some great news from my agent. She said she has a couple of publishers that seem extremely interested in my book. I am meeting with them today. I have a really good feeling about this, Brandy."

She abruptly stood up and took her empty coffee cup to the sink. With her back to him, she rolled her eyes and tried to restrain herself from letting out a big sigh. She really wanted to throw something at him. Why doesn't he see how much all his talk about his project irritates her to no end?

He walked up behind her and wrapped his arms around her waist. She instinctively stiffened in his embrace, but he did not seem to notice. That only made her even more tense.

"This is all going to come together; you just wait and see," he said against the side of her head.

She pulled his arms apart and stepped out of his embrace. She turned to face him, her brows knitted together in a scowl.

"Has it ever occurred to you that there is more to life, to our lives, than you getting your book published? You don't talk to me about anything else, and I'm tired of being overlooked, Bobby. You seem to forget that quitting your job majorly affected our lives, and you never thought to include me in that decision. Now, you expect me to go along with your crazy plan with a smile on my face and my mouth shut! I can't...I just can't deal with this...with you...right now!"

She quickly walked out of the room and into the formal dining room, but Bobby was hot on her heels. He reached out and grabbed her arm.

"Brandy, wait. You know how important you are to me, and it's certainly not my intention to make you feel second-class. I really wish you would see how important this is to me and stand beside me with your support."

"Oh, you want me to stand by you when you abandoned our relationship by making a HUGE decision without even talking to me about it? Obviously, I'm not that important to you," she said, raising her voice.

"I know what our family and friends think about me. That I am mad at you because of the big change in our finances. And yes, I am mad about that, but I am more pissed at the utter disregard you had for my opinion and input in our lives. We are supposed to be part-ners, Bobby... PARTNERS!! Now I see that I have been a damn fool believing that during all these years, we have been married. Obvi-ously, I ain't shit. So, do you know what? Your book ain't shit to me!"

She stomped all the way upstairs and slammed the bedroom door shut. She was breathing heavily and was on the verge of crying. "He better not even come up here! I might really lose it if he does!" She sat on the edge of the bed and pulled out her phone to call a cab. She just needed to get as far away as possible from Bobby. She noticed she had a voicemail. She pressed the button to listen to the message.

"Hey, Brandy. This is Timmoreia." Her heart skipped a beat, and a smile slowly spread across her face. "I know I should not be calling you, but I just wanted to apologize again for what happened yesterday. I mean, I am not sorry I kissed you. But I am sorry if it was something you did not want," he paused before continuing. "I gotta say, though, it did not feel like you did not like it. I am just hoping that you liked it. I know I certainly enjoyed it," she heard his soft chuckle. It sent chills down her back.

"Anyway, I just wanted to let you know that I was thinking about you. I hope you have been thinking about me. Talk to you later... I hope."

She sat there with the phone to her ear and a smile on her face, for who knows how long it had been since she snapped out of it and called a cab. She heard the front door open and close. Good, Bobby was smart and didn't come looking for her. She checked her makeup and changed her clothes again. Rather than the jeans and casual t-shirt she was wearing, she decided to wear a nice skirt with a sleeveless blouse and some open-toe slingback heels. She waited in the bedroom until the cab arrived, just in case Bobby came back. Then she quickly walked downstairs, out the door, and jumped into the cab with a sense of relief.

As Brandy exited, she pulled out her phone and dialled Meeka. With each ring, the weight of her conflicting emotions grew heavier, threatening to overwhelm her.

"Meeka," she said, her voice trembling slightly when her friend answered. "I'm on the cliff about a lot of things, girl. I really am. My moral compass is fading, and I feel like I just need to do some shit, you know?"

"Yeah, girl, I understand," Meeka replied, her tone a mix of concern and urgency. "Listen, I need to finish this meeting with my political team. I have decided to run for that district attorney's seat I told you about. I'm so sorry, Brandy, but I will call you as soon as I can."

"Listen, Brandy, whatever you do, don't do anything stupid that you will later regret. Every risk we take has its consequences. Be careful. I've got to go. Love you, girl."

"Love you too, Meeka," Brandy said, her voice barely a whisper as she ended the call.

She stood there for a moment, feeling the emptiness of the quiet street around her. Meeka's words echoed in her mind, a reminder of the precariousness of her situation and the importance of staying grounded. With a heavy sigh, Brandy slipped her phone back into her pocket and started walking, each step a battle against the urge to let her frustrations and fears dictate her actions.

As she walked, she tried to focus on the things that mattered —the people who cared about her, the goals she had set for herself, and the future she still believed she could build. Meeka's voice, filled with determination and purpose, gave her a glimmer of hope. If Meeka could push forward and chase her dreams, then maybe, just maybe, Brandy could find her way through the darkness, too.

But for now, she had to take it one step at a time, keeping Meeka's advice close to her heart: "Be careful and think about the consequences." With that in mind, Brandy squared her shoulders and continued down the street, determined to find a way to navigate the tumultuous path ahead.

Bobby's arrival at his agent's office had been marked by optimism, a shimmering hope that dissolved like mist as he emerged from the building into the bright sunlight. A gentle breeze, usually welcoming, now seemed to carry the weight of his escalating predicament. Seeking refuge on a desolate bench along the sidewalk, he attempted to clear his mind, only to find the shadows of his recent encounter with Brandy looming large.

The conference call with the major publishing house had initially painted a rosy picture. The prospect of his novel's success was within reach, with minor tweaks required to secure a deal. However, the elation crumbled beneath the burden of Brandy's recent words—words that left him wounded and questioning the foundation of their relationship.

As Bobby replayed the call in his mind, the reality of his situation unfolded. A month was given for revisions, a daunting task he believed he could accomplish with focused determination. Yet, the looming cloud of Brandy's discontent cast a pall over his aspirations.

Lost in the maze of conflicting emotions, Bobby grappled with the realization that pursuing his dream might come at the cost of his marriage. The once unbreakable bond between him and Brandy was now strained under the weight of unspoken disappointments and shattered expectations.

In a moment of vulnerability, Bobby sought solace in the company of Fleet, a friend who had always been a source of camaraderie. The cab ride to Fleet's house became a journey away from the heavy atmosphere at home, an attempt to escape the impending storm.

As Bobby approached Fleet's door, relief washed over him at the sight of Fleet's truck in the driveway. A faint hope lingered that the familiar warmth of friendship could provide a temporary respite from the tempest brewing in his personal life.

However, the door that opened to Fleet's home was not just a portal to refuge but also an unwitting gateway to a cascade of unexpected revelations. Fleet, initially caught off guard, welcomed Bobby with a mix of surprise and amusement, setting the stage for a candid exchange.

As the two settled into patio chairs with beers in hand, Bobby's burden spilled forth. The once tranquil yard, adorned with rustling leaves, became a witness to the unraveling of a man's world. Fleet, with genuine concern, probed into Bobby's personal crisis, only to discover a tale of financial ruin that echoed louder than the breeze through the trees.

"Yo, I have to tell Brandy something that is really going to piss her off. I do not even know how to bring it up." At that moment, Bobby looked utterly defeated.

"It can't be that bad," Fleet said, trying to instil some hope in Bobby. "I mean, how bad can it be, man?"

"Shi...," Bobby paused. "Man, I lost the house! I have enough in our savings to cover rent someplace for a few months, but not enough for our huge house payment. I do not know why we bought such a big house when it is just the two of us," Bobby said, shaking his head. "But that does not matter now because we don't have the money for the mortgage. Getting this book published is taking a lot longer than I thought it would."

"Damn, Bobby! So now what?"

"Well, I already talked to Christine to see if she could put us up for a while. I'll pay her rent, of course. She was kind enough to agree to it, but now I have to tell Brandy."

"Whoa! Man, she is gonna be more pissed that you told her sister before you told her what's going on," Fleet exclaimed loudly. "Ooooh, she's gonna have yo ass!" Fleet laughed into his closed fist that he held to his mouth.

"Wait... what?" Bobby's face was full of confusion. "What do you mean?"

"You should have told Brandy about the house situation first and then asked Christine about staying with her. I betcha Brandy is going to feel embarrassed knowing that her sister knew about her living situation before she did. I mean, come on now, Bobby! Think about it! Then she is going to be mad at her sister for not telling her right away about this 'arrangement' you set up. So, your ass is grass, my man!" It was not comforting the way Fleet was rolling with laughter at the mess he had created.

Bobby's confession revealed the imminent loss of his house, a blow that would undoubtedly shake the foundations of his marriage. Fleet's reaction, a mixture of shock and laughter, only added to the complexity of the situation. The misstep of confiding in Christine before Brandy cast a looming shadow over Bobby's already fragile state.

As Fleet handed Bobby another beer, the weight of the impending storm settled on his shoulders. The comforting warmth of friendship could only do so much to shield him from the tempest of consequences that awaited him at home. The shadows of unraveling dreams and fractured relationships loomed large, and Bobby could only brace himself for the storm that was about to unleash its fury.

"I get what you're saying about losing the high-rise condo, Bobby. Not to bring it up again, but you did share it with me," Fleet thought, entertaining the idea of suggesting, "Why not just take the $1.5 million and pay off the condo? Then you could focus on your book and wait for things to settle down?"

But deep down, Fleet knew he could not make that recommendation. If Bobby were foolish enough to get into this mess, then maybe his loss could be someone else's gain. So, Fleet stayed silent, sitting with Bobby as he sobbed, both of them contemplating the gravity of the situation.

"Echoes of Resilience"

The oncologist's waiting room felt like a place of quiet tension as Brandy, with fifteen minutes of uneasy calm, checked herself in. She sat down among others, all of them sharing a similar sense of anxiety. As she looked around, her eyes met those of a woman in her early fifties, sitting alone with a scarf carefully wrapped around her head.

There was an unspoken question in Brandy's mind as she glanced at the woman's covered head. They shared a brief, curious connection before Brandy, feeling uneasy, looked away. However, the woman named Susan noticed Brandy's glance and got up, walking purposefully toward her.

Brandy silently hoped Susan would walk past, but instead, Susan sat down next to her. The room buzzed with unspoken tension as these two strangers, connected by their shared vulnerability in the waiting room, teetered on the edge of an unexpected conversation.

Breaking the silence, Susan extended her hand with a friendly smile and introduced herself. Brandy, reluctant and wanting to be left alone, gave a brief handshake and a quick "Brandy," trying to end the interaction. She sought the comfort of solitude, hoping to be alone with her thoughts in the face of the uncertain future.

But Susan didn't let Brandy's coldness stop her. She sighed softly and, folding her hands in her lap, gently asked about Brandy's treatment. The question hung in the air like a delicate tremor, and Brandy responded with an eye roll and an audible sigh, clearly not wanting to talk about her private struggles.

Forced to engage, Brandy gave a forced smile, her eyes betraying the inner turmoil she was trying to hide. The tension between them grew, a shared vulnerability that was waiting to surface. In that waiting room, where the weight of medical diagnoses felt like a dark cloud, Brandy and Susan were standing on the edge of a journey that would bind them in ways they couldn't yet see. Their silent exchange set the stage for a shared experience through the uncertain times ahead.

"Well, you're in good hands with Dr. Thomas," Susan said, offering some reassurance that echoed through the sterile atmosphere of the room. "He's very knowledgeable and capable."

"Good to know," Brandy replied, her eyes seeking escape in a far-off corner. But Susan, sensing the shared vulnerability that hung in the air, leaned in closer, bridging the gap between two strangers connected by the looming threat of illness.

"Do you want to see?" Susan whispered as if sharing a secret. Brandy's head snapped back in surprise, caught off guard by the unexpected offer.

"What? See what?" "You know...see what's under my scarf. I'm not shy. If you're curious, I'll show you."

Brandy, initially shocked, felt a mix of curiosity and unease. The offer lingered, a choice wrapped in vulnerability. "Umm... Susan, right? Uh, that's really not necessary. I'm sorry if I was staring, but no... no, I don't want to see anything. It's none of my business," Brandy stammered, the words spilling out quickly.

A soft hand landed on Brandy's arm, and Susan bestowed upon her a sincere smile as Brandy noticed her striking sea-water blue eyes, surrounded by the purest white she had ever seen, welling with tears that spoke volumes of shared experiences. There was a pause of familiarity that entered into Brandy's mind for a brief moment as if she had seen this woman before. In a voice steeped in empathy, Susan unraveled the complexities of the human psyche in the face of a cancer diagnosis.

"Listen, my dear. I remember all too well how I felt when I was first diagnosed. All the questions that bombarded my mind regarding treatment, quality of life, and the possibility of death. But what I've realized is that human beings are prisoners of physical appearance. Now, I'm not saying we're shallow or vain, no, no! But we feel good about ourselves if we feel good about how we look."

Her gaze unwavering, Susan continued, "With all the questions about life or death, my initial concern came down to 'Am I going to lose all my hair? Will I still feel like a woman if I have to have a mastectomy? Will my husband still find me attractive?' It's human nature to have those thoughts and concerns. I just wanted you to know that if you're curious about what 'all that' looks like, I will be happy to show you. It's really not as bad as you might imagine. Well, the hair loss, anyway. The other side effects of the treatments are really bad, big time!"

To Brandy's surprise, she found herself laughing. The unexpected humor broke the tension, and for a moment, they shared a genuine laugh, easing the heavy burden they both carried.

As their laughter faded, a nurse called Brandy's name, interrupting the moment. Brandy, wiping away a tear of joy, stood up and impulsively took Susan's hand. Their eyes met, and in that look, unspoken gratitude flowed.

"You don't know how much I needed that laugh," Brandy confessed, her voice heavy with unspoken sorrows.

"Oh, I think I do," Susan replied, her hand squeezing,

conveying a silent understanding. Laughter had created a bond between these two women, both facing the unknown.

To Brandy's surprise, the nurse led her not to an exam room but to the doctor's office. Dr. Thomas stood up and offered a formal greeting. Brandy shook his hand, her mind preparing for the news to come.

"It's good to see you, Mrs. Pope. Please have a seat," Dr. Thomas said, guiding her to the chair in front of his desk. Brandy, determined to stay focused, took out a small notebook and pen, ready to take notes on her treatment plan. She knew that her emotions might overwhelm her once the consultation ended.

Dr. Thomas flipped through a folder, carefully reviewing the test results. Brandy's heart raced as she waited for him to speak. The mammogram image held her attention, a silent signal of what was to come.

Finally, the doctor spoke, his words offering hope. "Well, we have some good news, Mrs. Pope. It looks like we caught breast cancer very early."

Relief washed over Brandy, but the road ahead was still uncertain. The doctor explained her options: a lumpectomy, radiation, or possibly a mastectomy. Each choice carried its challenges and sacrifices.

Brandy, pen ready, felt the weight of these decisions. The future, full of unknowns, stretched out before her, each option requiring its own kind of strength. As she thought about what she might have to give up to survive, the room seemed filled with whispered decisions, and the doctor's words echoed in the quiet space.

Dr. Thomas, sensing Brandy's anxiety, got up from his desk and moved closer, resting a gentle hand on her shoulder. "Mrs. Pope, please know that you're in good hands. Everything I've told you will be printed out for you. We'll send you home with some helpful brochures," he reassured her, his voice calm and comforting. "We're going to recommend an oncologist who will guide you every step of the way so you'll always know what's happening and what to expect."

Dr. Thomas's words were full of promise, and he introduced the key figure in Brandy's journey—Dr. Weimer. The mention of the upcoming appointment with the oncologist made the situation feel even more serious. Brandy, trying to juggle brochures and her notebook, accidentally dropped her things. In that vulnerable moment, her emotions threatened to spill over.

"I don't have any questions right now. I'm sure I'll think of something later," Brandy said, her voice shaky as the weight of the information settled on her.

Dr. Thomas, concerned, offered her a break. "Are you sure you're okay? Just sit for a minute. I'll have the nurse bring you some water."

Brandy, grateful for the pause, sat down and put her face in her hands. The room became a quiet space where she could process the path ahead. The nurse brought her a bottle of water, offering a small but welcome relief.

As Brandy drank the cold water, the room felt more balanced. Dr. Thomas, understanding the fragile line between vulnerability and strength, encouraged her to take all the time she needed. His departure marked the start of Brandy's deep thinking.

The receptionist, polite and respectful, helped her with the next steps. As she handled the paperwork, a handwritten note from Susan caught Brandy's eye. Susan, now a connection in this shared journey, had offered to share more of her experiences. The personal touch of the note felt especially meaningful in the clinical setting.

Stepping outside into the warm sunlight, Brandy felt a small but growing sense of optimism. It was like a delicate bloom in her soul. Thinking about what to do next, she decided to visit the theater—a place where her past and present often came together. The cab ride offered a brief escape, carrying her toward a place that had been both her refuge and her stage.

As Brandy traveled through the city, she reflected on the weight of the decisions ahead. The theater, her safe space, waited for her arrival, unaware that within its familiar walls, a new leading lady was about to take the stage—someone deeply connected to Brandy's heart and the essence of her safe place.

"Echoes of the Past"

Brandy walked into the dimly lit theater, a place that had been her sanctuary for many shows. The cool air wrapped around her, bringing with it familiar smells that hinted at the theater's long history. The scent of stage makeup and the faint musk of worn costumes welcomed her like old friends. In the distance, she could hear the rhythmic sounds of hammering as stagehands worked hard to get everything ready for the upcoming performance.

Brandy walked through the winding halls, gently running her hand along the textured walls, each touch reminding her of the many memories held within the theater's structure. She arrived at the common area, a space filled with chairs, loveseats, and racks of costumes, all arranged in a charmingly messy way. The lighted makeup mirrors hinted at the transformations that happened backstage, ready for the actors between scenes. To her left, a hallway led to private dressing rooms, and to her right, the entrance to the backstage awaited her.

Laughter and conversation echoed from deep within the building, tempting Brandy to join the lively atmosphere. However, she held back and headed toward what used to be her dressing room. She picked up a forgotten box in the hallway, knocked on the door out of courtesy, and then carefully stepped inside.

"Hello, is anyone here?" Brandy called out, her voice echoing in the empty room. Only silence greeted her. As she looked at the neatly packed box, a mix of emotions welled up inside her. She felt grateful for the help but saddened that her departure seemed so quick and without ceremony. As she sifted through the box's contents, she realized that her replacement had already started making their presence known.

Fingers delicately traced the contours of a familiar sweater casually draped over a chair. The fabric sparked a distant recognition that she hastily dismissed. The room bore the signs of transition, and the sight of the new actress's belongings fueled Brandy's sense of displacement.

Driven by curiosity, Brandy moved toward vanity and discovered a script for the current play. As she flipped through its pages, she noticed handwritten notes in the margins, the writing familiar but just out of reach in her memory. Setting the script aside, she opened the drawer and found only traces of her past life there. But it was the sweater she found that made everything click into place.

She held up the sweater, bringing it close to her face and breathing in a scent that was deeply familiar, wrapped in the fabric of her memories. Confusion and disbelief washed over her as she tried to make sense of it all. Placing the sweater back where she found it, she picked up her box and headed toward the voices she heard in the distance, ready to face whatever awaited her.

Brandy stepped into a larger room, where comfortable chairs surrounded a communal table that reminded her of the Knights of the Round Table. The occupants of the room were deep in conversation, their laughter and chatter filling the space. As Brandy's gaze swept across the room, her eyes locked onto the one person she had suspected might be there, laughing and fully immersed in the group. The realization hit her hard, making the air feel thin as she struggled to breathe, her heart shattering with the weight of the moment.

The lively room fell silent as Christine looked up and met Brandy's intense stare. The laughter died in Christine's throat, replaced by a sudden, overwhelming breathlessness. It took several agonizing seconds before she managed to find her voice, her greeting hesitant and uncertain.

"Brandy! Hey..." The words felt weak, their hollowness echoing painfully in Christine's ears.

A heavy silence fell over the room, marking the sudden shift in atmosphere. Brandy, who had once been part of this group, now felt completely out of place. The actors, unsure how to react, offered her half-hearted greetings, their glances quick and uncomfortable. Brandy, overwhelmed by a mix of emotions, found it difficult to speak. She wanted to brush off the encounter, but her feelings betrayed her. A slight shake of her head signaled her refusal to accept the situation, and she felt her cheeks flush with heat. The threat of tears loomed large, and without saying a word, she turned and hurried away.

She heard hurried footsteps behind her, and Christine's voice broke through the tense silence. "Brandy! Brandy, please stop! Let me explain... please." The desperation in Christine's voice was clear as she tried to close the gap between them. Brandy quickened her steps, determined to avoid the confrontation. But Christine's hand grabbed her arm, stopping her in her tracks, and Brandy turned, her gaze cold and unforgiving.

"What could you possibly say, Christine? Why didn't you tell me you were working here?" Brandy's voice shook with a mix of anger and embarrassment, her chest rising and falling with the intensity of her emotions. Christine tried to guide her to a quieter spot, but Brandy yanked her arm away, resisting the attempt.

"Please, just calm down and let me explain," Christine

urged, her tone pleading. "I never meant to hurt you or make you feel embarrassed. You know that's not who I am. I was planning to tell you tonight when I brought the rest of your things over." Christine's words came out in a hurried whisper, reflecting the tension of the moment.

"Please, just come in here and talk to me. No one else needs to know all our business," she implored.

Reluctantly, Brandy followed Christine into what was now her dressing room. Habit led her to the chair before the makeup mirror, where she sat, hands clasped defiantly in front of her, anger smoldering in her gaze.

"So? What have you got to say, Christine?" Brandy's voice, low and steady, hinted at the potential for escalating tensions. The room brimmed with unspoken grievances, and the sisters stood on the cliff of a confrontation that could shatter the unstable bonds between them.

"Okay, okay," Christine stammered, her voice trembling as she nervously wrung her hands. Despite their close age, Brandy's imposing presence always reduced Christine to the role of a timid little girl. She despised feeling so easily intimidated by her sister.

"Remember how much we loved singing in church? We had our different styles but a shared passion. However, much of that light dimmed when Mama Lella May died. Singing brought me joy, but I couldn't bear to do it without her. You command attention, Brandy, and for a long time, I was content to watch you from the sidelines."

In the dimly lit room, Christine's words hung in the air like a delicate confession. The weight of unspoken emotions and suppressed aspirations lingered, casting shadows on the walls. As she uttered those words, there was a bittersweet tone to her voice, an emotional admission that she had willingly assumed the role of a silent observer in the grand theater of Brandy's life.

Christine's eyes were locked on Brandy, filled with a mix of admiration and a longing that had never quite been fulfilled. The room seemed to hold its breath, as if waiting for the complexities of their relationship to unravel.

"You have a way of commanding attention, Brandy," Christine continued, her voice tinged with the weight of years spent in the background, always in the shadows. There was a tone of resignation in her words, a hint of unspoken dreams and unvoiced desires. It was as if she had always been an observer, watching and applauding Brandy from the sidelines while she took center stage.

The air was thick with tension, the room charged with emotions that neither of them had fully acknowledged until now. The shadows on the walls seemed to dance around them, reflecting the intricate dynamics of their unspoken feelings. Christine's admission wasn't just a simple statement; it was a confession of her silent struggle, a bittersweet recognition of a life lived through Brandy's spotlight.

For a moment, the room seemed to pause, capturing the deep emotions written on Christine's face. The flickering light highlighted the scene, casting shadows that reflected the mixed feelings in the room.

As Christine's words hung in the air, Brandy's strong presence became even more pronounced, reminding them both of the dreams Christine had never fully pursued. The room echoed with the weight of unspoken hopes and hidden stories, creating a poignant backdrop to the complex emotions between the sisters.

"After a health scare, I realized life was slipping away from me. I wasn't really living—just going through the motions." Christine hoped Brandy would understand, but her sister's anger remained, showing little sympathy. "And with my health issues, Bobby started talking about his novel, and..."

"Bobby? What the hell does he have to do with any of this?"

Brandy's screech took Christine by surprise, making her step back.

"Nothing! I'm saying his passion for his dream inspired me to step out of my box and do something unexpected. When I saw the open audition, I got excited at the thought of us performing together again," Christine explained with enthusiasm. However, confusion clouded her face as she continued.

"Then I found out you left the theater for personal reasons. You never said a word about it to me. Why, Brandy? I'm here for you, Sis; you know that."

Brandy's steely glare intensified, and her next words caught Christine off guard.

"Oh, so you find my husband inspiring and exciting, do you?" Brandy's voice was ominously flat.

"What are you talking about? Why are you twisting it like that? I'm telling you about my feelings and my decision to enjoy life. I'm not taking what the Lord blessed me with for granted," Christine replied sharply, growing weary of Brandy's emotional aggression.

"But Bobby was your inspiration, right? How long have you had those feelings for my husband, huh, Sis?" Brandy's voice escalated, but Christine refused to back down.

"Now he's your husband? Forget all the years he supported you while you pursued your dream. As long as he does it for you, it's all good. But the minute the focus isn't on you, you act like a big-ass baby," Christine retorted, raising her voice in defiance. The room crackled with tension as the sisters confronted years of unspoken grievances and misunderstandings.

Brandy's eyes widened in profound shock, not only at the unexpected revelation from Christine but also at the uncensored profanity that escaped her sister's typically composed demeanor. The room, once a sanctuary for shared confidences, now reverberated with the echoes of a storm that had been unleashed.

"What the hell did you just say? You think Bobby is so damn

supportive and wonderful?" Brandy's incredulous tone hung in the air, a stark departure from their usual sisterly discourse. The tempest of emotions brewed, fueled by a truth Brandy hadn't anticipated.

"Yeah, he got you fooled. If he was so damn supportive, he would not have just up and quit his damn job without discussing it with me first," Brandy's voice reached a crescendo, each accusation landing like a painful blow. The room seemed to tighten with the intensity of their confrontation, creating an atmosphere thick with unresolved tension.

Christine, undeterred by the rage of her sister's fury, countered with a heated defense. "But he does love you! And he wants to take care of you in any way he can!" The words hung in the charged air, a feeble attempt to temper the impending storm.

The gravity of Christine's revelation hung heavy in the air, each word a seismic tremor that shook Brandy to her core. The weight of her sister's disclosure bore down on her, leaving her stunned and disoriented in the face of an unexpected tempest.

"That much was obvious when he came by the other day and asked if you two could stay in my extra bedroom," Christine's voice carried a mixture of sympathy and concern, a plea for understanding in the midst of familial upheaval. Her encouraging smile, a fragile attempt to soften the blow, was met with the silent disbelief etched across Brandy's face.

Brandy stood frozen, her mouth agape, as the reality of Christine's words settled like a gloomy cloud. "What the hell did Christine just say?" The question hung in the air, pregnant with an astonishment that bordered on disbelief. They had lost their house, and Bobby, in a desperate bid for shelter, turned to Christine, telling her the depths of their despair.

"The fuck you say? We lost our house?" Brandy's voice vibrated with a volatile blend of fury and hurt. The revelation unfolded like a cruel plot twist, unraveling the fabric of their stability. To compound the shock, the realization that Bobby sought refuge from Christine first painted a stark picture of their deteriorating circumstances.

"And he asked you to let us stay with you?" The words spilled from Brandy's lips, each one carrying the sting of wounded pride. The reality of the situation weighed heavily on her, turning what once felt like solid ground beneath her feet into a shaky, unfamiliar terrain filled with emotional challenges.

The room, once a place of comfort, was now charged with unspoken truths and tension. Brandy's sense of security, once anchored by the certainty of home, was now drifting in the storm of financial instability. The bonds that tied them as a family were stretched thin, on the verge of breaking under the weight of their collective struggles. The air was thick with unresolved emotions, leaving Brandy to face the harsh truth that her once-stable world had shattered, and the pieces of her life were scattered by the winds of change.

When the full impact of losing their house hit Brandy, her anger erupted with force. "What do you mean we lost our house?" Her voice shook the room, the intensity of her rage revealing the deep cracks in the foundation of their family bonds.

The torrent continued each word a relentless downpour of resentment. "If I hear about that fucking book one more time, I'm gonna catch a case!" Brandy's hands clenched into tight fists, her physicality mirroring the emotional tempest that consumed her.

"Brandy, calm down. It's not that bad," Christine implored, a lone voice trying to navigate the storm she had inadvertently invoked.

"Christine... just shut up! You don't know shit about marriage or being in a relationship. Keep your damn nose out of mine!" Brandy, snatching up her box, seemed poised to storm out, but an abrupt pause preceded a final act of defiance.

"You know what? Since you think so highly of Bobby, you

take him, then. I'm done with him, his book, with you... done with all your asses!" The door slammed violently behind her, sealing the wounds inflicted upon their sisterly bond. Suddenly, the door sprang back open. "Oh, by the way," she said as she reached over to the sweater, "give me my damn sweater," and she snatched it up and stomped out the door.

Left alone in the turbulent aftermath, Christine crumpled to the floor, her sobs echoing in the once-hallowed space. Hot tears streamed down her cheeks, each droplet a testament to the shattering of familial bonds. After a deluge of emotions, she reached for her cell phone, the device a lifeline in the tempest of despair.

The phone rang four times before the voice on the other end answered, "Hello?" Christine's sobs spilled into the receiver. "Bobby... I messed up, and I'm so sorry."

"Where are you? I'll be there as fast as I can," he replied, his concern palpable.

"I'm at the theater... at Brandy's theater. I'll explain everything when you get here," she said, attempting to regain control of her emotions.

"I'm on my way," Bobby's reassuring words promised a glimmer of hope amid the wreckage of fractured bonds as the theater walls echoed with the remnants of familial strife.

Bobby arrived at the theater shortly after Brandy had left. He sprinted to the dressing room where Brandy would normally be, his heart pounding with urgency and concern. Upon reaching the door, he hesitated for a split second before pushing it open. Inside, he found Christina draped over the dressing table, her body shaking with sobs.

"Hey, Christina, are you okay? What happened?" Bobby asked gently as he placed a comforting hand on her shoulder.

Christina looked up, her tear-streaked face filled with remorse. "Not this time, Bobby. I really messed up. Brandy came by to pick up her things from the theater because she had quit the production due to medical reasons. I still don't know what that means or what's really going on with that, but that's what she told them."

Bobby's brow furrowed in confusion. "Wait, what? Her replacement? What do you mean?"

Christina took a deep breath, trying to steady herself. "Once I heard about your changes and the fact that you were chasing your dream, it motivated me. After seeing this ad online for auditions to sing and act, I decided that I was going to try it out. It was time for me to step out and go after my own dreams and aspirations. And I have you to thank for motivating me to do that."

Bobby nodded slowly, encouraging her to continue.

"The problem is," Christina said, her voice breaking, "when Brandy came here, I hadn't told her that I actually auditioned and got the role, which happened to be hers. But honestly, Bobby, I didn't know it was hers in the first place. She came here, and it got tense. She felt like I wasn't listening to her reasoning, and she started bullying me like she always did when we were kids. I just got angry and snapped at her. I told her that you had come over to ask if you could stay because you guys had lost the condo."

Bobby's eyes widened in disbelief. "Oh man, no, you didn't, Christina," he said, shaking his head.

"Yes, I did, Bobby. And that's not all. I told her that you were the one who motivated me to step out and pursue my dreams of singing."

"Oh wow, this is not good," Bobby muttered, running a hand through his hair. "Not good at all. Where is she now?"

"I don't know," Christina said, her voice small and defeated. "She took my sweater, the one she had given me years ago, and stormed out."

Bobby sighed deeply, feeling the weight of the situation pressing down on him. He looked around the dressing room, the mirrors reflecting his troubled expression. "Okay, we need to fix this. First, I need to find Brandy and talk to her. Explain everything."

Christina nodded, wiping her tears. "I'm so sorry, Bobby. I never meant for this to happen."

"I know, Christina," Bobby said softly. "But right now, we need to focus on making things right. I'll handle Brandy. You focus on your role and make the most of this opportunity. It's what you wanted, and you deserve to follow your dreams, too."

Christina managed a small, grateful smile. "Thank you, Bobby. I really appreciate it."

Bobby gave her shoulder a reassuring squeeze before heading out of the dressing room. His mind raced with thoughts of how to approach Brandy, how to make her understand the situation, and how to repair the damage that had been done. He knew it wouldn't be easy, but he was determined to try.

As he stepped outside into the crisp evening air, Bobby pulled out his phone and dialled Brandy's number, hoping she would answer and give him the chance to explain.

"Decisions of the Wounded"

Brandy stormed into the house, her anger palpable in every step, her emotions crashing against the walls like a relentless storm. The mere thought of seeing Bobby, the person she held responsible for her world falling apart, intensified the turmoil inside her. With a determined pace, she headed upstairs, seeking refuge in the space that once felt like a sanctuary but now seemed tainted by betrayal.

Entering the bedroom, she didn't hold back, throwing open the closet door with a force that mirrored her chaotic feelings. The Louis Vuitton suitcase, once a symbol of luxury and happy memories, now felt like a container for her frustration as she tossed it onto the bed. Brandy, driven by a need to regain some control, quickly grabbed clothes from the dresser and closet, her movements mechanical but determined.

Despite her hurt and anger, she refused to let the chaos within her take over completely. Each item she packed into a large tote bag was chosen with purpose, a small act of defiance against the crumbling reality she faced. She threw in matching shoes and a tan purse, chosen carefully to go with the clothes she had hastily selected. This was her way of holding on to some semblance of order in the midst of the emotional storm.

In the chaos of her emotions, Brandy struggled to process Christine's revelations. The condo, once a symbol of her dreams and hopes, now felt like an empty shell, a reminder of a life unraveling before her eyes. As she paused amidst the turmoil, she took a moment to look around the room she had decorated with such care, feeling the sting of irony in all the sacrifices she had made for Bobby's elusive dreams.

Her gaze drifted to the top shelf of the closet, where she spotted a small, familiar box—an artifact from her past decorated with painted macaroni noodles from her childhood. She carefully retrieved it as if it were a fragile piece of her former self. Inside, she found something she had hidden away long before Bobby entered her life: an account card, her secret financial safety net.

With the debit card in hand, Brandy quickly called the bank, navigating the automated system to check her balance. The account wasn't overflowing with wealth, but it offered a small glimmer of hope in the darkness. She tucked the card back into her wallet, placing the box in her suitcase as a reminder of her independence before the chaos.

She packed her toiletry bag—a small token of her daily routines now thrown into disarray—signaling her readiness to leave. As she finished packing, she glanced out the window, anxiously awaiting her ride. She hoped to be gone before Bobby returned, and the confrontation she dreaded could begin.

Finally, the car arrived, offering a brief moment of relief. Brandy, her emotions heavy, hurried to load her things into the vehicle. Ignoring the driver's offer of help, she moved with determination, her actions a mix of anger and sorrow as she prepared to leave behind the life she had known.

Sitting in the car, Brandy's emotions churned as the driver, sensing her turmoil, waited for her to give the destination. Struggling to find her voice amidst the chaos of her thoughts, she finally recited the address of the hotel where she planned to take refuge. The driver gave a silent nod of understanding and began driving, leaving the house—and everything it represented—behind in the distance.

As the familiar sight of her home faded in the rearview mirror, Brandy couldn't help but reflect on the life she was leaving behind. The house had once been a place filled with love, joy, and dreams, but now it felt like a monument to everything that had gone wrong. How had her marriage, once so full of promise, deteriorated into this? Why had Bobby kept her in the dark about his career change, something that had turned their world upside down? The security she once felt had vanished, replaced by a void that seemed to grow with every passing mile.

Lost in her thoughts, Brandy barely noticed when they arrived at the hotel. The driver, courteous and efficient, opened her door and helped unload her bags. At the reception desk, she quickly secured a room, paid the driver, and followed the bellboy to the elevator. The ride to her suite was quiet, but inside, her mind was anything but.

Once alone in the suite, Brandy looked around at her expensive luggage, the tangible remnants of a life now in shambles. The sight only fueled her anger, prompting her to order a bottle of pink Moscato. She hauled her suitcase into the bedroom and changed into comfortable pajamas, choosing solace over style. Unpacking could wait; she needed a moment to breathe, to find some sense of normalcy in the midst of chaos.

In the bathroom, she went through her usual beauty routine, clinging to the familiar as everything else seemed to spin out of control. Back in the bedroom, she found a hair tie in her purse and pulled her hair back, a small act of defiance against the storm raging inside her. When room service delivered the wine, she barely registered the act of kindness, too absorbed in her own pain.

Sitting on the sofa, her legs curled beneath her, Brandy took a deep drink of the wine, but the warmth did nothing to ease the ache inside. Finally, the weight of it all became too much, and she broke down, tears streaming unchecked down her face. In the quiet of the hotel room, she let herself cry, the unanswered question reverberating in her mind—"Why?"

Why did Bobby have to decide to abandon his job and plunge into writing? Why keep his literary aspirations hidden from her for so long? And why the silent descent into financial ruin without a single word, leaving her unaware of their precarious situation until the house was lost? The unanswered questions plagued Brandy—a relentless onslaught of confusion, frustration, and fear.

Her mind raced, grappling with the looming uncertainty of covering medical expenses without the safety net of Bobby's job. Above all, the betrayal cut deep—why had he confided in Christine before her, stripping away the semblance of partnership in their marriage? As the weight of her unanswered questions pressed upon her, Brandy sank into the sofa, a river of tears and wine offering no solace.

The empty bottle brought a jolt of irritation; her inebriated state was a strange mix of numbness and chaotic emotions. Attempting to regain composure, she contemplated a facial cleanse, only to find herself hilariously unsuccessful at standing. Laughter bubbled from her, a twisted acknowledgment of her intoxicated state. "Damn, girl. I think you might be messed up," she chuckled, measuring her inebriation with a pinched gesture.

The room swayed as she crawled to the bathroom, where a splash of cold water did little to dispel the intoxication. A feeble attempt at brushing her teeth followed each move a testament to the day's neglect. Collapsing against the sofa, she reached for the remote, craving the solace of music.

. . .

Classic R&B filled the air as Brandy found her rhythm, contemplating another bottle of wine. A chirping phone brought her back to reality, revealing a cascade of missed calls from Bobby and unread texts from Christine. Amidst the familiar chaos, Timmoreia's name appeared, sending a tingle down her spine.

"Oh, Timmoreia. Timmoreia, Timmoreia, Timmoreia, Timmoreia, wherefore art thou, Timmoreia," she giggled, unable to resist the playful wordplay. The decision to call him hung in the air, a tipsy resolve to connect with a familiar presence.

"F**k it, I'll just call him instead," she declared to no one in particular, pressing the dial button with inebriated determination. As the phone rang, she teetered on the edge of hanging up until Timmoreia's voice finally greeted her. "Hey, Brandy! I was hoping to hear from you."

"Well, aren't you a lucky boy," she slurred, the words dripping with a peculiar mix of inebriation and candor. "I was sooooo happy to see that you texted me," she drawled, the elongated syllables a testament to the waves of wine coursing through her.

"Are you okay?" Timmoreia's voice echoed through the phone, genuine concern lacing his words. Brandy, however, was riding the unpredictable waves of intoxication, responding with a playful retort before bursting into laughter. Timmoreia's worry heightened; something wasn't right.

"Brandy, are you drunk? Where are you?" Timmoreia's inquiries poured through the phone, each question carrying the weight of genuine concern. Brandy, caught in the whirlwind of emotions, declared the loss of her home with an abrupt sob.

"Hey, baby. It's okay, don't cry. Where are you? I'll come to you right now if you need me," Timmoreia reassured, his voice cutting through the chaos of emotions. Brandy, in a mixture of vulnerability and desire, admitted, "Oh, yeah, I need you. I need you so badly, Timmoreia. I need to feel you."

"Where are you?" Timmoreia pressed a tinge of impatience in his tone. Brandy, immersed in her tipsy reality, revealed she was at the hotel where they almost had lunch, the room number rolling off her tongue in a sing-song cadence. She hung up abruptly, sprawled on the floor, cautiously closing her eyes to subdue the room's disorienting spin.

Reality hit her with a sudden realization. "Oh, shit. I look like shit!" With a clumsy attempt to stand, she lost her balance and fell onto the couch, a momentary pause before regaining her feet. The bathroom became her sanctuary, a place for a hasty makeup rescue mission.

"Lipstick, mascara, and laughter ensued until a loud knock disrupted her makeover. Timmoreia's urgency escalated, demanding answers. In a frenzy, Brandy opened the door, revealing a mascara mishap. Timmoreia's anger melted into concern, but confusion still lingered."

"Did he hit you?" Timmoreia's grip tightened, inspecting her smeared eye. Brandy, initially frightened, explained through laughter that it was just mascara. The tension subsided as Timmoreia struggled to comprehend the emotional rollercoaster Brandy was on.

"I'm sorry, Timmoreia. I didn't mean to cause you any worry. I just had to get away from Bobby... from everything," Brandy confessed, her voice a rush of words seeking understanding. Timmoreia's laughter, gentle and genuine, reassured her. But as he cleaned her face with a wipe, Brandy's vulnerability spilled out along with her tears.

"What brought all this on?" Timmoreia asked, wiping away the makeup and tears. In the comfort of his arms, Brandy began recounting the theater incident, her voice carrying the weight of heartbreak and disappointment. Timmoreia held her, a silent pillar of support, allowing her to cry until no more tears remained.

They remained on the plush couch, the soft glow of the muted TV casting a gentle light on the room. Brandy, now resting with her head against Timmoreia's chest, had surrendered to a peaceful slumber. Timmoreia, a silent guardian, gently carried her to the bedroom, ensuring she was tucked under the covers. Returning to the living room, he hesitated before choosing to immerse himself in the realm of news, a feeble attempt to ward off the looming silence that awaited her if she awoke alone.

As the television channels flickered in the background, Timmoreia reflected on the unexpected twist his life had taken. His initial plan, fueled by revenge against Bobby, seemed to be unraveling. The months spent plotting against Bobby, aiming to dismantle his life and dreams, now felt like a futile endeavor. The downfall Bobby faced seemed self-inflicted, a consequence of his own choices.

Timmoreia, once successful and now stripped of everything, pondered the collateral damage of his vengeful pursuit. He had lost his savings, his home, and even his family—all due to a misguided revenge plan. The irony was stark: while he aimed to ruin Bobby's life, his own had crumbled in the process.

His original scheme involved seducing Bobby's wife, but when Brandy unveiled the aspirations of Bobby's book, Timmoreia decided to crush that dream as well. The plan was to exploit the superiority of high society, using their penchant for gossip and criticism to tarnish Bobby's literary aspirations.

Yet, the plan took an unexpected turn when Brandy entered the picture. He hadn't foreseen the depth of her vulnerability, the mesmerizing beauty that radiated from her, or the unexpected flashes of humor that sparkled through the gloom of her recent experiences. As he delved deeper into her world,

Timmoreia discovered facets of Brandy that transcended his initial perceptions.

Her talents, like a hidden trove of treasures, unfolded before him. A stage performer with a profound ability to captivate, she wasn't just a victim of circumstance but a resilient force driven by an unyielding determination to survive. Her voice, both as a singer and a woman navigating the complexities of life, resonated with a richness that went beyond the superficial.

In Timmoreia's research, he had stumbled upon Brandy's performances online and on YouTube. One night, captivated by her talent, he spent hours watching her sing and perform. To him, her discovery was nothing short of a revelation. She was amazing; her talent was world-class, and her presence on stage was mesmerizing. Her voice, powerful and soulful, resonated deeply with him, and her ability to connect with her audience was extraordinary.

Brandy was a jewel, a rare talent that deserved to shine brightly. This realization made the follow-through of his plan incredibly challenging. The more he learned about her, the more he admired her strength, resilience, and undeniable talent. She wasn't just another performer; she was a beacon of inspiration, someone who had the potential to achieve greatness.

Timmoreia's admiration for Brandy grew with each performance he watched. Her dedication and passion were evident in every note she sang and every emotion she conveyed. It became clear to him that she wasn't just performing; she was living her dream, pouring her heart and soul into her craft. This made his mission even more complex, as he couldn't bring himself to undermine someone so deserving of success.

As he sat in his dimly lit apartment, surrounded by the remnants of his past, Timmoreia found himself at a crossroads. His original plan, fueled by anger and resentment, now seemed tainted by the respect and admiration he felt for Brandy. The inner conflict was intense, pulling him in different directions.

He knew he had to find a way to reconcile his feelings and figure out a new approach. Brandy's performances had shown him a glimpse of what true talent and determination looked like, and it was something he couldn't easily ignore. She had become more than just a target in his scheme; she had become a symbol of what he aspired to be—someone who turned their struggles into strength and their dreams into reality.

Timmoreia took a deep breath and closed his laptop, the images of Brandy's performances still vivid in his mind. He needed to rethink his strategy and find a way to achieve his goals without compromising his newfound respect for her. It was a difficult path, but one he was now determined to navigate with care. Brandy had unknowingly shown him the power of true talent and perseverance, and it was a lesson he couldn't afford to forget.

Timmoreia found himself spellbound by this revelation, realizing that Brandy was more than a pawn in his revenge game. She was a multifaceted gem, adorned with talents, resilience, and a drive to overcome the challenges fate had thrown her way. The revenge plot that once seemed straightforward now appeared tangled in the intricate threads of her existence.

His weakening demeanor became a complicated factor, casting shadows over his meticulously laid plans and undermining the disciplined façade of a soldier. In the intricate dance of emotions, he found himself entangled in a web of unexpected feelings, threatening to shatter the demonic resolve he had once wielded so effortlessly.

Falling for her was a dangerous descent into uncharted territory, a journey that unraveled the tightly wound threads of his calculated approach. Reflections of his own vulnerabilities echoed loudly, raising doubts about the path he had chosen. The goal, once crystal clear, now appeared blurred and elusive.

Though he stood exactly where the mission dictated, he felt worlds away from the detached, demonic agent he had aspired to be. The paradox lay in the internal conflict—a battle between duty and desire, between the place he needed to be and the place he secretly yearned to linger. The internal struggle intensified, threatening to compromise the very essence of the mission he had sworn to fulfill.

The mission stood as the linchpin to a grand design, a meticulously crafted plot destined to extractexact revenge on Bobby and settle the debts owed to those who eagerly awaited the culmination of the financial aspects of the plan. It was not merely a task; it was a vendetta, an intricate dance of fate where every move had a purpose, and every step was calculated.

This undertaking bore the weight of Timmoreia's past grievances and financial obligations, a convergence of personal vendettas and pragmatic necessities. The culmination of this operation would not only dismantle Bobby's world but also serve as the financial remedy that would placate the looming creditors, each hungry for their share of the orchestrated retribution.

The complexity of the plan was shrouded in shadows, its success hinging on precision and flawless execution. It wasn't just about revenge; it was a journey toward liberation from the burdens that had shackled Timmoreia for far too long. Every detail, every nuance of the mission carried the weight of his past —a past that demanded retribution and redemption.

As Timmoreia delved deeper into the intricate layers of his scheme, he felt the palpable tension building—a crescendo of anticipation and determination. The revenge he sought wasn't a mere act; it was a cathartic release, a settling of scores that went beyond the financial realm. It was personal, a vendetta woven into the very fabric of his being.

The mission wasn't just a means to an end; it was the narrative of a man seeking justice and closure, a tale that would unfold with every meticulously calculated move. The shadows of the past danced in the background, casting an ominous glow over the unfolding drama, and the stage was set for a reckoning that would transcend the boundaries of mere vengeance.

The fire of revenge, once burning fiercely within him, began to wane as he witnessed Brandy's pain and despair. The goal of destroying Bobby's dreams seemed less enticing in the face of the genuine hurt inflicted upon Brandy.

He found himself captivated by her, a desire awakening within him that went beyond revenge. The fire coursing through his veins was no longer fueled by retaliation but by an intense longing to possess her—emotionally and physically. The realization struck him as he delicately wiped away her makeup and tears.

"What the fuck am I doing?" Timmoreia questioned himself abruptly. The sudden surge of self-awareness prompted him to stand up, feeling the need to distance himself from Brandy. He believed that clarity would return with distance, allowing him to reenter the realm of revenge.

He considered quietly checking on her first, just to ensure she was okay. Stepping quietly to the bedroom door, he opened it slowly. To his surprise, she was sitting up against the headboard, her eyes locked on his. He froze in his tracks, not knowing what to say. Actually, he was not able to speak because she took his breath away. The moon illuminated her soft skin. Her eyes shimmered with unshed tears. The blanket fell away from her torso, exposing the cotton tank top. Her braless form, with breasts heaving beneath the thin fabric, beckoned his attention.

In a slow, deliberate motion, she extended a hand, inviting him into her space. Overwhelmed, he ventured further into the room, standing in uncertainty. Her beckoning gesture encouraged him to take her hand. As he delicately brushed her fingertips, she grasped his hand, never breaking eye contact.

Attempting to speak, he was silenced by her finger placed gently against her lips, shushing him. The pull of her hand urged him closer until he stood at the edge of the bed. Tilting her head upward, she exposed her slender neck, a vulnerable gesture.

In the softest of whispers, she uttered, "I need you." Rising to her knees, she explored his chest and arms, reaching his waist to unfasten his shirt. The belt followed, and with her eyes inviting a kiss, he succumbed to the allure of her eager lips.

She removed his shirt, taking a moment to appreciate his presence. It was evident that words were not necessary; this encounter was about a shared sense of connection, guiding them into an intimate space.

His jeans yielded to her touch, falling to the floor as he shed his shoes and socks. Standing in front of her in briefs, the unspoken desire hung in the air. She retained her tank top, pulling it down with a subtle elegance. Brushing against him, she skillfully invited a connection.

Stepping behind him, she engaged in a shared moment of vulnerability. Her hands reached around a silent expression of unity. A tender kiss hinted at the impending connection. In a slow dance, she traced her lips along his body, exploring every inch.

The shared intimacy unfolded without explicit details, a dance of emotions and connection. The unspoken understanding between them conveyed a mutual desire for closeness and shared pleasure.

He was deeply immersed in the pleasurable sensations she bestowed upon him when she gently nudged his shoulders with both hands, silently indicating her desire for him to lie down on the bed—on his stomach. Complying with her unspoken request, he adjusted himself, and at that moment, his arousal reached an unprecedented intensity. Brandy climbed onto the bed, straddling him, aligning herself skillfully; the warmth and moisture of her contact against his skin created an intimate connection. She began to move, a rhythmic motion pressing against him, starting slow before gaining momentum. The act seemed to serve as a release for her, and he could hear her moans and breath quicken as she moved faster.

Suddenly, she halted, disengaged, and rolled him over. Straddling him once again, she took control, guiding him into an intimate connection. The sensation of heat and moisture enveloping him nearly overwhelmed him. Glancing up at her beautiful face, her closed eyes and head thrown back, she rode him with deliberate slowness, her breasts gently bouncing with each movement. Satisfied with her moment, he felt it was time to reciprocate.

Sitting up, he took hold of her breasts, indulging in a less-than-gentle manner. She moaned in response, still working her hips against him. She wrapped her legs around him, and as he stood, still connected to her, he turned around and gently placed her on the bed. Unexpectedly, he flipped her onto her stomach, pulling her hips up so she rested on her knees, exposing herself in a vulnerable pose. She reached back, inviting him to explore further.

Without hesitation, he gave her what she desired, sliding in and relishing the tightness. The rhythm started, and her moans filled the room as he explored various movements. The intensity increased as he withdrew, spreading and squeezing her cheeks with each thrust. Her passionate pleas and encouraging words fueled the fire.

Timmoreia shifted positions, maintaining the connection but adjusting the dynamic. He slapped her ass, and she responded with pleasure, arching her back and pushing against his every move. Holding her by the hair and spanking her, he felt her reaching climax.

As the waves of pleasure surged, Timmoreia let go of her hair, grabbed her hips, and intensified his thrusts. The mutual ecstasy reached its peak, echoed by their loud moans. He held himself deep within her as the spasms of pleasure reverberated between them.

. . .

After the peak subsided, he released her hips and slowly withdrew. The cool air of the room surrounded him, contrasting with the heat of the intense encounter. Brandy lay flat on the bed, still on her stomach, arms stretched out over her head, slowly returning to a normal breathing pattern. Timmoreia lay down next to her on his back, turning his head to observe her.

Her eyes remained closed, yet tears streamed down her face, a complex mix of emotions etched across her features.

"Desperate Search"

Bobby's desperation intensified as he frantically sought Brandy. The mystery of her disappearance weighed heavily on him, with Christina being the last known person to have contact with her. Balancing comforting his sister-in-law and scouring the places he thought Brandy might be, Bobby faced the daunting challenge of the unknown.

Even among Brandy's supposed theater "friends," silence prevailed, an unusual and unsettling void. Staring dejectedly out of the breakfast nook window, Bobby grappled with the realization that he had mishandled the situation. Regret flooded him as he acknowledged the lack of attention he'd paid to the evolving dynamics between Brandy and himself. He had naively assumed that once she adjusted to his aspiration of becoming an author, she would embrace it, especially as it became clear how crucial it was to him.

Did he not share his dream with her back in college? The details puzzled him, and the urgency of the present situation overpowered such thinking. Finding Brandy's safety became his sole focus. Attempts to extract information from hotels proved futile, leaving Bobby frustrated and helpless. Meanwhile,

Christina bombarded his phone with texts, seeking updates every fifteen minutes. Bobby, overwhelmed, eventually called her, requesting she cease the barrage of messages, assuring her he'd inform her the moment he had any news on Brandy.

Seated at the table, Bobby grappled with the uncertainty, contemplating the alleged 22-hour waiting period before filing a missing person's report. The ticking clock echoed the seconds slipping away as he faced the reality that every moment counted in the desperate search for his wife.

Meanwhile, back at the hotel, Brandy abruptly rose from the bed, hastily donning her clothes while using her hands to wipe away the lingering tears on her face. Avoiding eye contact with Timmoreia, she struggled to process the intensity of their encounter. Sensing the shift in dynamics, Timmoreia quietly mirrored her actions, both dressing in an uncomfortable silence that hung heavily between them.

In the aftermath, Brandy grappled with the mortification of her unrestrained behavior. Despite knowing it was a boundary she shouldn't have crossed, a peculiar desire lingered, tempting her to indulge once more. How could she face herself in the mirror? How would she confront Bobby, her mind replaying the vivid memories of her and Timmoreia entangled in each other's desires?

The remnants of the wine's effect seemed to dissipate, leaving Brandy in a state of conflicted emotions. Moving out of the bedroom, she hesitantly settled on the couch, uncertain of how to interact with Timmoreia. Tingles lingered from their passionate encounter, creating an internal conflict she couldn't easily shake off. Her self-reflection led to the realization that an apology to Timmoreia was necessary for entangling him in her personal chaos.

Unable to meet his gaze, she contemplated the tears threatening to resurface, realizing they were more for herself than for the impact on Bobby. The internal struggle intensified as she grappled with the reality of her actions, never envisioning herself in the role of an "adulteress."

With her head in her hands, Brandy emitted a sigh filled with remorse, creating an atmosphere charged with tension. Timmoreia, understanding the complexity of the situation, stood beside her. Restraining himself from intruding on her personal space, he wished to offer comfort and assurance. Sometimes, life took unexpected turns, and the aftermath required understanding rather than judgment.

Choosing to sit on the floor next to her, Timmoreia gently rubbed her forearm, seeking to convey understanding. "Hey, listen, Brandy," he began, addressing the unspoken turmoil. He expressed his enjoyment of their shared moment and emphasized the impact she had on his life beyond the physical encounter.

He clarified his stance, recognizing her commitment to Bobby and respecting the boundaries that existed. Timmoreia assured her of his continuous availability, no matter the magnitude of her needs. Tenderly kissing her fingertips, he conveyed the sincerity of his sentiments.

Moved by his words, Brandy felt herself drawn into his eyes, his soul. Their connection deepened as she kissed him lightly, expressing gratitude. Walking him to the door, their silent exchange lingered, neither eager to part ways. A gentle goodbye kiss sealed the intense encounter, leaving Brandy to navigate the aftermath and confront the choices that lay ahead.

"Yearning Echoes and Timmoreia's Rage"

In the wake of their recent encounter, days passed without a word from Brandy, leaving an unsettling void in Timmoreia's world. The boundaries they once set now seemed like distant echoes, fading away in the intensity of their newfound connection. The intimate entanglement had laid bare the depth of their feelings, exposing a longing that refused to be ignored.

Eagerly and intensely yearning for Brandy, Timmoreia found himself consumed by an insatiable desire. Her touch, her presence, her taste—the mere thought of her haunted his existence. Within the confines of his small and disheveled apartment, he paced restlessly, stumbling over objects misplaced in his distracted state. An internal rage simmered, fuelled by the overwhelming need that now dominated his every waking moment.

Timmoreia was now consuming more and more alcohol to help cope with the intense feelings he had developed for Brandy. As he stood there in his dilapidated apartment, he found himself struggling just to stand up. The room spun around him as he staggered aimlessly, his balance failing him. Eventually, he fell to the floor, momentarily unable to get up.

Lying there, he was haunted by the passion he both felt and experienced with Brandy. The memory of her touch, her voice, and the moments they shared together was a tormenting contrast to the reality of his current state. He knew in his mind that the game had changed. His emotions were no longer just a distraction; they were an overwhelming force that he couldn't control.

His mind started to play tricks on him. In the haze of his drunkenness, he began to hear and recall the pivotal meeting with Bobby—the meeting where Bobby had closed the deal that ultimately cost him everything he had. The scene replayed in his head like a haunting echo.

Timmoreia remembered Bobby's confident smile, the way he effortlessly convinced everyone in the room that the deal was a good idea. He could hear the chatter, the laughter, and finally, the moment of realization when he understood what he had lost. The betrayal and the financial ruin that followed were crushing, and the pain of it all felt fresh again.

In his alcohol-fueled stupor, Timmoreia's anger and regret mixed with his feelings for Brandy, creating a chaotic storm in his mind. The walls of his apartment seemed to close in on him, and he felt trapped by his own choices and circumstances. The alcohol that once numbed his pain now intensified his anguish, and he couldn't escape the tormenting thoughts.

He managed to crawl to a nearby chair and pull himself up, his body trembling from the effort. He sat there, breathing heavily, staring at the empty bottles scattered around the room. Each one was a testament to his attempt to drown out the past, but the past was relentless, always resurfacing no matter how much he drank.

Timmoreia knew he had to find a way to regain control, but the path forward seemed impossible. The love he felt for Brandy was real, but so were the consequences of his actions and the shadows of his past. He closed his eyes, trying to steady himself, but the images and voices continued to plague him.

Lying in his chair, Timmoreia fell into the memory of that pivotal moment when he and Bobby executed the trade. The room seemed to echo with the weight of undisclosed truths and hidden motives. The flickering lights in the office mirrored the uncertainty of the market they were entering.

"Okay, just a little more paperwork, and we can have this done," said Bobby. "Jay T., if you don't mind, what is the 'T' for?" asked Bobby.

"Well, it's a sort of funny name, and I really haven't used it much since I was a kid in grade school. The students used to tease me about it. So, let's just leave it at 'T.' Thank you."

"Okay, no problem, Mister Jay T. Willabee, it is," Bobby replied, a smirk playing at the corners of his mouth.

"I need you to understand this, though, Mr. Pope," said Jay, his voice tinged with urgency. "I've got a lot riding on this. And I mean a lot."

Mr. Pope leaned back in his chair, steepling his fingers thoughtfully. "Well, Jay, all I can tell you is that in life, everything we do, every step we take, is a mechanism of change. And change never happens unless we take some risks. But you should also know that with every risk, there can be consequences—sometimes good and sometimes not so good. It's completely up to the one who takes the risks."

Jay nodded; his expression was curiously tinged with concern. "I understand that, Mr. Pope. But this... this feels different."

"This could change everything for me—for the better," Jay repeated, his voice a mix of hope and desperation. The phrase seemed to hang in the air, reverberating with the significance of the moment.

"This could change everything for me—for the better."

"This could change everything for me—for the better."

"This could change everything for me—for the better."

"This could change everything for me—for the better."

The cry repeated itself over and over again in Timmoreia's mind. It vibrated throughout the walls of his apartment like an echo that just wouldn't stop. The memory of that conversation, the stakes involved, and the haunting words of his past intertwined with his present turmoil, creating a relentless loop in his consciousness.

As he lay there, the line between his past and present blurred, the weight of his choices bearing down on him. The realization of how much he had gambled and how little he had gained gnawed at him, a constant reminder of his failures and the life he could have had. The echoes of his desperation filled the room, a relentless reminder of the risks taken and the price paid.

By this time, Timmoreia's conscience had taken over the chaos, and it began to speak to him through the alcohol. "Look at you, Jay. You ain't shit. You're lying out here looking like a two-dollar hoe. What happened to the grind in you, man? What happened to the hustler in you...?"

"Oh, I know—you let that pretty ass girl put that thing on your ass. Now look at you. You are pathetic! If I was real, I would spit on your punk ass. You're gonna get us killed, Jay! I'm telling you, you're gonna get us killed!" You hear me Jay...Hey, --- --------Jay, you hear what I said! ------ You're gonna get us killed, Jay!

His conscience's harsh words echoed in his mind as his consciousness faded away.

Things were now real, and there was no doubt; the game had indeed changed, and Timmoreia was struggling to find his place in it. The battle was no longer just external; it was within him, a relentless fight between his desire for redemption and the weight of his past mistakes. And in the midst of it all, Brandy was the beacon he couldn't ignore, even as his world crumbled around him.

It felt like Timmoreia's past, like when he was struggling with addiction, feeling the familiar pull of withdrawal and the intense desire for a "high" to alleviate it. Yes, no doubt she was now his desired high. This shit reminded him of his past struggles with addiction, particularly during his time with Crack. Unfortunately, in his desperation to satisfy his cravings then, he was willing to resort to harmful actions, potentially causing harm to others in the process. It's a stark reminder of the grip that addiction can have on a person's life and the lengths they may go to in order to feed it. He was, no doubt, finding her presence.

As he paced, the urgency to find common ground with Brandy grew. She had vocalized their connection, and he believed her feelings mirrored his own. In his conviction, he was certain that her love for him surpassed any ties to Bobby. The tempest of tempting passions within him birthed a new plan, and the strategic thinker Timmoreia took a back seat to Jay Willabee, the Hustler. In his mind, the cloak would come off, but in his plan, he would still need to remain a "wolf in sheep's clothing."

Driven by a relentless pursuit of his desires, Timmoreia grappled with the rationality of risks and the potential consequences. The boundaries between his calculated moves and impulsive decisions blurred, with the hustler mentality taking charge. The internal conflict unfolded, and Timmoreia found himself navigating the turbulent waters of love, lust, and the tangled webs of his own making.

The phone's harsh ring pierced the silence, a stark reminder of the intricate web of deception Timmoreia had woven. It was the orchestrator of their divine plan, the accomplice who held the strings to the clandestine operations that danced in the shadows. As Timmoreia answered the call, the weight of their scheme hung heavily in the air.

"Hey man, I haven't heard from you since our last check-in. How are we looking?" inquired the accomplice, his voice a blend of urgency and scrutiny.

Timmoreia hesitated, a fleeting moment of internal struggle as he grappled with the complexities that now tainted the once-clear blueprint of their plot. "We're good, man," he replied, attempting to conceal the newfound challenges that threatened the seamless execution of their plan.

"What's that sound I hear in your voice, man? Are you okay? Why do you sound distressed and out of sync?" questioned the accomplice, probing deeper into Timmoreia's apparent unease.

"Oh, shit. Don't tell me you slept with her. Damn, man, I told you not to touch her. She's like poison," the accomplice admonished, his voice sharp with frustration. "Now you're all messed up in the damn head. This is not good, man. I need to know that you can get this done."

The shadows of uncertainty loomed over their once-unshakable alliance, threatening to unravel the carefully laid threads of their deceitful plot. The room felt colder, the air thick with tension and mistrust.

"Look, there ain't no turning back on this," the accomplice continued, his tone deadly serious. "You mess it up, you die. Hell, we both die."

The words hung in the air, a stark reminder of the high stakes they were playing for. The gravity of the situation was unmistakable. There was no room for error, no second chances. The plan had to be executed perfectly, or it would mean the end for both of them. The bonds of their partnership, once strong and unwavering, now felt fragile under the weight of this new betrayal.

The accomplice's eyes bore into him, searching for any sign of weakness or hesitation. "Can you do this?" he demanded, the urgency in his voice leaving no room for doubt. "We've come too far to let it all fall apart now. Get your head straight and focus. This is life or death."

The tension was palpable, and the silence that followed was filled with unspoken fears and unresolved tensions. They both knew that the path they were on was perilous, but there was no other choice. The stakes were too high, and failure was not an option. They had to see it through to the end, no matter the cost.

"I said I'm good," Timmoreia retorted defensively, a thin veil of frustration masking the underlying turmoil within.

Timmoreia, feeling the weight of his past debts, replied with a sharp edge, "I don't need you throwing receipts in my face. I know the deal. It's just that things have gotten complicated, and we need to reset and get it done."

"Reset? What the hell do you mean, 'reset'?" demanded the accomplice, the tension in his voice palpable.

"Things have turned a little bit," Timmoreia confessed cryptically, careful not to divulge the newfound entanglements that had emerged. The mention of complications triggered the accomplice's concern.

"Look, Timmoreia, Jay, or whatever the hell your name is today, you need a reality check. People are out there with a thirst for your blood, and if we can't pull this off, death is the only certainty you face," declared the voice, each word heavy with the weight of past alliances and debts.

As memories of their shared prison days resurfaced, the voice continued, "Back in prison, you stopped me from meeting my end at the hands of those skinheads. I felt a debt, an obligation to keep you breathing. But I also know the ones searching for you, and they're not playing games. If this plan doesn't unfold the way it needs to, death will be knocking on your door, and I won't be far behind. So, pull yourself together, put on your damn cape, and make sure this shit happens. We don't have a choice."

The shadows of impending doom cast long twists over Timmoreia's every thought as the voice delivered a final ultimatum. "I'll give you three days. If something hasn't happened by then, you're on your own. I'll finish this shit myself; consequences be damned." The countdown to his fate had begun, and in the echoing silence that followed, the gravity of his predicament pressed upon Timmoreia like a suffocating weight. The shadows of retribution loomed ominously, and time was rapidly slipping through his grasp.

The metallic click sound of the phone hanging up reverberated through Timmoreia's dimly lit apartment, leaving behind a profound silence that mirrored the turbulence within him. Seated in his dilapidated recliner, the worn-out fabric seemed to absorb the weight of the choices that now confronted him—a stark dichotomy between the relentless pursuit of self-preservation and the chaotic longing for love and escape.

His gaze, burdened with the echoes of the conversation, fixated on the peeling wallpaper that bore witness to the struggles etched into his existence. The room seemed to close in, the shadows dancing to the dissonant melody of despair and agony that resonated in his mind.

The lazy boy chair, a relic of better days now marred by time, cradled him in a cocoon of conflicting emotions. In the corners of the room, fragments of shattered dreams lay scattered, embodying the broken pieces of his past and the uncertain shards of his future.

Timmoreia's hands clenched, fingers digging into the frayed armrests as if seeking an anchor in the storm of choices before him. The air hung heavy with the scent of indecision, a strong aroma that saturated the room, mixing with the dusty memories he couldn't escape.

The shadows, cast by the feeble light filtering through

tattered curtains, danced on the walls, embodying the contrast of his predicament. One path led to the harsh realm of survival, where danger lurked, and debts demanded payment. The other whispered promises of love and freedom, a chance to break free from the shackles of his turbulent existence.

As the seconds ticked away, each choice echoed with consequences that vibrated through the very core of his being. The phone call had left him at the crossroads of his own narrative, and the weight of the decision he now faced pressed down upon him, a relentless force shaping the flight of his uncertain future.

"Shattered Ties"

Brandy's mind raced as she left Timmoreia's presence, her heart pounding in her chest. She knew she was wrong in so many ways, but the aftermath was a storm for which she had no answers. The weight of her decisions bore down on her as she hurriedly exited the condo, desperate to avoid a confrontation with Bobby. In her rush, she left behind her medication, an oversight that would soon become significant. As her mind and body rebelled, she felt an overwhelming urge to find something—anything—to take the edge off.

Christina embarked on an emotional journey to unravel the mystery of Brandy's disappearance. Her footsteps echoed through the stillness of the night as she approached Brandy and Bobby's house. Her heart pulsated with worry, each step a rhythm echoing the uncertainty that hung in the air. Brandy, her sister, was missing, and the gravity of the situation compelled Christina to abandon the worry of waiting and seek comfort in action. The narrative unfolded like a chilling play, revealing Brandy's struggles and the persistent specter of her early trauma that continued to exert its wicked influence.

· · ·

In the annals of Brandy's life, Christina recognized the recurring motif of cocaine's insidious grasp and the mental scars inflicted by her chaotic relationships, notably with Carl and the looming figure of Silvia, her mother. The impact of these relationships, like shadows, lingered, leaving Brandy to navigate a complex web of trauma and substance abuse. The tendrils of Silvia's influence, a lethal remedy for resolve, manifested in Brandy's life, especially in moments of despair when options failed to align with her expectations. A subtle hint of schizophrenia added another layer to her challenges. Voices reminiscent of Silvia's relentless whispers led Brandy down treacherous paths, pushing her toward resolutions that promised nothing but self-inflicted harm.

Christina unbuttoned her coat, revealing a mixture of determination and concern in her eyes. She followed Bobby into the sitting room, where the heavy air bore witness to the unspoken tension that filled the space. Bobby slumped into an overstuffed chair. Weariness etched into the lines of his face.

"So, no word from her yet?" Christina inquired, attempting to navigate the fragile terrain of their shared worry.

"Not a damn thing. No text, no voicemail, nothing," Bobby replied, frustration tainting his voice. The weight of Brandy's absence pressed upon him, and the mystery of her whereabouts fuelled his distress.

Christina, her own emotions intertwined with an unspoken truth, tried to offer comfort. "She probably checked into some hotel to work things through in her mind," she suggested, the unspoken tension hanging heavily between them.

"Yeah, I know I messed up on that part. But to be mad at you for whatever imagined feelings she thinks you have for me? Come on, that's just crazy!" Bobby expressed, inadvertently shining a light on the unspoken and complex undercurrents between them.

Embarrassment tinged Christina's face as she stood, unable to meet Bobby's eyes. The room became her refuge as she paced, the inner turmoil threatening to breach the surface. The unspoken feelings she harbored for Bobby remained hidden, like a delicate secret she dared not unveil.

"Have you talked to Meeka? Maybe she knows something," Christina asked, trying to redirect the conversation.

Bobby shook his head. "Meeka's been working so hard on her campaign that she hasn't even been around lately. I'm sure she doesn't know."

"Maybe you're right," Christina conceded, "but if she's not here soon, I will call her, and the two of us will go out and look for Brandy while you wait here in case she comes home."

Attempting to further redirect the conversation, Christina asked about Brandy's friends, hoping for a lifeline in their search. Bobby's response revealed a solitary existence—a stark reality that heightened their concern.

With uncertainty lingering, Christina suggested waiting, and with Bobby's consent, she sought refuge in the kitchen, the rhythmic sounds of making coffee a feeble attempt to drown out the echoing silence.

As the minutes crawled by, the room bore witness to Christina's internal struggle, and Bobby, burdened by the unknown, yearned for Brandy's return. The oppressive stillness was shattered by the insistent ring of Bobby's phone, an unexpected lifeline cutting through the anguish. His heart raced as he grasped the device, his voice laced with a fusion of yearning and anxiety, "Brandy?"

A gentle yet resolute voice emerged on the other end, "Yes, it's me, Bobby." The relief that surged within him was intense. "Brandy, where are you, baby? You have both me and your sister worried sick." Her sister? The revelation added an unforeseen layer of complexity to the situation.

"Your sister," he reiterated, the gravity of their shared

concern casting a shadow over his words. "We're both going crazy trying to find you. Brandy, what's going on?" The urgency in his tone underscored the depth of his apprehension.

In a moment of poignant candor, Brandy dismissed the details that had driven a wedge between them. "Look, it doesn't matter anymore, whatever it is. All that matters is that we—I need you to come home." The plea echoed through the phone, laden with unspoken emotions and a longing for reconciliation.

Brandy's response, laden with a promise, lingered in the air. "I'll be there shortly. There's something I need to tell both of you." The cryptic revelation added an air of suspense, intensifying the emotional currents at play. "Okay, babe, please hurry home," Bobby implored, a potent mixture of anticipation and worry etched across his face.

As the call ended, the promise of imminent revelation hung in the air, setting the stage for a reunion fraught with emotions, secrets, and the undeniable gravity of the untold story that awaited both Bobby and Christina.

"Let me talk to her," Christina said, her voice trembling with emotion. Bobby handed her the phone without hesitation.

"Brandy, it's me," Christina began, her voice soft but firm. "Look, Brandy, you're my sister, and I love you so much. I am so sorry for everything that's going on with you and for being so selfish not to tell you what was going on with me. Sis, I just want you to be as proud of me as I am of you. Please come home so we can talk."

There was a long pause on the other end, filled with the silence of Brandy's contemplation. The weight of Christina's words hung in the air—a bridge extended in the hope of reconciliation.

Finally, Brandy's voice came through, fragile yet resolved. "I'll be there soon, Christina. I promise." The line went dead, but the promise lingered, a beacon of hope in the darkness.

Meanwhile, in the quiet solitude of Brandy's sanctuary, she

grappled with her own turmoil. Alone with her thoughts, she contemplated a future riddled with uncertainty, her health hanging in the balance. The weight of her decisions pressed upon her, and the need to confide in Bobby and Christina became an urgent priority assoon as she reached for her phone, a journey into the unknown awaited her—fraught with shattered ties and the prospect of rebuilding what was broken.

As Brandy crossed the threshold of her home, an eerie silence greeted her, replacing the once-familiar cocoon of comfort. The security that used to envelop her when entering was visibly absent. Bobby's revelation that Christina was already at the house heightened an underlying irritation, amplifying the enigma of why her husband and Christina were alone in her sacred space. She suppressed the surge of jealousy but could feel it simmering beneath the surface, an unstable feeling.

Within the hushed mood, Brandy found them both seated, silently gazing into coffee mugs, a scene of anticipation hidden in a disguise of casual normalcy. The abrupt rise from their seats upon her arrival mirrored their unpreparedness for her presence. Christina's eyes, glinting with unshed tears, betrayed her concern, slowly dissolving the walls of defense Brandy had erected. In a moment of vulnerability, Christina approached, and a spontaneous embrace shattered the passive exterior Brandy had clung to. Unrestrained, a cry leaks out, marking the unraveling of carefully guarded emotions.

Amidst the charged atmosphere, Brandy grappled with pacing—a nervous ballet that mirrored her internal turmoil. Attempting to articulate the confusion within, she confessed to a sudden escape, an urgent need for clarity amid the storm in her mind. Seated in an armchair, she rocked back and forth, reluctant to verbalize her reality outward. The admission of her critical diagnosis hung heavy in the air, the fear of the looming struggle evident.

Bobby, guilt-ridden for recent decisions, attempted to bridge the emotional split with an outstretched hand, only to be met with rejection. As Brandy paced, the specter of guilt about Timmoreia compounded her internal strife. The room became a battlefield of emotions—anger, fear, and guilt interacting in a complicated waltz.

In the dimly lit room, Brandy's restless footsteps painted an abstract masterpiece on the canvas of her internal turmoil. Each movement carried the weight of an unspoken guilt, a specter that loomed large in the corners of her consciousness. The dance of shadows around her mirrored the intricate choreography of regret, a silent acknowledgment of the choices made and the consequences left unattended.

"Christina," witnessing Brandy's unfiltered vulnerability, raised her voice in concern, breaking the accustomed composure that defined Brandy. "I have cancer. They say we caught it early at the stage 2 level. I was diagnosed yesterday, and I will need to make some decisions about my treatment options." The revelation of Brandy's stage 2 breast cancer plunged the room into an unsettling stillness, punctuated only by the comically frozen expressions of disbelief on Bobby's and Christina's faces.

"Baby, are you gonna be alright?" Bobby replied, highly disturbed. "Brandy, I just went through something similar last month. But they said I would be fine and that the test I took produced a false positive. Well, damn. Don't we have a lot of shit going on up in here?" Brandy said, shaking her head. "See, this is the problem; we are all running around here with too many damn secrets between each other," said Brandy in a subtle and disturbed voice.

Questions about the veracity of the diagnosis, the potential treatments, and the collateral damage sought answers in the midst of escalating fear. Brandy's attempt to focus on the actionable plan brought a momentary respite from the emotional turmoil.

As the trio confronted the harsh reality, the weight of the

situation settled, and exhaustion replaced the initial shock. The decision for Christina to stay overnight marked a collective acknowledgment of the emotional toll that had been exacted.

In the private sanctuary of the kitchen, Brandy and Bobby confronted the widening gap between them. The request for separate sleeping arrangements, a tangible manifestation of Brandy's unaddressed pain, left Bobby grappling with the stark truth. The night concluded with Bobby retreating to a solitary guest room, wrestling with the haunting prospect of an uncertain future and the tumult of emotions that accompanied it.

Brandy's phone rang, and it was Dr. Thomas delivering unexpected news. The surgery date had been moved up to two weeks, the 18th at 7:00 am. Hearing the news, Christina quickly reached out and called Meeka. Meek, hearing the news over the phone while still driving, with her calming presence, insisted they all ride together to the hospital the day of.

As the plans unfolded, Brandy hesitated but ultimately welcomed Meeka's support. The prospect of a waiting room entourage almost made her laugh—almost.

Exhausted after the day's events, Brandy attempted to clear the table, but Bobby intervened, urging her to relax and take a hot bath. Despite his caring gesture, Brandy felt a twinge of irritation, questioning his sudden concern for her well-being.

Upstairs, Brandy grappled with conflicting emotions. She considered dismissing the bath suggestion but conceded to its allure. As the soothing scent of lavender filled the bathroom, Brandy reflected on her weariness and the strained communication with Bobby. Their conversations had been superficial, avoiding the issues that truly mattered.

Bobby, meanwhile, took care of the chores downstairs, eager to support Brandy in any way he could. After completing the tasks, he headed upstairs, knocked on their bedroom door, and offered his assistance. Brandy declined, citing fatigue, and closed the door, leaving Bobby with a sense of helplessness.

In his own room, Bobby resolved to bridge the emotional gap between them. Tomorrow, he vowed to make Brandy talk or, at the very least, listen. The commitment they made to each other, "for better or for worse, through sickness and in health," would be a reminder of the enduring bond they shared. The surgery, now just two weeks away, added an urgency to their need for understanding and connection.

Bobby rose early the next day, entering the kitchen with the intention of preparing breakfast. To his surprise, Brandy was already seated at the kitchen nook, sipping her coffee. Bobby joined her, casually making his own cup, and inquired about her night's rest.

"I got a few hours in," she replied, hastily standing up from the table. An obvious attempt to leave the room was thwarted as Bobby walked around the island, positioning himself in front of her. Annoyed, she uttered, "Umm... excuse me."

"No, Brandy. We need to sit down and talk, and I mean really talk," he said firmly, determined to address the underlying issues.

"Bobby, this isn't the time," she protested, attempting to evade the conversation. Bobby, however, blocked her path, insisting that now was precisely the right time to have an open and honest discussion.

"Of 'OUR' lives? I think you mean MY life, Bobby. You're not the one with some disease eating you up from the inside. You're not about to be sliced and diced and sewn back together like the fucking bride of Frankenstein! You're not the one that still might end up dying even after having all this shit done to your body! IT'S HAPPENING TO ME, BOBBY! TO ME," she screamed, her emotions pouring out with tears.

In response, Bobby did the only thing he could—he enveloped her in a tight embrace. She resisted, pushing and punching, trying to break free until she finally collapsed against him, sobbing.

"Why, Bobby? Why is this happening to me?" she questioned, not expecting an answer but finding some solace in his comforting hold.

"Baby, I can't answer that, but we are in this together, you hear me?" he affirmed, speaking softly. "I need you here by my side. Don't you know that? Can't you see how my heart is hurting for you?"

Bobby pulled away, looking into her eyes with determination. "I know I messed up, but I promise you here and now that we are partners in everything. I will do whatever is needed to get you back to your best health. But I need you to talk to me. Tell me what you need. Tell me what you're afraid of, and I will chase those monsters away. Do you hear me, babe? Do you understand that you are not alone?"

She met his gaze, recognizing the familiar determination that drew her to him. She felt his conviction and knew he would be successful in whatever he set his mind to, including his aspirations as an author.

For a moment, her mind visualized that cool "you" Kappa Brother standing on the porch in college, gaming me by knowing I was checking him out but trying to hide the fact that he knew. He has always been the smoothest brother she had ever met. Even more than that, his level of ambition is what got both of them to where they are. He had never cheated on her, he had never disrespected her, he had only treated her like a Queen and that made the internal guilt of what she had done feel all the more damaging in her mind.

"Do you accept that?" Bobby asked again.

She nodded gently, whispering, "Yes, I accept that. I do."

He pulled her close once more, offering the strength and comfort she desperately needed. In that moment, surrounded by his embrace, everything felt right. It felt good.

"Echoes of Redemption: Unveiling the Lettered Confession"

In the hushed interlude between the storms that raged within Brandy's soul, a fleeting calm settled over her world. The weight of her impending battle with stage 2 breast cancer had been laid bare before Bobby and Christina, and, for a moment, the storm of their lives found a brief break. With Bobby running errands and Christina immersed in the world of rehearsals, Brandy found herself alone, a lone watch awaiting the unfolding chapters of her fate.

In the calm moments between the emotional storms raging inside Brandy, a brief peace settled over her life. She had recently shared her struggle with stage 2 breast cancer with Bobby and Christina, and for a moment, they all found some respite. With Bobby out running errands and Christina busy with rehearsals, Brandy found herself alone, waiting for the next chapter of her life to unfold.

Drawn to the neglected mailbox, a container of everyday correspondence and overlooked bills, Brandy walked across the damp grass, still wet from the night's rain. As she retrieved the armful of mail, a single letter slipped from her grasp and fell to the ground. The blurred address suggested it was more than just another bill or legal notice. Curious and uneasy, Brandy picked up the damp letter.

Opening the letter, she noticed the handwritten words, simple yet filled with an eerie familiarity. The childlike penmanship carried profound regret. "Hello," it began, immediately setting a somber tone. The letter asked for Brandy's attention, hinting at a tale of remorse and sorrow.

The letter unraveled an unspeakable past, a confession from someone deeply regretful for the mental anguish they had caused Brandy and her late mother. The author shrouded in anonymity, painted a haunting picture of despair and guilt, expressing a wish to bear the consequences of their actions.

In a twist, the writer expressed a wish to absorb Brandy's pain, pleading for divine intervention. They spoke of transformation during twenty-two years of confinement, suggesting a soul reborn within prison walls. As Brandy read, a chill crept up her spine, mixing fear with curiosity.

Brandy dropped the letter, recoiling as a scream escaped her lips. The paradox of terror and fascination gripped her, stirring long-dormant memories. An inexplicable force urged her to confront these tangled threads of her past, leaving her torn between uncovering the truth and protecting herself from old ghosts.

Amidst the shadows of remorse and the echoes of a tormented past, Brandy found herself grappling with a letter that bore the weight of a fractured soul seeking redemption. Staring at the handwritten words, she sensed the tremors of an admission that carried both the heavy burden of guilt and a flicker of remorseful hope.

The room, bathed in the dim glow of a solitary lamp, became a sanctuary where Brandy confronted the specter of her father's confessions. Her hands trembled as she traced the contours of the letter, each word etched with a mixture of pain and penance. The silence in the room mirrored the hushed confessions of a man burdened by the wreckage he had left in his wake.

Carl's words unfurled like a tragic tapestry, weaving the narrative of a man whose sins had eclipsed the innocence of a once-young daughter. Brandy's eyes traversed the lines, each sentence delivering a blow to her heart, the inked expression of a soul striving to break free from the shackles of its own malevolence.

"Brandy, you bear the blood of my veins, and what I have done to you, how I have negatively shaped the course of your life with memories of tragic accounts and destructive nightmares, cannot be taken away. But I want you to know that for every negative thing I have done to you and through you, you have done the opposite for me."

As the words etched themselves into Brandy's consciousness, a torrent of emotions swirled within her. The room seemed to contract, its walls closing in on the secrets that had remained dormant for too long. Carl's plea for forgiveness echoed in the stillness, a poignant symphony of regret that reverberated through the air.

"I have watched your life grow through the magic of your voice and the joyful beauty of who you have become. I will not bother you again, but I want you to know that I could not be prouder of who you have become."

The penultimate paragraphs struck a chord deep within Brandy's wounded heart. The promise to silence the echoes of a remorseful past, the commitment to shield others from a fate mirroring her own, emerged as a testament to the complex metamorphosis occurring within Carl's incarcerated soul.

"I will watch and cover you with my prayers. I pray for your continued strength in life and in the purpose of who you are."

The final lines, an earnest prayer for Brandy's well-being, lingered like a benediction in the quietude. Brandy's eyes, clouded with tears, sought solace in the notion that perhaps, beyond the ink-stained pages, a man once ensnared by darkness sought redemption in the only way he knew how.

Brandy sat, and instead of reading it sporadically, she read it in its entirety.

My Dearest Brandy,

I hope this letter finds you in a place of peace, though I know that peace has been hard for you to come by, especially with all the pain I've caused. I'm writing to you from a place of deep reflection and with a heart full of regret yet also filled with pride for the woman you've become.

There's so much I need to say, and I'm not even sure where to begin. How do I ask for forgiveness when I know I've hurt you so deeply? How do I explain the years of silence, the missed birthdays, the absence of a father's love that you deserved so much? I've thought about these questions every day in this cell, and though the answers still don't come easily, I know I have to try.

"Brandy, I am so, so sorry. I'm sorry for the monster I became when I let drugs and my past take over my life. You deserved better—a father who was strong, present, and loving— but instead, you got a man who was broken and lost. The things I did, the choices I made—they haunt me. But the worst part is knowing how my actions hurt you, my beautiful daughter, who did nothing to deserve the pain I brought into her life."

I want you to know that the man I am now, the man who writes you this letter, is not the same man who failed you all those years. Prison has been a place of reckoning for me, a place where I've been forced to confront the demons I ran from for so long. The horrors I faced as a child, the abuse, the darkness—I carried those wounds into my adulthood, and instead of healing, I let them fester. I turned to drugs to numb the pain, but all they did was make me numb to the love and responsibility I should have felt for you and your sister.

But even in my darkest days, Brandy, I watched you. I saw you grow; I saw your strength, your resilience, your kindness. I saw you become everything I could have never imagined for myself—a strong, independent woman who shines despite the shadows I cast over your life. I am so proud of you, more than words could ever express. You have become a beacon of light, a woman of grace and courage, and that is something no one can ever take from you.

I wish I could have been there to tell you this in person, to hold you and let you know how much you mean to me. But even though I can't, I want you to know that I will always have your back. I know I didn't protect you when you needed me most, but I'm here now, watching over you in the only way I can. And I will continue to do so for the rest of my life.

You don't owe me anything, Brandy, least of all your forgiveness. But if there's any part of you that can find it in your heart to forgive me, know that I will carry that grace with me every day. And even if you can't, I will still be here, loving you, proud of you, and praying for you.

You are my daughter, and I will always be your father. And no matter where life takes you, I will be watching over you, proud of the woman you've become and thankful for the second chance you've given me to be a better man, even if it's from a distance.

With all my love and deepest regret,

Brother Carl

"Shadows of Betrayal"

Timmoreia stood under the dim light of a streetlamp just outside Brandy and Bobby's condo in downtown Chicago. The night air was cool, and a sense of unease settled over him as he watched the softly glowing windows. His mind was a storm of emotions—conflict, resentment, and a dangerous mix of love and hate. He was torn between disappearing into the night and facing the painful truths that haunted him.

As he stared up at the condo, he felt the weight of the hidden gun pressing against his side, a cold reminder of how his once orderly life had spiraled into chaos. He glimpsed movement through the slightly parted curtains and recognized Bobby's figure. The sight of him stirred a whirlwind of emotions within Timmoreia—betrayal, possessiveness, and deep, consuming anger.

Bobby, unaware of the eyes watching him from the shadows, moved out of view, leaving Timmoreia gripping the weapon tightly, the tension within him growing by the second. He was lost in thought when something unexpected happened—a woman appeared inside the condo, someone Timmoreia didn't recognize. Her presence added fuel to the fire of suspicion in his mind.

Timmoreia strained to hear their conversation, but the distance and the murmur of the city made it impossible. Then, he saw something that made his heart race—a brief, unexpected embrace between Brandy and the woman. It was enough to push Timmoreia to the brink. His hand moved instinctively to the gun at his side, fingers brushing the cold steel as his emotions threatened to overtake him.

A war raged inside him. Was this betrayal real, or was it something his mind had twisted into existence? He couldn't tell where the truth ended, and his fears began. The night seemed to grow darker, filled with the tension between confronting what he believed to be true or letting his anger consume him.

As he sat in his car, Timmoreia's thoughts spiraled further. The rain pattered against the windows, matching the turmoil in his heart. He gripped the steering wheel in one hand and the gun in the other, the weight of both grounding him in his chaotic reality.

A voice—his own, yet somehow separate—whispered cruelly in his mind. It taunted him, reminding him of everything he had lost, everything that had been taken from him. He saw images of his daughter, of a life that could have been, now shattered by what he believed to be Bobby's betrayal. The voice grew louder, more insistent, weaving a narrative that Bobby had been the one to orchestrate his downfall.

"You were supposed to be stronger, smarter," the voice hissed. "And now look at you, crumbling like a fool." Is yo bitch ass crying...? his conscience spoke loudly to him. Man..., take yo ass home..., before you catch a case out here with yo..., simple ass.

Timmoreia's grip on the gun tightened as the voice mocked him, calling him weak, a shadow of the man he once was. It urged him to act, to reclaim what was his, to stop being a victim.

The rain outside mirrored the tears that slid down his face, mixing with the anger and despair that consumed him.

The glow of the city lights outside the car was a stark contrast to the darkness inside. As a patrol car slowly drove down the street, Timmoreia's pulse quickened. He fumbled through the car's contents, pretending to search for something, all the while keeping a close eye on the passing officer. For a brief moment, their eyes met, and Timmoreia gave a subtle nod—an unspoken acknowledgment of the troubled past that had led him to this point.

As the patrol car disappeared down the street, Timmoreia was left alone with his thoughts, the night pressing in on him. He was at a crossroads—faced with a choice that could change everything. The question that lingered was whether he would confront the demons that haunted him or let them drive him to a point of no return.

The officer, a guardian of order, saw in Timmoreia a resident of the neighborhood, a face familiar in the community's nocturnal choreography. A brief wave, a gesture of neighborly recognition, sliced through the tension-laden air. Timmoreia reciprocated, the muscles in his face contorting to form a façade of normalcy.

The patrol car ambled on, its red and blue lights fading into the canvas of the night. The officer's acknowledgment lingered, a spectral presence in the rearview mirror. Timmoreia, now alone with the echoes of the encounter, gathered the fragments of composure.

He ignited the engine, a mechanical growl punctuating the silence. The car inched forward, a vessel carrying the weight of unresolved conflicts. As he navigated the labyrinthine streets, Timmoreia mumbled words to himself—a quiet vow beneath the hum of the engine.

"This is not the time," he muttered, the words dissolving

into the rain-soaked night. "But I will finish this and put an end to it all."

The car turned, leaving the patrol officer behind, disappearing into the shadows that clung to the edges of the city. In the opposite direction of the law's fleeting gaze, Timmoreia embarked on a journey toward an uncertain resolution, the rain bearing witness to the tempest within.

Timmoreia's thoughts churned as he walked away, the night's tension still lingering in the air. He knew deep down that tonight wasn't the right moment to push things further. Perhaps, if he gave her the space she needed, she would eventually come to see things his way. "Patience," he reminded himself. If he just waited a little longer, everything might fall into place, just as he had envisioned. There was still time and with it, the hope that their paths would realign.

"Ripples of Change"

As Meeka walked into the house, she felt a mix of excitement and nerves bubbling inside her. She had big news to share with Fleet and couldn't wait to see his reaction. "Honey, are you home?" she called out, her voice carrying a hint of anticipation.

"In here, babe," Fleet responded from the living room. Meeka found him sitting on the couch, and without hesitation, she wrapped her arms around him, kissing him softly. Their connection was undeniable, and anyone who saw them together could feel the deep love and passion they shared.

Fleet had always wanted to make Meeka's life perfect. He dreamed of being the man she could look up to, but his past constantly weighed him down, making him feel inadequate. Even though Meeka reassured him time and again, telling him how much she believed in him and how she loved him no matter what, Fleet couldn't help but feel that he needed to prove his worth.

"What's going on, babe? You look like you're bursting with something to tell me," Fleet said, sensing her excitement.

Meeka's eyes sparkled with pride as she finally shared her

news. "You're looking at the new Assistant District Attorney for the City of Chicago!"

Fleet's eyes widened with surprise and pride. "No way! Baby, that's incredible! I'm so proud of you. You're going to be the best AD this city has ever seen," he said, pulling her close.

"And that's not all," Meeka continued, her excitement growing. "You remember the financial firm Bobby used to work for? I'm going to be leading the team on a major fraud investigation involving that company. It's huge, but I can't go into details just yet."

Fleet's smile faltered slightly, his mind racing with a mix of emotions. He couldn't shake the feeling of unease. "That's big news, babe. But... should you tell Bobby?"

Meeka shook her head, her expression serious. "I can't, Fleet. It's too sensitive, and Bobby isn't involved anymore. Everything should be fine. Now, let me make us some dinner."

As Meeka moved toward the kitchen, Fleet's thoughts grew darker. He knew this investigation could bring up issues for Bobby, and he wasn't sure how to protect his friend without betraying Meeka's trust.

Meeka, still riding of high on her promotion, thought about calling Brandy. Lately, they hadn't been in touch much, and Meeka missed her best friend. She knew Brandy was dealing with her own challenges—especially with the recent health issues she had confided in her about. Brandy had been diagnosed with stage 2 breast cancer, and Meeka suspected that her silence was due to the overwhelming stress and fear Brandy must be feeling. Determined to reconnect, Meeka decided she would reach out to Brandy soon to share her news and offer her support during this tough time.

As Meeka prepared dinner, she couldn't help but feel a sense of accomplishment. Yet, beneath the surface, she sensed the storm clouds gathering—clouds that would soon challenge her relationships, her career, and the fragile balance of her life.

"Ripples of Change"

Brandy was determined to make things right. After all the secrets and tension that had surfaced, she felt an urgent need to support her sister, Christina, and patch things up with Bobby. She decided to host a small gathering at her home—a chance to bring everyone together and restore some sense of normalcy.

Brandy called Christina first. The upcoming event was meant to celebrate Christina's new role in an off-Broadway production. Despite the recent turmoil, Christina hesitated only briefly before agreeing to come. The bond between sisters was strong, and Brandy hoped this night would help heal some of the wounds.

Next, Brandy reached out to Meeka, her close friend, inviting her and Fleet to the celebration. She promised they would catch up on recent events and work on rebuilding their strained relationships. Brandy was determined to strengthen the connections that had been tested by recent events.

As Brandy finished her calls, her phone buzzed again. The name "Timmoreia" flashed on the screen—a reminder of a chapter in her life she was trying to close. Part of her wanted to answer, to address the unresolved issues, but she pushed the thought aside. Tonight was about family and healing, and she was committed to that.

However, Timmoreia was persistent. The calls turned into texts, and the tone shifted from apologetic to aggressive. He started sending threats, trying to force Brandy into meeting him. But Brandy was focused on the evening ahead. She ignored the distractions, determined to reclaim some peace and unity.

The house, despite being on the brink of foreclosure, felt alive and warm as guests arrived—a reminder of better times with Bobby. Brandy gathered everyone together for a toast to Christina, but there was an undercurrent of tension in the room. Unspoken issues lingered, but everyone played along, masking their unease for the sake of the gathering.

"Okay, everyone, gather around!" Brandy called out, stepping into her role as hostess. The group gathered in the living room, where champagne waited for them. Brandy's voice was bright as she spoke about Christina's new role, expressing pride and excitement. The room seemed to relax as glasses were raised in a toast, and for a brief moment, the tension eased.

But just as the mood lightened, the doorbell rang. Brandy excused herself, her heart pounding as she approached the door. A sense of dread washed over her, and the laughter from the living room faded into the background. When she opened the door, her fears were confirmed—Timmoreia stood there, his expression dark and intense.

"Brandy, we need to talk," Timmoreia said, his voice a mix of urgency and resolve.

"This isn't the time, Timmoreia. How did you find out where I live?" Brandy's voice was firm as she blocked the entrance. The warm light from inside cast shadows on Timmoreia's face, highlighting the tension in his features.

"I'm worried about you, and there are things we need to

settle," Timmoreia pressed, his voice betraying the tension he tried to hide.

"I'm fine, and whatever needs to be settled can wait until later," Brandy replied, her gaze steady. She noticed the tightness in his jaw and the slight tremor in his hands—signs that his usually calm demeanor was slipping.

"But I can't wait," Timmoreia insisted, stepping closer. The space between them narrowed, and the air grew thick with tension. "You've been avoiding me, and we can't leave things like this."

Brandy's resolve hardened. "You need to leave. Now." Her voice was low but firm. She wanted to slam the door in his face and return to her gathering, but she knew that dismissing him might only make things worse.

Timmoreia's eyes searched hers, looking for any sign of weakness. Finding none, he took a deep breath. "Please, Brandy. Just a few minutes. It's important."

The moment stretched out, heavy with unspoken words and unresolved issues. Finally, with a glance back at the gathering inside, Brandy stepped outside, closing the door behind her. The cool night air was a sharp contrast to the warmth inside. "Talk, then," she said, her voice cautious.

Timmoreia's words came in a rush—apologies, explanations, a desperate plea to start over. But Brandy's thoughts were on the laughter and light she had left behind in the living room and the stark contrast with the darkness that Timmoreia brought with him.

"I can't let it end like this. We need to start over, no matter what," Timmoreia said, his desperation growing. The intensity in his eyes was unnerving, casting a shadow over the warm glow of the porch light.

The distant sound of laughter drifted through the closed door, a reminder of the life Brandy had moved on to—a life Timmoreia seemed determined to disrupt.

"Is that your husband?" Timmoreia asked, his voice sharp and jealous. He tilted his head, listening to the sounds inside. The question hung in the air, dangerous. Before Brandy could respond, Timmoreia's hand moved to his coat, revealing a gun tucked into his belt. The sight of the weapon turned the atmosphere from tense to dangerous.

"Timmoreia, what are you doing?" Brandy's voice sharpened with fear. "You need to leave now. This isn't the way."

But Timmoreia's desperation had already tipped into something darker. "No, I need to settle this—with him," he insisted, nodding toward the laughter inside. His hand hovered near the gun, a silent but clear threat.

Brandy felt a wave of fear wash over her. She quickly tried to find a way to calm the situation without putting anyone inside in danger. "Listen to me, Timmoreia. This isn't you. You don't want to do this," she pleaded, her voice a mix of calm and urgency.

Timmoreia's eyes were clouded with pain, betrayal, and a determination that seemed immovable. "I've lost too much already, Brandy. I can't lose you too—not to him," he said, his voice breaking with emotion.

Brandy realized how far Timmoreia had fallen into despair and how dangerous his mistaken belief had become. "Pulling a gun isn't going to bring me back to you, Timmoreia. It will only push me further away," she said, her eyes locked on his, trying to reach him.

Brandy's voice trembled with a mix of fear and anger as she spoke. "See, I knew I shouldn't have messed with you. I could tell you were one of those crazy, gray-eyed, manipulative men. I really thought you were different, a good guy, but now look at this mess. You're here to ruin my life and threaten my guests? Just turn around and leave before I call Bobby in here, and he and Fleet start whooping your ass."

Timmoreia's frustration was evident as he glared at her. "Oh, there she is. Mrs. Pope, all tough, standing in her nice, soon-to-be-foreclosed house, acting like she's got everything under control. That's fine. It'll make it all the more satisfying when I blow your pretty little head off, you slippery, pretty-ass bitch. And to think I fell for you quick and deep, and this is how you play me. That's alright because now I'm gonna have to kill a couple of motherfuckers up in here."

He pressed the gun to her head, and everything froze. In that instant, Brandy knew she had taken the wrong path, risked too much, and now the consequences had come to collect.

The standoff continued every second heavy with potential disaster. Brandy knew she had to keep him talking to prevent him from doing something irreversible. "Let's put the gun away and talk this through, Timmoreia. There's a better way to handle whatever you're feeling."

Behind the door, the gathering continued, unaware of the dangerous drama unfolding just outside. Brandy's heart pounded with the hope that she could defuse the situation before it spiraled out of control.

After what felt like an eternity, Brandy managed to convince Timmoreia to lower his gun and follow her back inside. As they stepped through the door, the festive atmosphere in the living room vanished. Conversations stopped abruptly, and the laughter died as all eyes turned toward Timmoreia. His entrance, with the heavy door closing behind him, seemed to seal the room in a thick, oppressive silence.

Bobby, standing near the fireplace with a glass of champagne, squinted at the newcomer. His usually friendly face tightened with confusion and concern. "Can I help you?" Bobby asked his voice firm but cautious, trying to maintain control despite the sudden disruption.

Timmoreia's eyes locked onto Bobby's with a cold, accusatory gleam. "Oh, you don't remember me, Mr. Pope?" he asked, his tone mocking and bitter. The use of "Mr. Pope" felt formal and out of place, adding to the tension already filling the room.

Jay's mind fell back to that moment:

Bobby Pope, a seasoned and principled broker, glances up from his desk as Jay T. Willabee nervously enters. They exchange handshakes, the atmosphere tense with anticipation.

Bobby gestures for Jay to take a seat, his mind already grappling with the ethical dilemma looming over them.

Mr. Pope leaned back in his chair, steepling his fingers thoughtfully. "Well, Jay, all I can tell you is that in life, everything we do, every step we take, is a mechanism of change. And change never happens unless we take some risks. But you should also know that with every risk, there can be consequences—sometimes good and sometimes not so good. It's completely up to the one who takes the risks."

Jay nodded; his brow furrowed with concern. "I understand that, Mr. Pope. But this... this feels different. This could change everything for me – for better or for worse."

Mr. Pope regarded Jay with a sympathetic expression. "I get it, Jay. Taking risks can be daunting, especially when so much is at stake. But sometimes, you have to trust your instincts and take that leap of faith. Who knows? It might just be the best decision you ever make."

A flicker of determination crossed Jay's face as he absorbed Mr. Pope's words. "You're right, Mr. Pope. I can't let fear hold me back. I've come too far to turn back now."

With a reassuring smile, Mr. Pope clasped Jay's shoulder. "That's the spirit, Jay. Remember, fortune favors the bold. Now, go out there and seize the opportunity that's waiting for you."

Feeling emboldened by Mr. Pope's encouragement, Jay straightened his posture and squared his shoulders. With a newfound sense of purpose, he strode out of the office, ready to face whatever challenges lay ahead.

Bobby's confusion deepened. He took a step forward, trying

to place the face in front of him. "I'm sorry. Do I know you from somewhere?" His question hung in the air, genuine and puzzled, but it was met with only a smirk from Timmoreia.

The room, already tense, seemed to tighten as guests exchanged uneasy glances. Whispers started among the group, trying to make sense of the connection between Bobby and this imposing stranger.

Bobby, standing across from Jay, clenched his jaw. The memories came flooding back—a period marked by heated debates and sleepless nights, where the risk of investing in volatile microchip stocks was weighed against potential monumental gains. Bobby had initially been a deterrent, considering the move too risky, but circumstances and persuasive arguments had shifted his stance, ultimately encouraging Jay to proceed.

"Jay, I advised based on the information available at the time. It was a gamble, one that you decided to take," Bobby replied, his voice firm, attempting to keep the conversation rooted in rationality despite the undercurrent of personal upset.

Jay chuckled darkly, stepping closer, his eyes narrowing. "A gamble you persuaded me into, Bobby. And let's just say it didn't quite pan out as you had suddenly become so optimistic about." The bitterness in his voice was unmistakable, as was the blame he cast in Bobby's way.

The guests, previously murmuring among themselves, now watched in rapt attention, drawn into the unfolding drama. Fleet's expression was particularly grave. He had known of Bobby's involvement in Jay's financial decisions but had never anticipated it would resurface in such a volatile manner.

Brandy, feeling a mix of anger and protectiveness towards her husband, intervened. "Timmoreia, whatever happened with that investment was business. Bringing it here, into our home, isn't going to change the past. What are you really after?" Her tone was both pleading and defiant, seeking to steer the confrontation away from mere accusations to uncover Jay's true intentions.

Jay paused, the smirk fading slightly as he considered Brandy's words. His gaze shifted around the room, landing on each of the attendees before settling back on Bobby. "What am I after?" He repeated her question, his voice dropping to a menacing softness. "I'm here to reclaim what I lost because of that investment, and maybe a bit more."

The threat was subtle but clear, sending a shiver through the room. Christina, who had been quietly supporting Brandy, stepped forward. "And what would that be, Jay? Money? Satisfaction? You're disrupting lives over a business risk that you took willingly."

Jay's eyes flicked to Christina, appreciating her boldness. "Maybe all of the above. Or maybe something a little more personal. We'll see how the night unfolds." Besides, "Bitch, did I ask you to talk?" Jay said as he pointed his gun at her.

As Jay's cryptic threats hung in the air, the once celebratory gathering had definitely turned into a scene of a high-stakes drama, with each person caught in the web of Jay's vengeance. Bobby, realizing the depth of Jay's bitterness and the potential threat he posed, knew he needed to find a way to defuse the situation before irreparable damage was done to the lives entwined in his and Brandy's home.

The revelation unfolded like a sinister plot twist, casting a shadow of disbelief and betrayal over the scene. The room, already thick with tension and disbelief, found itself thrust into deeper turmoil as Brandy's accusations and revelations spilled forth, each word slicing through the previously unspoken truths. "You played me," Brandy accused Timmoreia, her voice laden with hurt and betrayal, the words heavy with the weight of realization. "You, gray-eyed devil, you a simple mother fucker!" she yelled, her fury palpable as she confronted Timmoreia, now revealed as Jay T Willabee.

Her actions, bold and unflinching, demonstrated a break from the fear that had once restrained her. As she pushed Jay, her bravery resonated through the room, reflecting the depth of her betrayal and her refusal to be intimidated any longer. The sudden silence that followed her outburst was a thick, heavy blanket over the room, punctuated only by Brandy's breathing, harsh and rapid from her exertions.

"So, you manipulated and fucked me just to fuck over my husband. Is that what it is, Timmoreia?" Brandy's voice broke through the quiet, the accusation stark, leaving no room for misinterpretation. The room's atmosphere shifted substantially; the air was charged with a new, raw edge.

Bobby, his face a mask of hurt and disbelief, echoed her words. "You... you were with him?"

Brandy's eyes filled with tears. "It was a mistake, Bobby. I was lost, and he took advantage."

"Brandy, what the hell!" Christina's shock was evident; her words were sharp, slicing into the tense silence that followed Brandy's revelation. Her voice was a mixture of disbelief and confusion, trying to grasp the scope of what had just been disclosed.

Bobby's reaction was visceral, his voice a mixture of hurt and disbelief as he echoed, "Baby, what did you just say? You fucked him?" The pain in his voice was unmistakable, a raw display of his heartbreak. "How could you do that to me?" he added, the betrayal etching deeper lines into his already strained expression. He turned away, the action a physical manifestation of his need to distance himself from the hurt, sinking into his chair with a heavy thud, the sound echoing his emotional collapse.

Brandy, seeking any semblance of support, turned to Christina, her eyes brimming with tears, her voice cracking as she attempted to explain herself. "Christina, I just lost myself, you know? There was a lot going on, right?" Her plea was desperate, seeking an ally in her sister amidst the wreckage of the revelations.

Christina, however, could only shake her head, her actions a silent testament to her disappointment and inability to immediately reconcile the sister she knew with the actions disclosed.

Amidst the family's turmoil, Timmoreia—Jay, as they now knew him—tried to salvage the situation, his voice cutting through the tension. "Look, baby, we don't need this; just get your shit and let's go," he said, attempting to pull Brandy away from the wreckage he had helped create.

"Do you really believe that I would leave this man for yo-ass? I mean, really?" Brandy shot back, her voice a mix of scorn and defiance. Even in her emotional turmoil, her loyalty to Bobby, despite her transgressions, remained clear.

"But, baby, I know what it looks like, but I fell in love with you. I don't give a damn about all this; I just want you," Timmoreia confessed, his declaration of love a stark contrast to the manipulative figure they had come to see him as. His words, meant to be reassuring, seemed only to add fuel to the fire, highlighting the complexity and depth of their entanglement.

The room, now steeped in a cocktail of shock, betrayal, and wounded hearts, looked on. Christina's and Bobby's faces, mirroring each other in disbelief and disappointment, summarized the collective reaction. The revelations had not only exposed infidelities and manipulations but had also laid bare the vulnerabilities and fractures within their relationships.

Now, everything in the room had shifted irreversibly. The risks Brandy had taken, driven by whatever justification or moment of weakness, had crystallized into this moment—the theatrical stage of consequences, where each character was forced to confront not only the actions of others but also the truths about themselves.

In the midst of the unraveling chaos and heightened emotions, Brandy stood, a mixture of defiance and vulnerability etched across her face. She wiped the tears away, her gesture one of reclaiming control over the situation, even as her personal secrets spilled into the open. "Okay, well, my shit is out there now," she declared, a note of resignation lacing her voice, acknowledging the exposed truths.

"Brandy, what the hell is going on with you? How come you didn't talk to me? I'm your best friend?" Meeka interjected, her voice tinged with hurt and confusion. Her stance was one of support yet underscored by a personal sense of betrayal. As someone who had been part of Brandy's life through the formative years of college and beyond, Meeka's shock was deep.

"I know, Meeka, but you've got a lot of shit going on, too," Brandy replied, her voice softening as she addressed her friend. "You're running for office, deep into your campaign. It happened really fast, and I felt like I couldn't put that shit out there." Brandy's explanation, while heartfelt, hinted at her isolation in dealing with her burgeoning problems.

"But this brother came at me fast," Brandy continued, her eyes darting toward Jay, who stood with a façade of composure that barely concealed his role in the drama unfolding. "Just when I was dealing with all this new shit that Bobby had put on me— him quitting his job, losing the house, and all kinds of other things, you know. And this convenient motherfucker right here," she pointed accusingly at Jay, her anger resurfacing, "here he comes."

Pausing, a curious and suspicious thought crossed her mind. "Wait a minute," Brandy said, her eyes narrowing as she fixed her gaze on Jay. "I just gotta ask one thing," her voice rose in accusation, "how did you know so much shit about my life? What I liked to eat, what music I liked, and what to say to me about my life at the right time?" Her pointed finger moved from Jay to herself, emphasizing the personal nature of the information he had used to ensnare her.

Turning to Meeka, her eyes filled with a mix of suspicion

and desperation, Brandy voiced the thought that had suddenly clicked into place. "Wait a minute, the only one who would know me like you came at me would be... Meeka." The room's attention swivelled to Meeka, the atmosphere charged with the implication of her possible involvement.

"Really, Brandy?" Meeka responded her voice a mix of shock and anger. "After all we've been through together, you think I would do you like that?" The hurt in Meeka's voice was clear, and her disbelief at being considered a conspirator was evident in her expression.

"Naw, this gray-eyed motherfucker here got fuelled by somebody else, and it damn sure wasn't me," Meeka fired back defensively. Her denial was vehement, a strong refutation of any role in the betrayal that had so deeply wounded her friend.

The room fell into a tense silence, each person digesting the layers of deception and betrayal that had been peeled back. The accusations had not only exposed Jay's manipulations but had also thrown the nature of Brandy and Meeka's friendship into question. As suspicions and allegiances shifted, the group was left to confront not only the immediate revelations but also the deeper, more painful implications of trust broken and relationships potentially irreparably damaged.

The room, already thick with tension and revelations, now erupted into a full-blown familial and emotional confrontation. Christina, protective and incensed, stepped forward, her stance defiant as she addressed Jay. "Look,, Mister Jay, Tee Moe, or whatever your name is. I don't know what your intentions are here, but you're messing with the wrong ones up here. This is my sister, and Bobby is like a brother I never had, and we ain't about to let you come up in here and start no stuff now," she declared, her voice brimming with determination and loyalty.

Brandy, her emotions still high from the previous accusations, turned her frustration toward Christina with a sharp, biting retort. "Yo, sister, huh?" she scoffed. "Is that why you decided to take my role at the theater? Is that why you are always looking all thirsty and shit at my man?" Her accusations tumbled out, charged with years of pent-up feelings and perceived slights.

"Ever since we were little girls, all you have ever done with your quiet ass is walk into my life and take shit with that innocent-ass demeanor you've got. Always walking around like you're the victim. I found a foster family that loved me, and here comes your ass. I found a man that adores me, and here comes yo ass. I found a theater that damn near worshiped me, and again, here comes yo ass," Brandy continued, her voice rising with each recounting of her grievances. "Now that I'm knee-deep in some talk show shit, here comes your ass. My 'protective' sister," she finished, her words dripping with sarcasm and hurt.

Christina, visibly shaken by the onslaught, responded with a mixture of sadness and sincerity. "Brandy, you don't mean all of that. You know I would never hurt you. I had no control over any of those things, and I would never, ever involve myself with Bobby." "Yeah, I admire him; yeah, I think he's a wonderful man, and that's where it stops." "I love Bobby because of how he loves you, so if anything, for all these years, I have simply just lived in your shadow and stayed so proud of you that I never believed in myself. So now that I am trying to come out of my shadow, you're gonna make it seem like all that. That's cold, sister," Christina's voice broke, her plea tinged with both defensiveness and pain.

The exchange was interrupted by Meeka, who tried to bring calm to the escalating feud. "Damn, Brandy, what are you doing?" she interjected. "We're all here because we love both of you."

"Well, that's easy for you to say, Ms. Soon-to-be District Attorney. Your shit is intact, and you're doing your thing. My life, in the meantime, is fucked," Brandy shot back, her voice raw as she turned her hurt and frustration toward Meeka, lumping her in with the perceived betrayals of Christina.

The room fell into a heavy silence, the weight of Brandy's words settling like a thick fog. Each person present felt the sting of her accusations, reflecting not only the immediate crisis triggered by Jay's plots but also deeper, long-standing family dynamics and personal insecurities. The complexity of their relationships—saturated with love, rivalry, and deep-seated fears of inadequacy—was laid bare, exposing the fragile human elements behind their polished exteriors.

As they stood, confronted by the rawness of their emotions and the messiness of their ties, it was clear that the path forward would require not just addressing the immediate threat posed by Jay but also healing the wounds that had been festering, unnoticed or unaddressed, for far too long. The challenge was immense, but it was also an opportunity—to rebuild trust, to affirm their bonds, and to emerge stronger, both individually and together.

In the charged atmosphere of Bobby and Brandy's living room, the tensions escalated to a breaking point as accusations flew and long-buried secrets surfaced with jarring clarity. Bobby, his patience frayed to its limits, stepped forward, his voice resolute and commanding as he addressed Jay. "Look, man, you're gonna have to get the hell out of my house," he declared, his stance firm and unwavering. "Whatever happened in the past with the investments, I am truly sorry, but that's how investments go." "I tried to tell you then, and I'm telling you now—a risk comes with consequences. And the risk you're taking, coming up in here with all this shit and the things you've done, is going to cost you."

Bobby paused, his chest heaving with restrained anger. "Now I'm doing everything I can to stay off your ass, but you need to step out of here. And if that means that Brandy's leaving with you, then let's get that declared, because there are too many lives up in here for you to be playing with," he added, stepping even closer to Jay, his gaze unflinching.

Jay, seemingly unfazed by Bobby's confrontation, responded with a cold, calculated calmness. "Well, Mr. Pope, I hear you, but there are some other matters that need to happen before me and your lovely wife depart," he said, his voice dripping with condescension and veiled threats.

Brandy, her own anger flaring, interjected sharply, "Look, I have told you I'm not going anywhere with you," she snapped, standing her ground.

Fleet, who had been quietly observing, turned slightly away, his face unreadable as he took a long, slow sip of champagne. His reaction did not go unnoticed; several pairs of eyes flicked toward him, sensing that he knew more than he was letting on.

Fleet's reaction added another layer of mystery to the situation. His apparent knowledge of Timmoreia—or Jay, as they now knew him—hinted at a deeper connection that he wasn't ready to reveal. This secrecy only fueled the suspicions and whispers circulating among the guests.

Brandy, standing a step behind Timmoreia, her eyes wide with worry, tried to convey a silent plea to Bobby. Her look was one of concern, an unspoken warning that the man standing before him was more dangerous than he appeared.

As the tension built, threatening to explode, Bobby set his champagne down and addressed Timmoreia directly. "If there's something you need to discuss, let's hear it now. Why bring this here tonight?" His demand for clarity wasn't just for his own understanding but also an attempt to protect his guests and defuse the growing tension.

Timmoreia's response was cryptic and laced with implications. "Maybe we should ask Fleet why the past has come knocking tonight." His eyes briefly flicked toward Fleet, letting the insinuation hang in the air.

The room fell silent, everyone waiting for Fleet's reaction, which could unravel the mystery Timmoreia—now known as Jay—had brought into their midst. The tension grew thicker as the connection between past grievances and the current situation tightened, pulling the evening closer to an inevitable revelation. Ensure that Jay has already revealed his name first.

In the charged atmosphere of Bobby and Brandy's living room, the once joyful celebration had become a minefield of secrets and hidden agendas. Everyone in the room—Bobby, Brandy, Fleet, Christina, and the newly revealed Jay—was now part of a web of betrayal and deceit that threatened to change their lives forever. rewrite

"Look, man, I never wanted you to make that deal," Bobby said, his voice firm. "I tried to tell you in so many words not to go through with it, but you were so eager that the caution I was trying to give you just didn't sink in. So, reluctantly, I closed the deal for you. But afterward, I tried to reach out to offer my support if you wanted to change your mind, and I couldn't find you."

"The hell you did, Mr. Pope," Timmoreia snapped back, his tone dripping with disbelief.

No, Timmoreia, or whatever your damn name is, he did. Brandy intervened, her voice carrying a note of desperation as she tried to protect Bobby. "He told me about the deal that night when he came home. I was devastated and really concerned that he couldn't find you. Bobby has always been like that whenever he felt he didn't do right by someone."

Timmoreia's eyes narrowed as he sneered, "Well, well, well, speaking up for your man. You weren't speaking up for him the other night, were you now?" The room went silent, the weight of Timmoreia's words hanging heavy in the air. Everyone turned to look at Brandy, their eyes filled with shock and betrayal. How could you, Brandy? their gazes seemed to ask.

Brandy felt a chill run down her spine. The man she had known as Timmoreia, who had once brought her comfort, was now revealed to be Jay Willabee, a name entangled with darker chapters of their past. The trust she had once freely given felt shattered.

Fleet, whose earlier shock had morphed into a cautious detachment, turned fully to face Jay. His expression was unreadable, but his eyes betrayed deep knowledge—perhaps complicity—in the secrets Jay was beginning to unravel before them all.

Christina, ever the observer, drew closer to Brandy, her protective instincts flaring up. She watched Jay with a critical eye, trying to reconcile the friendly face with the sinister implications of his true identity. Her mind raced to understand how this revelation could alter not just her relationship with Brandy but also the dynamics of their entire circle.

Jay, sensing the rising alarm and confusion, decided to press his advantage. "You see, Bobby, our paths have crossed more significantly than you remember. Or perhaps you chose to forget?" His tone was accusatory, each word dripping with double meanings and veiled threats.

Bobby, feeling the weight of all eyes on him, cleared his throat. "Jay, if that's what you prefer to be called, I think you owe everyone here, especially me, a clearer explanation. What is it that you believe I've forgotten?"

The room tensed further as everyone waited for Jay's response. His smile was tight and knowing as he prepared to dive into a past that would unravel the carefully constructed present, promising that none of their lives would remain the same by the end of the night.

Jay's voice was steady as he recounted their shared history, a history that Bobby had hoped to leave behind. Jay revealed how Bobby had been involved in a high-stakes investment that had gone wrong—one that had led to Jay losing a significant amount of money. The bitterness in Jay's voice was intense, as was the blame he cast in Bobby's direction.

The room descended into chaos as old wounds were

reopened and new ones inflicted. But amid the storm, Jay's plan continued to unfold, pulling everyone deeper into the web of secrets, lies, and betrayals that threatened to tear them all apart. As the night wore on, it became clear that the truths revealed tonight would change their lives forever. And as the sound of approaching sirens filled the air, everyone knew that nothing would ever be the same again.

Fleet finally spoke up, his voice tense. "Put that damn gun down, J Will," he ordered. "With yo bitch ass. I told yo ass not to fall in love with this hoe." "What the hell did you call me, Fleet?" "You heard me, bitch. Bobby has ridden your ass all these years, and look what you do at the first sign of trouble, but it's all good because it makes the plan so much easier."

"I'm not putting shit down, Wood," Jay retorted, his voice cold and defiant.

"Oh, is that right?" Fleet responded as he slowly pulled out his own gun, locking eyes with Jay.

"So, it's like that, Wood? You're gonna do me like that over these motherfuckers, after all we've been through?" Jay's voice wavered slightly, though he kept his gun aimed at Fleet.

"Naw, I ain't gonna do shit if you put down that damn gun. Don't forget, we got business. We're in this shit together," Fleet said, his tone calculated, trying to defuse the situation.

Those words seemed to give Jay a sense of comfort, and he slowly lowered his gun. But the tension in the room only thickened.

"What do you mean, y'all are in this together?" Bobby asked, confusion and betrayal evident in his voice.

"Oh, I'm sorry, Bobby," Fleet replied, his voice dripping with sarcasm. "This is my real friend. We spent time together in prison, and we always had each other's backs. Unlike you, Bobby —where you dropped me like a dog when I went to prison. No calls from my supposed best friend, no cash drops, not even a few damn dollars to help a brother out. Nothing, not even a damn postcard. You just abandoned me. So now, my brother and this brother are gonna need that $1.5 million you got stashed, and we'll move on for good."

"$1.5 million?" Brandy echoed in disbelief. "What $1.5 million?"

"Oh, that's right, your boy didn't tell you," Jay sneered. "He's got over a million stashed from those crooked brokers he was working for. It was a bonus he got for that bad 'Microchip' deal he did with Jay and others over there."

"Damn, Bobby, for real?" Brandy asked, her voice filled with shock.

"Wait a minute, Fleet," Meeka interjected, her voice trembling. "What is wrong with you? See, Ashton must be about to come out from behind one of these walls and say, 'Y'all been punked,' right?"

"Naw, baby, that shit ain't gonna happen, and neither are we," Fleet said coldly. "And just so you know, I did it. I really did kill that old dude, and you, my pretty little queen, helped me beat the case."

In the midst of the chaotic scene, Meeka desperately tried to reach the man she thought she knew. "Fleet, what did I mean to you? Who have you become? We were supposed to get married!" Her voice was filled with disbelief and pain as she struggled to understand the stranger standing before her, armed and dangerous.

As the standoff continued, the room's dynamics shifted dramatically. Trust was frayed, alliances were questioned, and the presence of the gun introduced a deadly seriousness to the proceedings. The revelations had not only unearthed hidden truths but had also set the stage for a confrontation that none could have anticipated, least of all Bobby, who now found himself facing the twin threats of betrayal and physical danger in his own home.

In the thick tension that filled the room, voices and accusations collided, creating a discord of betrayal and desperation. Bobby, grappling with the unraveling of his friendships, turned to Fleet and Meeka with a desperate plea for clarity. "Are y'all together on this? What the hell is this all about, Fleet?" Bobby's voice cracked under the strain of disbelief and betrayal.

"Hell no, Bobby, now you know me," Meeka responded swiftly, her tone mixing shock with indignation. Her loyalty to Bobby was clear, distancing herself from any conspiracies or hidden agendas.

Fleet, whose demeanor had shifted from quiet to confrontational, finally broke his silence with a bitterness that surprised everyone. "It's about you, brother. You and the fact that Bobby always got his shit together. Bobby is doing all the right things; Bobby is the man. He's so successful. Truthfully, Bobby, that shit irks me. I've been struggling since we were teens, man, and I don't really get shit to show for it."

"Yeah, Fleet, but that ain't got nothing to do with me," Bobby responded. "You made your choices in life, and I made mine. I busted my ass to get where I'm at, and I always told you to do the same. But all you wanted to do was hang out and be a thug. You always got caught up with the wrong dudes, doing the wrong shit. But I knew that who I hung with would shape my life and the direction I wanted to go in."

I mean, look at this sorry, gray-eyed nigga over here. This is who you say is your boy? And y'all come up in here with a bitch-ass plan to take money that ain't even legally mine because of all the investigations going on with that company. But here y'all are, pointing guns at each other, and I'm not a real friend? See, that's always been your problem, Fleet—always in the wrong place at the wrong time with the wrong crew.

And as for that "send you money" shit, I wrote to you one time and asked for information on how to come see you and do a little shit for you every now and then. The next thing I knew, you were sent to another place because you were in there trying to kill inmates. After that, I didn't know where you were or what the hell you had going on.

And let me remind you of something—a matter of fact, let me remind all y'all, your boy and Brandy. You know me, that quiet and professional brother Bobby, but you also know Bobby Pope. And I ain't never been accused of being soft just because I live a soft life. So y'all must've forgotten—I will whip all y'all asses up in here. And Fleet, you know, because I've whipped your ass plenty of times coming up. "So if you and your boy are real men, then put down those guns, and I promise I'll be the only one walking out of this motherfucker. Y'all have done too much, and now Bobby Pope is ready to put some hurt on y'all's asses."

"Well, damn, Bobby, why do you get all that hostility up in your voice? Don't be so sensitive, my brother," said Fleet. "I know your capabilities, and that's exactly why I'm not putting down this gun."

"Man, Fleet, we should whup this dude's ass."

"Look, J Will, Bobby will fuck you up in approximately seven seconds, and that ain't no speculation. All your bitch ass needs to do is keep that gun on his ass until we get this money."

"Nice try, Bobby, but I'll pass on that option," said Fleet. "Yeah, I figured you would take that option," said Bobby. He then turned to Brandy, his voice steady despite the tears in her eyes. "And Brandy, don't let these tears fool you. "What you did was foul." "Just like I told this dude, in life, everything we do, every step we take, is a mechanism of change." "And change never happens unless we take some risks." But you should also know that with every risk, there can be consequences—sometimes good, sometimes not so good. It's completely up to the one who takes the risks."

Bobby's voice grew firmer as he continued, "And I think you're gonna have to do some figuring out about which way this is gonna go because consequences are like snake venom—

once it gets into your veins, reversing the effects is almost impossible."

Brandy put her head down, knowing she had broken him, as Bobby's words hung heavily in the air.

Meeka, stunned by Fleet's raw envy and resentment, shot back, "What the hell do you mean you ain't got shit to show for it? I have given you everything and every opportunity to be somebody better, including getting your black ass out of jail!"

Meeka, who was getting more and more disturbed by the minute, once again interjected, her voice filled with pain and disbelief. "And what about us? We were going to be married." Her plea was cut short by Fleet's cold dismissal: "Well, Mr. Pope and Ms. Meeka, things have changed."

Jay, observing the fray with a calculating gaze, couldn't help but sneer at the chaos he had helped create. "I can't believe y'all went for that shit from this brother," he said, mocking Fleet's duplicity. "Fleet ain't nothing but a hustler."

"Shut your ass up; I can speak for myself," Fleet snapped back, now completely abandoning any pretense. "Here's what we're gonna do right now: Bobby, I need you to unass that money, all of it. And we're gonna make our way outta here. But if not, somebody dies." Fleet's voice was cold, more threatening than ever.

Jay, amused by the turn of events, looked at Brandy with a twisted smile. "Damn, he is colder than I am, ain't he, baby?" he taunted, his tongue flicking out in a disturbing gesture.

"You two bastards," Brandy spat out, her voice thick with disgust and resignation. Despite her loathing, she couldn't help but express her shock at Fleet's betrayal. "Damn, I didn't see this one coming, Fleet. But I told my girl you weren't shit when she almost lost her career getting yo-ass out of jail."

The room fell into a stunned silence following Fleet's chilling confession. His words, delivered with a cold nonchalance, shattered the fragile semblance of normalcy that Meeka had clung to amidst the chaos. "And just for the record," Fleet continued, his tone harshly calm, "yeah, I did it. Baby, you were brilliant in the way you handled that case. Now, it's time for me to move on." The stark finality in his voice cut through the tension like a knife.

Meeka, her face pale and her eyes wide with shock, struggled to process the enormity of Fleet's betrayal. The man she had loved and defended with fierce loyalty was admitting to heinous crimes with an airy jokiness that chilled her to the bone. Fleet's readiness to abandon their relationship as if it were nothing more than a convenience left her reeling. The realization that the person she thought she knew was merely a facade crumbled around her, leaving her feeling isolated and betrayed in a room full of people.

"Wow, see, the problem, Fleet, is you've got me mistaken for some soft bitch. But let me assure you, if you think back to the day I came up and met your ass at that prison, there wasn't a damn thing soft about me. You've been plotting this shit since day one. Motherfucker, I will blow your damn head off." Just as she said that Meeka quickly pulled a gun out from behind her suit jacket. "See, as the new District Attorney, I'm also licensed to carry and licensed to correct a motherfucker—and your ass is about to get corrected."

Fleet was immediately shocked. He quickly pointed his gun at her, and now they were both staring down the barrels of each other's weapons.

"Damn, baby, you a bad bitch. See, that's what attracted me to your pretty little ass," said Fleet as he moved around, trying to gain an advantage.

The callousness of Fleet's confession did not just affect Meeka; it sent ripples of discomfort throughout the room. Bobby, who had trusted and supported Fleet as a brother, felt a deep sense of betrayal and disappointment. The fact that Fleet had used Meeka, manipulating her professional skills for his own gain, only deepened the sense of outrage.

Brandy, already dealing with her own whirlwind of emotions and revelations, looked at Meeka with a mix of sympathy and sorrow. The solidarity of shared betrayal briefly united them, even as the chaos continued to unfold around them.

Christina interrupts, "Look, everybody needs to just calm down. We've got three guns pointed in different directions up in here, and just so y'all know, I don't want one pointed at me. This is a no-win situation. Fleet, if you know Bobby, you should also know he ain't stupid enough to have one and a half million dollars just sitting around this house. So clearly, the money ain't here. Why don't you and Gray Eyes here just pack up and leave, and nobody has to lose anything?"

Jay, irritated, snaps back, "Look, lady, I told your ass once already that I didn't need your damn advice. Sit your ass down," as he turns his gun on her. Christina recoils backward with her hands up and repositions herself strategically in the room.

Jay, observing the unraveling bonds with a detached interest, seemed to take a perverse pleasure in the destruction he had helped catalyze. "Damn, this shit's getting crazy up in here," he muttered, almost amused by the chaos.

"Yeah, you're right, Fleet," Jay continued, his tone dripping with sarcasm. "You told me everything I needed to know to get to her, but you didn't mention she had that 'catch a nigga' cat down there. Screw you, Timmoreia—or J Will, or Jay T Willabee, or whatever the hell you go by," Brandy snapped, her voice laced with venom. "That's why your bitch ass is running around here all messed up. And just for the record, I might have been good, but you were well below average," she added, her sarcasm cutting deep.

Jay's earlier confrontations and provocations had set the stage for this moment of raw, painful honesty. He watched as the tension in the room thickened, every word exchanged like a knife twisting in the wound.

Fleet's gaze shifted around the room, meeting the eyes of his former friends and allies. His expression was one of resigned acceptance as if he had made peace with the path he had chosen, regardless of the destruction it caused. The cold detachment with which he viewed the fallout of his actions was a stark departure from the man they all thought they knew.

Meeka, her initial shock giving way to a profound hurt, found her voice amidst the silence. "How could you?" While still pointing the gun at his chest, she whispered, her voice trembling, "How could you do this to us, to me?" Her question hung in the air, a touching echo of the betrayal that had just been laid bare.

Amid the chaos and the raw exposure of hidden agendas, Meeka's voice trembled as she reached out to Fleet, her despair cutting through the tension that filled the room. "Fleet, what on earth did I mean to you? Who have you become? We were supposed to get married, for crying out loud!" Her voice wavered each word a plea from deep within her soul. "Look, I'm trying to give you an out before I'm forced to bust a cap in your ass. Find a way to tell me you don't want this to end like this," Meeka pleaded, her hand steady but her heart breaking as it hovered over the trigger.

Her plea wasn't just a question; it was a heart-wrenching call to the man she once loved, an attempt to reach whatever remnants of that man might still exist beneath the cold exterior he now presented to her. She desperately searched his eyes for any sign of the person he used to be, hoping against hope that somewhere inside him, there was still a flicker of the love they once shared.

Fleet sighed, his voice heavy with resignation. "You know what, Meeka? I owe you this much. Yeah, I was deep for you, no doubt about that." "I can't deny how good that thing you got is." But the problem is, I am what I am, just like Bobby said.

"I'm a brother, misguided and out of control, still running from a past that won't let me go until I'm dead." "Baby girl, I've got people looking for me." "I owe a lot of folks money for some stupid shit I got caught up in, and I needed a way out." So, when Bobby came and told me about the money he had stashed, and this nigga Jay wanted to get revenge on Bobby, it all just came together. And once the clock started ticking and the stakes got high, I had to go back to the me I know—the me that could get me out of this shit."

"Fleet, I could have helped get you out of this," Meeka said, her voice trembling with emotion.

"Well, that's not gonna work now because it is what it is. So, if you want to shoot me, then shoot me, 'cause there will be a few dead people in here after that."

Bobby spoke up, his tone calm yet tinged with disappointment. "Fleet, why didn't you just tell me that? It wouldn't be the first time I helped you get out of some deep shit."

Meeka, confused, asked, "What does that mean, Bobby?"

"Meeka, I'm the one who arranged for you to take Fleet's case," Bobby explained. "I went to your firm because I knew you were rising to the top, and they praised you so much that I asked your boss—who I'd helped make a lot of money in the past—if he could recommend one of his attorneys to help my friend. He recommended you, and I thought that was great because you and I are great friends."

Meeka's eyes widened in disbelief. "Wow, you did this? You sidelined me and hooked me up with this nigga? Well, damn, maybe I should shoot both y'all asses," she said, turning the gun toward Bobby.

Brandy quickly intervened, "Meeka, don't point that gun at Bobby. He's not the problem here. Meeka, you've been my sister since the day we met. All I ever wanted was to see you prosper," Bobby said. "Hell, that's all I ever wanted for all of us. I was the one always pushing the buttons to help all of y'all with your growth and progress. A lot of people in this town owe me, and I wouldn't hesitate to use those I.O.U.s if it was to benefit my family. And Meeka, you have always been a part of my family."

Bobby turned to Christina. "And as for you, Christina, I'm the one who called in and set up the audition for you—not for Brandy's part, but for a supporting role. The problem is, I didn't know Brandy was declared out. So when they heard your voice, they fell in love with you immediately and wanted you to take her place. They told me it might be temporary until Brandy decides what she wants to do," Bobby explained.

"Well, damn, Mr. 'Hook a Bitch Up,'" Brandy said sarcastically. "All I got was a lost house, cancer, a repossessed car, and a nigga standing here right now trying to kill me. Thank you very much, Bobby."

Bobby's voice was thick with emotion as he responded, "Damn you, Brandy. I gave you everything—support, prosperity, hope, opportunity to shine in doing what you love. Yeah, I know the cat that owns the theater, too. But most of all, I gave you unconditional love and loyalty. I gave you everything that a man could have shared with a woman he loved as much as I loved you, Brandy. And damn if that wasn't enough."

The words seemed to hang in the air, dense with betrayal and a pleading undertone. Meeka, her eyes searching Fleet's, struggled to reconcile the disparity between the partner she had known and the man who now stood before her, armed and dangerous, his motivations laid bare in the most painful way.

Fleet, meeting Meeka's gaze, his expression unreadable for a moment, finally responded with a chilling indifference. "Marriage was never really in my plans," he admitted starkly, his voice devoid of warmth. This admission was not just a denial of their planned future but an unraveling of the narrative Meeka had believed in so fervently. The revelation was a brutal cleaving of the future she had envisioned. Her dreams of domestic bliss and partnership shattered irrevocably.

Reeling from the shock, Meeka pressed on, her voice thick with emotion. "After everything we've been through, all we've shared, how can you say that? Doesn't our past mean anything to you?" Her words were a desperate clutch at the threads of their shared history, hoping to awaken some flicker of the man she believed he was, to stir a memory of their intimacy and pull him back from the brink.

Fleet, however, remained resolute, his next words cutting through the tense air. "Look, Meeka, what we had was real; at least, it was to me at the time. But people change, and situations change. I'm in survival mode now, and that means making hard choices." His justification, cold and pragmatic, laid bare the harsh reality of his transformation—from a loved partner to a calculating stranger, driven by desperation rather than sentiment.

At that moment, the tension in the room reached its peak as the unmistakable sound of a Glock being cocked echoed through the space. Everyone froze, their eyes snapping to Meeka, who stood there, gripping the gun with a determined yet trembling hand.

"Meeka!" Christina's voice cut through the thick silence, sharp and pleading. "Don't throw everything away by killing that motherfucker. He isn't worth it. Let those crooked bastards who are after him deal with his ass." Christina's voice was filled with a cold resolve, surprising everyone with its edge.

"Oh, he's gonna get what's coming to him," Christina added, her tone dark, promising retribution that was both unexpected and unsettling coming from her. Even in the midst of the chaos, the room fell into stunned silence as all familiar eyes turned to her, shocked at the transformation they were witnessing.

Christina, usually the calm and composed one, was now speaking with a fierce, almost ruthless certainty. Her words hung in the air, heavy with the implication that something far worse than a bullet from Meeka might be waiting for their betrayer. It was clear that the events of the night had pushed everyone far beyond their limits, revealing sides of themselves that they hadn't even known existed.

"Aww, your weak ass is finally growing up. About time you came out of your little timid shell," Jay taunted, his voice dripping with mockery. "Oh yeah, your sister told me all about your psycho, jealous ass—always wanting to be like her but too scared of your own shadow."

Christina's eyes narrowed, anger flaring in her chest. "Well, damn, she told you all that, huh? Just for the record, I might be in my shell, but you can't shoot all of us at the same time. And when you have to choose, if it ain't me, I'm gonna be on your ass, you bitch-ass nigga," Christina shot back, her voice strong and defiant. "Oh, and just so you know, this is going to escalate sooner or later tonight, and I will not hesitate to kill a mother-fucker over my sister—plus or minus where we stand in our relationship that day. Believe that." She shook her head, her eyes rolling with a mix of determination and disdain.

The room felt colder at his words, the shift intense as everyone absorbed the stark transformation in Fleet. Meeka, her heart breaking, was left grappling with a profound sense of loss —not just of the future she had envisioned but of the man she had loved, who now seemed as distant as if he had never existed.

Fleet, with a shrug that felt like a physical blow to Meeka, turned away, signaling the end of not just their relationship but of the trust and camaraderie that had once defined their group. As he faced the consequences of his actions, the room was left to grapple with the harsh reality of betrayal, deception, and the painful cost of secrets finally brought to light.

Meeka, overwhelmed by betrayal and shock, lunged at Jay in a desperate attempt to seize control. "Give me that goddamn gun; I am gonna blow this brother's head off," she screamed, her emotions spilling over.

Jay, quick to react, pushed her away, causing her to fall to the floor. "Yeah, that's right, Ms. District Attorney," he mocked, stepping back to maintain distance.

Meeka, witnessing the chaos, declared defiantly, "Well, y'all better kill me then 'cause I'm gonna put both you mother-fuckers under the damn jail."

Fleet, unyielding, pressed on. "Look, enough games. The shit is what it is, Bobby. Where is the money?"

"Look, man, you, of all people, should know that I wouldn't keep that kind of money here," Bobby responded, his voice strained with frustration.

Suddenly, the tension was interrupted by a ringing phone. Alexa picked up the phone, and it went on loudspeaker. "You have a call from an inmate. This call is for Brandy Pope," the automated voice announced. The inmate then added, "The inmate says he's your father."

"What?" Bobby exclaimed, his voice a mixture of confusion and disbelief. "Damn, are there any more secrets to be revealed here?" he asked, his frustration echoing around the now-silent room as everyone processed the latest unexpected twist in their already convoluted drama.

In the tense atmosphere that filled Bobby and Brandy's living room, the emotional stakes were at an all-time high. Brandy, already burdened by the traumatic weight of her cancer and the unraveling of personal relationships, sought a moment of honesty with Bobby amidst the chaos. She confessed a moment of vulnerability with Jay, emphasizing the absence of deeper feelings—a desperate attempt to salvage the trust between them. Her voice, heavy with sincerity, was meant to draw a line, to clarify the emotional landscape marred by Jay's misconceptions.

Jay, however, driven by a misguided belief in Brandy's affection for him, reacted with volatile indignation. His emotions, skewed by rejection and misunderstanding, manifested dangerously as he raised his gun, pressing it to Bobby's head with a threatening snarl, "Bitch, I will blow this nigga's head off."

As the tension in the room reached its peak, Christina saw her chance. With a vase in hand, she struck Jay from behind, knocking him unconscious. The gun he had been holding fell to the ground, and Christina quickly picked it up, aiming it at Fleet.

"Don't move," she warned, her voice steady despite the fear coursing through her. At the same moment, Bobby lunged at Fleet, wrestling with him for control of the gun. In the struggle, a gunshot rang out, reverberating through the room.

Fleet, now injured, rolled over in pain as Christina fired the gun she held, hitting him in the hip. The impact was enough to make him drop his weapon, but the damage had already been done.

Bobby, blood pouring from a wound near his heart, turned to face Brandy. The realization of what had happened settled heavily on everyone in the room. Bobby, accepting the tragic outcome, took responsibility for the events that had unfolded. His words, though weakened by the pain, were filled with a solemn acceptance of the choices that had led them to this moment.

As Bobby's voice faded, the room was engulfed in grief and disbelief. The weight of the situation was almost too much to bear, leaving those present to confront the fragility of life and the complex web of relationships that had unraveled before them.

Tears filled the room as the reality of what had happened set in. The sound of approaching police sirens in the distance hinted at the consequences that were yet to come, adding a final note of inevitability to the tragedy that had just occurred.

"Fortune's Whispers and Unwritten Letters"

Meeka returned home from another grueling day as the new District Attorney. Stepping into the familiar surroundings of her house, the words "Hunny, I'm home" lingered on the tip of her tongue, a habitual greeting that had become second nature. However, she caught herself mid-sentence, the weight of recent events pressing on her mind.

The silence that greeted Meeka was deep, emphasizing the absence of Fleet that she was still grappling with. The entryway, usually bustling with the warmth of shared laughter and the comforting scents of dinner, stood stark and uninviting. She set her briefcase down with a sigh, the sound echoing off the walls, underscoring the emptiness.

As she hung up her coat, her gaze lingered on the small, cluttered table by the door, a makeshift repository for keys, mail, and memories—mostly stuff left behind from Fleet; he was never one for putting things away. Among the usual detritus, a single, unopened letter lay prominently, its edges slightly curled. The handwriting was painfully familiar, a poignant reminder of words left unsaid and conversations postponed; in this case, it was forever.

Moving deeper into the house, the living room seemed frozen in time. The cushions on the sofa still bore the imprints of previous evenings spent together, between her and Fleet, an evening when the challenges of her new role as District Attorney had seemed manageable, buffered by support and shared resolve. The television was dark, a stark contrast to the nights filled with debate over news stories and decisions on which movie to watch.

Meeka's steps slowed as she approached the kitchen. The calendar on the fridge was still turned to the previous month, each day marked with meticulous notes of plans, appointments, and little reminders that now felt like relics of a different era. She reached out, tracing her finger over a date circled in red—the anniversary dinner they never got to have.

With a heavy heart, Meeka turned away, the reality settling in deeper with each step. She passed the small dining table, its surface clear except for two placemats still positioned across from one another. The scene was a silent testament to routines disrupted and spaces left unoccupied.

Upstairs, the bedroom door stood ajar. Normally a sanctuary, now it felt like the threshold to a shrine of what was lost. The bed was made neatly, her side smooth and untouched, the other side slightly rumpled, just as it had been left that morning —abrupt, like the goodbye. After the traumatizing night at Brandy's home, Meek had decided not to go back home until after the election and the case against Fleet and Jay was concluded. Make no mistake about itMeek used her status as a District Attorney to ensure that Jay and Fleet would not be home for a very long time. Yet now, she was finally facing her own reality of emotional loss and betrayal.

As night fell, Meeka found herself back in the living room, the dim light casting long shadows. She finally allowed herself to sink into the sofa, her mind replaying the days and decisions that had led her here. The responsibility of her role weighed heavily on her, yet it was the personal loss, the absence of her partner in both triumph and tribulation, that felt most acute.

In the quiet, Meeka whispered, "Hunny, I'm home," into the emptiness, a fragile attempt to bridge the gap between past comforts and her current reality. Her voice broke the silence, filling the room with sorrow too vast for words.

The court case that had consumed her attention ended earlier than expected, affording Meeka an opportunity for some much-needed mental rest. With Fleet and Jay behind bars, their prison sentences a consequence of a series of charges, Meeka was beginning to settle into the stark reality of her newfound solitude. The echoes of that chaotic night at Bobby and Brandy's house still haunted her, making it feel as if it were just yesterday.

The end of the trial brought a strange, hollow victory to Meeka. As she drove away from the courthouse, the last echoes of the judge's gavel seemed to reverberate through her, a stark reminder of the justice she had served, yet mingled with a deep-seated unease about what it had cost her personally.

Arriving home, the house felt unusually still. The silence was no longer just a physical absence but felt charged with the remnant adrenaline and tension of the courtroom. She wandered into the kitchen, where a stack of unsorted mail and neglected responsibilities awaited her, but her mind was elsewhere, trapped in the recollections of that night at Bobby and Brandy's house.

The night had been chaotic, a blur of flashing lights, raised voices, and urgent movements. She remembered how the situation had spiraled, from a simple gathering to an urgent, dangerous confrontation. The details were vivid in her mind: the sharp, acrid smell of spilled drinks, the sudden, shocking sounds of breaking glass and desperate shouts. Now, the silence of her kitchen seemed to amplify those memories, making them ring louder in her ears.

She made her way to the living room, her movements automatic. The couch invited her to sit, but instead, she paced slowly, her thoughts tumbling. The images of Fleet and Jay being led away in handcuffs replayed in her mind. The relief of their capture and conviction was undeniable, but so was the grief for the peace and normalcy lost along the way.

The mantle over the fireplace held photos that seemed to mock her current solitude—smiling faces at gatherings, holidays, and vacations. Each picture was a snapshot of happier times, starkly contrasting with her current state. She paused at one particular photo taken at a barbecue at Bobby and Brandy's—before everything went wrong. It was hard to reconcile the joy in those faces with the aftermath of that fateful night.

Feeling the walls closing in, Meeka stepped outside into the backyard. The garden, neglected and overgrown, reflected her inner turmoil. The air was crisp, and the sky was beginning to dim, with streaks of pink and orange bleeding into dusky blue. She breathed in deeply, trying to cleanse the courtroom air still lingering in her lungs.

The solitude was overwhelming, yet in this moment of quiet dusk, Meeka found a small, tender mercy—a chance to process, to grieve, and perhaps to start healing. The weight of her job, the losses she had endured, and the isolation she faced were daunting, yet the setting sun seemed to promise that even the longest, darkest nights eventually yield to the dawn. As she turned back to the house, the flickering lights seemed to whisper a tentative hope, a reminder that life, with all its trials and tribulations, still held moments of quiet redemption.

Her relationship with Brandy, once an unbreakable bond, had become strained and distant. The fallout from that fateful night had cast a lingering shadow over their friendship, creating an unspoken distance that seemed insurmountable. Meeka hadn't reached out to Brandy, and the silence between them spoke volumes.

In the midst of this emotional upheaval, Meeka found solace in attending one of Christina's performances. The powerful display of artistry provided a brief respite from the heaviness of her own reality. Though their interactions had become infrequent, Christina still reached out, and they shared occasional coffee dates, offering moments of connection amidst the prevailing distance.

As Meeka sank into a chair and kicked off her heels, the doorbell rang, shattering the quietude of her thoughts. She could hear muffled voices and peculiar noises from the doorstep. With hesitant anticipation, she opened the door, only to be greeted by a man exclaiming in a loud and celebratory tone, "Congratulations! You are the new winner of the Publishers Clearing House Sweepstakes."

Caught off guard, Meeka paused, skepticism etching her features. She questioned the legitimacy of the unexpected announcement, wondering if it could be some sort of mistake. The man confirmed her identity as Meeka Johnson, and with a triumphant grin, he declared her the winner. Still in disbelief, Meeka dared to ask, "What did I win?"

The man's response sent shockwaves through her being — she had won three million dollars. The revelation nearly caused Meeka to faint, and in that dizzying moment, a memory resurfaced. She recalled the day when she found Fleet earnestly praying over an envelope, urging her not to forget to mail it. In a legal maneuver, Meeka, being an attorney, reviewed the submission and, considering Fleet's situation, changed the entry name to hers. Back then, winning seemed like a remote possibility, but now, as she stood on the threshold of unexpected fortune, she looked up at the heavens and uttered a grateful acknowledgment: "You always know what you're doing. Thank you, Lord."

"Debts in the Mistaken Retobution"

Jay and Fleet had been convicted on multiple charges, each handed a significant prison sentence. Jay received a 35-year-to-life term, while Fleet faced a staggering 30 years to life. Fate, however, threw them an unexpected curveball when, due to prison overcrowding, they found themselves sharing the same cell. This stroke of luck, seemingly peculiar for seasoned inmates like them, raised suspicions about potential political influence or someone with significant sway orchestrating the arrangement.

Burdened by a substantial debt that lingered from their past endeavors, the duo braced themselves for the inevitable repercussions. They knew that payment was due, and someone would come to collect. In the confined world of the prison, Jay's charismatic persona, particularly his captivating eyes, had earned him favor among fellow inmates, both men and women.

Several weeks had passed since Jay and Fleet found themselves sharing the same tense airspace, their coexistence marked by an undercurrent of unease and suspicion. Despite their efforts to navigate the daily routines of prison life without incident, a palpable tension always lingered, like a silent third party to their interactions.

One day, this simmering tension burst into open hostility under the harsh, unforgiving lights of the prison shower room—a place where the law of the guards often gave way to the law of the jungle. It started subtly but unmistakably: inmates began filtering out of the shower area, their departure quick and silent, leaving behind a slick, echoing void. This sudden clearing of the space was an ominous sign well understood within the walls of the prison—a prelude to something grim and unavoidable.

As the last few stragglers hurried out, Jay and Fleet, now alone and exposed under the cold streams of water, sensed the shift in the atmosphere. Their worst fears were confirmed when eight sizable inmates, known enforcers in the prison's intricate hierarchy of power, methodically surrounded them. Each one was imposing in stature and demeanor, their faces set in grim lines, their intentions clear. The air thickened with tension, heavy with the weight of impending violence.

Just as Jay and Fleet braced for what seemed an inevitable confrontation, another figure emerged from the shadows, adding a chilling twist to the already fraught scenario. This figure moved with a deliberate, menacing grace, his presence alone enough to heighten the sense of dread that now dominated the room. His arrival was not just an addition to the numbers; it was a significant escalation, signaling a coordinated move that had been carefully planned.

Caught in this precarious encirclement, Jay and Fleet stood back-to-back, acutely aware of their vulnerability. The walls, lined with tile, reverberated with the sound of dripping water, each drop a reminder of the isolation of their position. As they faced their assembled adversaries, a complex mix of fear, defiance, and resolve played across their features. They knew that the next moments would be critical, not just for their immediate survival but for their standing within the prison's unforgiving social order. The air was thick with anticipation, every inmate holding their breath, waiting for the inevitable spark that would ignite the looming confrontation.

In the cold, echoing confines of the prison shower room, the unfolding drama gripped every inmate present with a tangible tension. As Brother Carl, the imposing leader of the Mussallem Organizational Movement, finished his initial declaration, confusion and a creeping sense of dread began to settle over Jay and Fleet. They were unprepared for the news that their debts had been acquired by someone so influential within the prison and that they were to remain cellmates under his directive.

Fleet, never one to shy away from confrontation, reacted with a mix of defiance and disbelief. "Hold on—what debts? What are you talking about?" he demanded, his voice echoing off the stark walls, seeking clarity in a situation that seemed increasingly complex and dangerous.

Brother Carl's response was measured, his tone chillingly calm as he delved deeper into the heart of the matter. "You may not have realized the full consequences of your actions outside these walls," he began, his eyes locking onto both Jay and Fleet with an intensity that commanded attention. "The couple you chose to victimize—manipulating them, exploiting their vulner-abilities—they weren't just nobodies. One of them was my daughter, Brandy, and the other, her sister Christina, whom you fortunately decided to leave unbothered."

The revelation struck like a physical blow, hanging heavy in the humid air of the shower room. The implications were imme-diate and severe; this was not merely a matter of prison politics or debts but a deeply personal vendetta that had ensnared them both. Brother Carl's use of "fortunately" was not lost on them—it implied a thin thread of mercy, a catastrophic situation that could have been even worse had they antagonized both of his daughters.

The other inmates, silent witnesses to this confrontation,

sensed the gravity of the situation. They understood that Brother Carl's reach and influence were extensive, and his personal stake in the matter added a dangerous edge to the already lethal politics of prison life.

Fleet, absorbing the weight of Brother Carl's words, could only exchange a bewildered look with Jay. Both men were suddenly acutely aware of their precarious position, caught in a web of their own making. The dynamics of power and survival in the prison had shifted dramatically with Brother Carl's disclosure. They were not only indebted to a powerful man but were also directly responsible for harm to his family.

As Brother Carl continued to outline the terms of their indebtedness and the expected recompense, Jay and Fleet stood in stifled silence, their future in prison now tethered to the whims of a man whose motives were fueled by paternal revenge as much as by the rules of the criminal code he governed. The room felt smaller, the stakes higher, and their path forward more treacherous than ever.

Unaware of the full scale of the consequences that their past actions had set into motion, Jay and Fleet found themselves scrambling to regain some semblance of control. Desperate to mitigate the dire situation they were now in, they quickly offered to perform any task or job that Brother Carl might require as compensation. They hoped that by showing a willingness to serve his interests, they might soften his approach to their punishment.

However, Brother Carl, whose motivations were driven by a deep personal vendetta rather than any practical need for labor or services, was uninterested in such offers. His response was cold and calculated, his eyes scanning Jay and Fleet with a dispassionate gaze that chilled the bone. "Your willingness is noted," he began in a low, menacing tone, "but it does not alter the nature of your debt."

He then outlined a plan that was brutal in its simplicity and terrifying in its implications. "Fleet will suffer a severe beating," Brother Carl declared with unsettling calmness. "It will leave him on the brink of death, barely able to walk. This will serve as a lasting reminder of the consequences of meddling with my family." His words echoed ominously in the damp air of the shower room, carrying a weight that was both a sentence and a warning.

The other inmates, who until now had been silent observers, shifted uncomfortably, their expressions a mix of fear and pity. The harshness of the proposed punishment was not just a message to Jay and Fleet but a clear signal to everyone within the prison about the lengths to which Brother Carl would go to protect his family and assert his authority.

Fleet, upon hearing his fate, felt a surge of fear that was palpable. His face drained of color, understanding that the retribution was not just about inflicting physical pain but about breaking him down completely, ensuring he would forever carry the scars of his transgression. Jay, standing beside him, felt a deep sense of dread for his friend and the irreparable damage that was about to be inflicted.

As Brother Carl concluded his chilling declaration, the gravity of their situation settled in. There would be no negotiation, no task or favor that could substitute for the physical retribution Brother Carl demanded. Jay and Fleet were left to absorb the harrowing reality that the consequences of their past actions were about to manifest in a painfully tangible way, altering the course of their lives within the prison indefinitely.

As for Jay, the punishment was equally harrowing. A fellow inmate known as Big John would become his cellmate, inflicting psychological torment by forcing him to submit every night. Brother Carl, unapologetic and resolute, emphasized the severity of the punishment. While acknowledging the savagery of their actions, he remarked that it was a slow and long punishment compared to what could have transpired for any man messing with his daughters.

With an unsettling farewell, Brother Carl departed, leaving Jay and Fleet at the mercy of the merciless hands of the prison's internal justice. The chilling screams that echoed through the prison walls bore witness to the beginning of a punishment that transcended the physical and delved into the dark realms of the prisoners' tortured minds.

It was the inaugural evening of the much-anticipated cell reassignment that had been arranged by Brother Carl at the correctional facility. As per the stipulations of this new arrangement, inmates Fleet and Jay Wilabee, who had a notorious and turbulent history, were placed in separate cells. This decision was brought on by a violent altercation earlier that day, one that left Fleet grievously injured, and consequently, he was rushed to the medical infirmary, his condition critical and his life hanging by a thread.

Meanwhile, Jay was placed in a cell with Big John, a man infamous not only for his formidable-sized manhood but also for his equally imposing reputation. That night, as Jay lay in the claustrophobic confines of the bottom bunk, he was acutely aware of Big John's presence just above him. The upper bunk groaned ominously under the weight of its occupant, the bed's frame bending inward so dramatically that it loomed a mere couple of feet above Jay.

The sounds filling the cell were unsettling, particularly the snoring of Big John. It was a jarring, primal noise, reminiscent of a lion in the throes of a bizarre, discordant mating ritual with a gorilla—demonic and raw in its tonality. Each snore echoed through the stark cell, reverberating against the cold, unyielding walls and amplifying in Jay's ears.

Lying there, Jay felt a growing sense of claustrophobia, fueled by the oppressive proximity of the sagging bunk above. The mere thought of the heavy frame potentially collapsing on him was intolerable. His mind raced with anxiety and simmering anger, pondering his predicament and the series of events that had led him to this moment, sharing a cell with a giant of a man whose very presence seemed to squeeze the air out of the small space. It was a long night for Jay, each minute stretching endlessly as he lay trapped under the shadow of Big John, driven to the edge by the cacophony and the fear of what lay above.

The prison had descended into an eerie silence as the clock ticked deeper into the night. What little sound did break this quiet was far from ordinary—it was the stuff of nightmares, not meant for sane ears. Distant, muffled screams punctured the stillness sporadically, each cry woven with threads of agony and desperation echoing down the sterile, cold hallways. These were not just sounds of routine disputes or the common clamor of incarceration; they carried a bone-chilling resonance of terror and pain of men caught in situations from which there might be no return.

As Jay lay there, the heavy snoring of Big John above him,, now a grotesque lullaby, made him feel an involuntary tremor in his left leg. It began as a mild shudder but soon escalated into a relentless shake, mirroring the tumult of fear and anticipation brewing within him. Translation: he was scared as hell and knew it was a matter of time before this big-ass dude came off that bonk to make a snack out of his ass.

Jay's previous stint in prison had already acquainted him with the notorious reputation of Big John, although seeing him up close was a starkly different and more intimidating experience. Big John was an imposing figure, not just in size but in the sheer aura of danger he exuded. His features were rough and fearsome, making him a figure of whispered tales and wide berths as inmates discussed his exploits in hushed, fearful tones.

Big John's influence extended throughout the prison. He was so fierce that during meals, other inmates would hastily offer up portions of their own food if he merely glanced their way.

The unspoken rule was clear: appease Big John or suffer dire consequences. Those who dared to defy him found themselves paying a steep price, particularly in the vulnerable solitude of the shower rooms, where Big John's rule was law, and his retribution was swift and harsh.

He stood 6 feet 10 inches and weighed 320 pounds, compared to Jay, who was 5 feet 9 inches and 165 pounds. He was known by many monikers—"Gorilla Ghost," "Sasquatch," and some even called him "The Black Loch Ness"—as if he were a mythical beast rather than a man. Each name carried its own legend, but all agreed on one thing: sharing a cell with him was a fate worse than any medieval punishment akin to burning at the stake. The air around him was charged with an unspoken threat, a constant reminder to all that his capacity for violence was as great as his massive frame.

Jay, now confined within the same cell as this feared behemoth, felt an overwhelming sense of dread. The stories he had heard didn't even begin to capture the palpable fear that now gripped him every moment he spent in Big John's shadow. As the night wore on, Jay lay there, the chilling reality of his situation sinking in deeper with every thunderous snore that rumbled from the bunk above.

The oppressive atmosphere of the cell, combined with the nightmarish soundscape outside, conspired to heighten his sense of vulnerability. It wasn't just the physical proximity of danger but the psychological foreboding of impending doom that gnawed at him.

Haunted by the echoes of his own past actions, Jay felt the weight of every decision he had made, each risk he had taken now circling back to him like a boomerang. He was acutely aware of the fragile line between retribution and survival in these walls, and tonight, it seemed the former was drawing inexorably closer. The prison, a behemoth of despair and lawlessness, felt as if it was closing in on him, the walls themselves whispering of consequences yet to come.

Jay's heart pounded against his chest. Each beat a loud drum in the quiet of the night as he lay paralyzed by the dual assault of sound and fear. The night was long, and the specters of his decisions loomed large, each second stretching into eternity as he awaited the unknown horrors that the dark might bring.

Suddenly, a voice as deep as a full-size bass drum being played by a fat kid in a band echoed through the cell. "You know you'll get used to it sooner or later," said Big John. Jay didn't respond, but his leg began to shake even faster. By this time, Jay was in a full sweat, like a baby wildebeest being chased by a lion.

"I hear your little scared ass down there. You know, it will get better after you steal some Crisco from the cafeteria. I highly recommend you take that route," continued Big John. "They don't just call me Big John because I'm big in height; they call me Big because of the size of my manhood," he added with a smirk.

"Is that you I smell? I bet you're all wet.... sweating, and shit... I like that..." Big John teased as he started singing in a deep Barry White-like voice. "Fee, Fie, Foe, Fum... I smell the booty of a bitch... ass bum."

Suddenly, the floor shook like a California earthquake. Big John hit the floor as he jumped down from the top bunk. Jay, shaking like a rabbit in heat, jumped back to the side of the bed against the wall, covering his face with the blanket to shield his eyes from the battle that was about to begin.

Big John chuckled, "Look at you all cute and shit." "Covers all damp. Damn, I like that shit. You know you got some sexy-ass eyes." "Timmoreia, Timmoreia, Timmoreia, Timmoreia, is that what they call yo little ass? You know you fucked up when you messed with Brother Carl's little girls, and now yo ass is assigned to me... you little wet noodle. Bring yo ass over here," shouted Big John.

Reaching in, Big John pulled Jay out of the bed like a mama picking up a newborn. Jay screamed like a white girl in a horror movie. After that night, he was never the same.

In prison, they called him only Timmoreia; it seemed to fit him better after becoming Big John's bitch. A month later, word came back to Brother Carl about the fate of his oldest daughter, Brandy, a carryover from the impacts of Jay and Fleet's actions. One night, during the session between Big John and Jay, he was beaten so badly that he never woke up the next morning. The reality of it is that he and Fleet had taken some risks, hoping that the outcome of those risks would settle without consequences. However, the spirit of consequence indebted them both for a price that ultimately took both of their lives.

"Veins of Desperation and Encounters of Consequences"

The dive into the deep hole of her own mind was relentless for Brandy, the uncontrolled emotions exacting a toll both on her psyche and her physical being. Shadows of a past she sought to bury had begun to etch themselves into the very fabric of her consciousness, turning the mysterious into something that now seemed to make a perverse kind of sense.

In the recesses of her belongings, Brandy harbored a number, a dark thread linking her to a college friend with connections to the illicit underbelly of substance abuse. The urge to resist this dangerous connection battled within her, yet the desperation clinging to her like a second skin drove her to make the call. They agreed to meet in the shadows of a downtown Chicago alley, an underground encounter that whispered danger and disguised secrecy.

Brandy, cloaked in the secrecy of an Uber, arrived at the designated location, instructing the driver to wait a moment while she ventured around the corner. There, amidst the darkness, emerged Blake—the dope man. A creepy reunion in an isolated alley, where echoes of their past connection lingered like ghosts in the shadows.

"Hey, how are you doing, girl? It's been a long time since we hooked up. What are you up to these days?" Blake greeted, his words laced with the detachment of the underworld.

"Look, Blake, I'm sorry. I know it's been a while, and we need to catch up, but I just need what I asked for, and I've got to make a move," Brandy explained, urgently underscoring her words.

"Okay, no problem," Blake replied, glancing around suspiciously, ever alert to the potential dangers of his trade. With caution, he reached into his jacket pocket, producing a package containing a white substance—the embodiment of Brandy's momentary escape. The exchange, a dance of secrecy and deceit, echoed with the ghosts of her mother's actions, memories etched into the canvas of her troubled past.

As Brandy handed him a tightly clenched fist of money, she felt the weight of her decisions pressing upon her. A swift retreat around the corner ensued, where the waiting Uber driver became her accomplice in this dark transaction. She slid into the back seat, heart pounding, instructing the driver to depart swiftly, leaving the shadows of the alley and the secrets contained within it behind.

In the quiet cocoon of the moving car, Brandy clutched the package, the substance within it a temporary antidote to the commotion in her mind. Yet, the echoes of the alley lingered, and she couldn't shake the feeling that this underground encounter had set in motion a series of events that would resonate through her life, leaving behind a trail of consequences she was unable to understand at the moment.

Blake, still feeling the effects of his own high, reached into his pocket and felt a cold wave of panic wash over him as he realized he had given Brandy the wrong bag. The stuff he handed her was laced—amped up for a heavy junkie who needed a stronger hit to feel the high. He fumbled for his phone but then remembered he had no way to call her, no way to warn her about the deadly mistake. Fear gnawed at him as he realized the gravity of what he had done. All he could do now was hope, hope that Brandy was strong enough to handle the potent mix he had accidentally passed her. But deep down, Blake knew the odds weren't in her favor, and that thought chilled him to the bone. Like any dopefiend he sold to, she had to understand the "risk of consequences that come when you ride that horse." Like any dealer, Blake knew he had to disappear for a while until it blew over. However, it blows over.

Unbeknownst to Brandy, as she hastily retreated from the concealed alley, the bustling urban canvas around her concealed an unexpected twist of fate. Nearby, a quaint café played host to an unlikely gathering—none other than her sister, Christina, immersed in an unusual outing with newfound cast members from the audition.

As Brandy sought refuge in the privacy of her Uber, Christina, engaged in animated conversation, sat mere steps away in the cozy ambiance of the downtown café. The laughter and chatter of the café patrons intermingled with the echoes of the underground exchange that had just taken place in the alley, creating an accidental symphony of contrasting worlds.

Christina, sipping her coffee, was blissfully unaware of Brandy's concealed transaction just moments ago. The chance of their nearness remained concealed, the strands of their lives intertwining without their knowledge.

In a strange and twisted way, their paths had diverged into two starkly contrasting journeys. Christina found herself on a road of self-growth and development, awakening to a new belief in herself and her future. She was beginning to embrace the world around her with a renewed sense of purpose and possibility. On the other hand, Brandy was spiraling down a darker path —a return to a life that could only lead to entrapment and self-destruction. She was shutting down, withdrawing from the world she once knew, and sinking back into a cycle that threatened to consume her entirely. Their lives, once intertwined, were now heading in opposite directions, each defined by the choices they made and the paths they chose to follow.

As Brandy's Uber merged into the flow of city traffic, Christina's gaze wandered toward the passing streets beyond the café window. Little did she know that the edges of her sister's world had briefly brushed against the very fabric of her own, leaving a trail of unspoken connections suspended in the urban air.

As the streets of the city embraced Brandy's speeding Uber and the café retained its lively atmosphere, the two sisters, unwittingly close yet worlds apart, continued their journeys through the unpredictable tapestry of life. The intricacies of their individual stories, unbeknownst to each other, unfolded against the backdrop of a city that bore witness to the silent interplay of destiny.

Brandy returned to the confines of her home, a specter of secrecy and shadows enveloping her every move. Like a prowler in her own domain, she surveyed the house with a sneakiness that denied the unrest within. The potent poison she now possessed, a dark elixir for her pain, was a secret she guarded fiercely, wanting no one to bear witness to the depths of her despair.

Satisfied that solitude reigned within the walls of her home, she tipped the Uber driver discreetly, slipping out of the car with a discretion that matched the illegal nature of her actions. The weight of her possession pressed upon her, a forbidden remedy for the agonies she bore.

Upon crossing the threshold, Brandy's purpose crystallized. The substance in her possession beckoned like a siren, offering relief from the burdens of the house, the car, the novel, the harsh reality of a stage 2 breast cancer diagnosis, and the image of

Bobby losing blood and life on the porcelain floors in the living room, his life slipping away before her very eyes. With desperate haste, she ascended the stairs, her mind consumed by the anticipation of the relief that awaited her in the confines of the bathroom.

Once behind the locked door, her refuge from the world, Brandy set the stage for her descent into oblivion. The mirror, already adorned with the powdered promise of escape, reflected the haunting echo of her mother's final moments. A chilling reminder, yet the allure of the substance drowned out any lingering doubts that might thwart her rendezvous with the "angel of numbness."

A razor, borrowed from Bobby's shaving kit, became the instrument of her descent. With methodical precision, she chopped and divided the powdery substance, preparing it for its journey into her bloodstream. In a moment of hesitation, the memory of her mother lying lifeless on a bed flashed before her eyes. The fear gripped her momentarily, but the echoing call of the substance resonated louder, drowning out the echoes of past traumas.

A set of old works that she had taken from her mother many years ago remained stashed away in her secret place. An instrument of self-destruction became her conduit to oblivion as it met the contours of her veins. Bowing down to the floor as the substance raced through her bloodstream, she began to experience a fleeting escape until the substance in the needle disappeared.

In the cold, solid mirror, a reflection of herself stared back— a brief moment of self-awareness that momentarily arrested her descent into the deep hole. The impending consequences cast shadows on the boundary of her consciousness, but she, undeterred, pressed forward. The illicit substance surged through her senses, a spiritual and intoxicating rush that momentarily eclipsed the encroaching darkness.

Brandy descended, not just along the bathroom wall but into another realm altogether. Her eyes rolled back, surrendering to the potent escape that had become a hazardous reality. The risk, once a distant specter, now coursed through her veins, leading her into a world where the weight of reality lifted and the pain melted away in the embrace of passing excitement.

As the heroin coursed through her veins, its intoxicating grip became a portal to a realm where time and reality blurred. In the vivid dance of her altered consciousness, the past manifested with a haunting intensity.

She lay there against the cool tiles of her bathroom wall, sinking into a place that felt like it had no return, held captive by its grips, strengthened by her decisions and choices.

"Momma, is that you?" As the substance in her veins began to take hold of her body, Brandy's voice trembled.

"Yes, baby, I'm here," her mother's voice seemed to echo from the very walls as Brandy melted into the effects of the venom. Tears streamed down her face as she spoke, her words slurred with the onset of the substance.

It was a feeling of escape, one that Brandy believed was only temporary, but this time, the intentions of the substance were much more gripping. Brandy knew something was wrong, but reversing the decision wasn't possible. It had begun to merge with her bloodstream, taking control of her heart.

"I miss you so much, Momma," Brandy said, her voice thick with emotion. She clutched her chest, her heart pounding faster and faster. "Momma, this hurts," she gasped.

"I know, baby, but it won't last long," the voice of her mother seemed to reverberate through the room. "Is this the cancer, Momma?" Brandy's voice trembled with intense fear.

"No, baby, it's the decisions you've made and the roads you've taken," her mother replied softly. "You're almost there. Reach for me, baby; take my hand."

"Momma, I'm scared," Brandy's voice shook with fear. At

that moment, her thoughts began to race, and memories flooded her mind. She remembered the day she first met Bobby, the warmth of his smile, and the first time they kissed. She recalled her parents' arguments and the nights she spent hiding under the bed, seeking refuge from their turmoil. She remembered the rush of adrenaline as she sang to an audience for the first time, the overwhelming sense of purpose it gave her. And she remembered Bobby, how deeply she loved him and how she never wanted it to end. It was like a movie playing in the channels of her mind, an account of every action and a glimpse of every scene.

Images materialized before her and every frame etched in the corridors of her mind. The recollection of that fateful night replayed with grotesque clarity—Bobby, lifeless on the floor, his body bathed in blood, and Jay standing over him, a maniacal laughter echoing through her thoughts. His words, both apologetic and perverse, reverberated in her mind like a horrific chorus.

Transported to the beginning of their love story, she witnessed Bobby standing proudly on the fraternity house porch, the very image of him etched in her memory. The scenes unfolded like a cinematic reel—Bobby's triumphant graduation, tears streaming down his face as he walked down the aisle on their wedding day, and the radiant joy when he learned of his prestigious position at the brokerage firm. The echoes of his love and pride were etched permanently in her mind.

Yet, amidst the joyous haze, the scene shifted suddenly. She confronted the moment of her own betrayal—the rehearsal night, the glint of the knife, and the revelation of her tryst with Jay. The pain in Bobby's eyes, a reflection of shattered trust, lingered like a ghost in the hallways of her consciousness.

In a surreal twist, the narratives of her life unraveled further, leading her to the tender years of childhood. A vision of herself as a little girl emerged, repeatedly calling out to her mother in a room shrouded in shadows. The haunting question, "Momma, are you okay?" echoed through the ages, and in the chilling silence, her mother turned, beckoning her to lay beside her.

As she approached her mother on the bed, a profound sense of comfort enveloped her. The warmth of her mother's embrace became a sanctuary, a refuge from the storms of life. At that moment, cocooned in the tender arms of her mother, she succumbed to the embrace of an unexpected, serene slumber. The surreal journey through time, love, and loss blended into an embroidery of emotions, leaving her suspended between wakefulness and dreams.

The house was unusually quiet when Christina burst through the front door, her keys jangling loudly in the silence. She called out, but only her echo answered, filling the emptiness with a sense of urgency. As she moved deeper into the house, the muffled sound of a voice drew her toward the bathroom. The door was ajar, soft light spilling into the hallway.

"Brandy?" Christina's voice trembled, pushing the door open with a hesitant hand.

Inside, she found her sister, Brandy, slumped against the tiled wall, her eyes glassy and her breathing erratic. Panic gripped Christina as she noticed the small, empty packet on the floor beside Brandy. Her heart raced as the terrifying reality set in— Brandy was in the throes of a critical reaction, her body succumbing to whatever she had taken.

"Brandy, what did you do?" Christina cried out, her voice cracking as she fell to her knees beside her sister. She fumbled for her phone in her pocket, her fingers clumsy with fear, and dialed 911.

"I... I love you so much, Brandy. Please, hold on," she sobbed into the phone, relaying their address to the dispatcher with a frantic urgency. "Please hurry," she pleaded, her voice a whisper of despair.

Brandy's dilated eyes met Christina's, a weak smile flickering across her face as she lifted a trembling hand to touch her sister's cheek. "You're my baby sister, and I am so proud of you," she whispered, her voice strained. "Momma always said you were the strong one of us, and she was right. Look at you; your life is just beginning, and here I am, lying here."

Tears streamed down Christina's face as she clutched Brandy's hand, the cold reality of the moment settling in her heart. "No, don't talk like that. You're going to be okay," she choked out, her voice thick with emotion.

"Go be the best you can be, sis. Make me proud," Brandy continued, each word slower and more laborious than the last.

Christina shook her head, her sobs growing louder and more desperate. "I need you, Brandy. Please."

Brandy looked past Christina, her gaze fixing on something unseen, a calm washing over her features. "I'm ready, Momma," she murmured, a tear escaping down her cheek.

Then, her hand slipped from Christina's grasp, her body going limp in her sister's arms. Christina's heart shattered as she felt Brandy's breathing falter and then stop. "Brandy!" she screamed, her voice echoing off the cold tiles, a stark reminder of her newfound loneliness.

The sound of sirens in the distance was a cruel irony as Christina cradled her sister, the room spinning around her. The first responders would arrive soon, but Christina knew it was too late. Her sister, her confidant, her heart, was gone. All she could do was hold Brandy, whispering words of love and regret until the medics pulled her away to make room for their urgent, futile efforts.

As the chaos unfolded around her, Christina felt a profound emptiness. Brandy's final words echoed in her mind—a touching reminder of the resilience that she must now find within herself to forge ahead. But in that tragic moment, all Christina could feel was the crushing weight of grief, holding on to the last piece of her sister that remained: the memory of her love and her final, selfless wish for Christina to live a life that would make her proud.

"Momma, don't leave me," she reached out, grasping at the mystical image of her mother wedged into her mind. "I'm not leaving, baby. I'm your escort, here to walk you through," her mother reassured her.

"Momma, I'm scared," she cried out, her body weakening and going limp.

"I know, baby, I know." A sudden flash of light pierced the darkness of her mind, and like a cursor in a text message, time sat there blinking, anticipating the next words to be written. But nothing came, and the cursor eventually stopped flashing. The only words that rained down were, "Bobby, I'm sorry..."

Suddenly, Brandy found herself being escorted by a woman as she was handed off from her mother. In the final validation of her life, Brandy looked into the eyes of the woman and felt a deep sense of recognition. "I know you," Brandy said softly. "You were with me at the doctor's office, and you were with me under my bed when I was hiding from my parents." "You were there with Bobby the day he couldn't find you after we left, and you gave him a gold coin." "You were with me in the bathroom that day, and I was feeling really bad. I know you—you have the most beautiful sea-water blue eyes, surrounded by the purest white I have ever seen."

The woman smiled gently and nodded. "Yes, baby, that's me. I've been with you for a long time, and now I'm here to take you home."

"Letters of Lost Love"

The small cathedral in downtown Chicago was filled with the quiet hum of people gathering, their footsteps muffled by the thick carpet. The air was heavy with the scent of flowers—lilies, roses, and carnations—carefully arranged around the casket at the front of the church. The room was dimly lit, the soft glow of candles flickering against the stained-glass windows, casting colorful patterns on the floor.

Christina stood near the front, her hands clasped tightly in front of her, trying to steady herself. The weight of the moment pressed down on her, and she took a deep breath, preparing herself for what she needed to say. The group of singers she had arranged began to perform the songs she had chosen, their voices filling the space with a gentle, haunting melody. The music was beautiful, a fitting tribute to the life they were here to honor.

When it was time, Christina stepped forward to speak. Her voice trembled at first, but she quickly found her strength. She spoke from the heart, sharing memories and expressing the love she had often kept hidden. She spoke of the impact Brandy had on her life, of the lessons learned, and of the moments shared. There was no need to say her name; everyone present knew they were here to honor "Brandy Pope," the woman who had touched their lives in profound ways.

Meeka followed, her voice steady and warm as she added her own reflections. She spoke of the light Brandy had brought into their lives, the laughter and the tears, and the legacy that would continue to shape them all. There was a sense of unity in the room, a collective understanding of the loss they were experiencing together.

The funeral procession to the Willow Creek Cemetery was led by two motorcycle police officers, their lights flashing silently as they made their way through the streets. The day was overcast, the sky a dull gray, and a light rain began to fall, adding to the somber mood. Mourners followed the hearse in a long line of cars, their headlights cutting through the mist.

As the entourage arrived at the gravesite, they were greeted by an awe-inspiring sight that none of them had anticipated. Standing at attention near the plot where Brandy would be laid to rest were sixty men, all dressed in immaculate black suits and bowties. These men, aligned in perfect formation, bore the solemnity and reverence typically reserved for high-ranking dignitaries. It was as though the presence of these soldiers transformed the cemetery into hallowed ground, a place where history and honor would soon converge.

The men were members of the Nation of Islam, and their presence was a powerful statement of unity, respect, and reverence for the life that Brandy had lived. Their stance was militant yet graceful, exuding an aura of strength and solidarity. As the hearse approached, carrying Brandy's casket, the pallbearers prepared to fulfill their solemn duty. However, before they could proceed, one of the men from the Nation of Islam stepped forward. With a respectful nod and a firm yet polite tone, he requested the honor of carrying the "queen" to her final resting place.

The pallbearers, recognizing the deep respect in the request, stepped aside, allowing the men to take their place. What followed was a beautiful and moving display that left all in attendance deeply touched. The sixty men formed a double line, creating a pathway that led directly to the burial site. As they carried Brandy's casket through this pathway, the men stood at military attention, their eyes focused straight ahead and their postures unyielding. The air was thick with the gravity of the moment, and those who witnessed it could feel the powerful sense of purpose and respect that emanated from the formation.

The casket was gently placed at the burial site, and just as the ritual was about to continue, a new development caught everyone's attention. A police car pulled up to the cemetery, and two officers stepped out, opening the door for a man they escorted from the vehicle. As the man walked toward the gravesite, the Muslim brothers saluted him, recognizing him as a figure of authority and reverence. He was dressed in simple yet dignified attire, his presence commanding respect without the need for words.

The man approached Brandy's casket, his steps measured and deliberate. Upon reaching it, he placed a hand on the polished wood, bowing his head in silent prayer before leaning down to kiss the casket. His gesture was filled with profound emotion, a final farewell that spoke of love, regret, and closure.

He then turned to Christina, who was seated in a chair near the gravesite, her face etched with grief and curiosity. The man knelt beside her, took her hand gently in his, and whispered into her ear, "Salaam alaikum, my black queen. My prayers are with you and the family."

Christina, though overwhelmed, managed to ask, "Who are you?"

The man met her gaze, his eyes filled with a quiet strength. "These men are here to protect you and your sister, to guide her on this side of her journey. If you ever need me for anything, I am here for you." Again, she asked, "Who are you?" As Brother

Carl leaned down, his voice barely above a whisper, he softly spoke into Christina's ear, "I'm your father." He knew this was a shocking revelation and felt the need to provide some kind of proof to back up his words. Gently, he placed a large envelope in her hands and said, "This will help explain everything."

With that, he rose to his feet, turned back toward the casket for one last look, then addressed the police officers, "I am ready." The sixty soldiers moved in unison with him as he was escorted back to the car. The sense of discipline and unity was palpable as they all departed, leaving behind an indelible mark on everyone present.

The entire scene was a testament to the respect and honor that Brandy had commanded in life, even as she faced her final rest. It was a moment that would be remembered by all who witnessed it—a poignant display of love, reverence, and the enduring power of family and faith.

At the burial site, the casket was slowly lowered into the ground. The rain had turned the earth soft, and the sound of dirt hitting the wood echoed in the quiet. Tears flowed freely as those closest to Brandy said their final goodbyes. Christina stood at the edge of the grave, her heart heavy with grief. She had always known this day would come, but knowing didn't make it any easier. The love she had often kept hidden, the admiration she had never fully expressed, now lay buried in the casket.

The theater, where Christina had found so much success, now felt different to her. The joy of performing was still there, but it was tinged with the sadness of knowing that Brandy, who had been such a big part of her life, was gone. She found herself thinking more and more about the things left unsaid, the opportunities missed, and the profound impact Brandy had on her life.

As the days passed, Christina continued to perform, but she was forever changed. Brandy's legacy lived on in her heart, guiding her, inspiring her, and reminding her of the love that had shaped her into the person she had become. The loss was deep, but so too was the love that remained—a love that would continue to influence her for the rest of her life.

In the aftermath of the funeral, Christina found herself immersed in a profound sense of solidarity yet surrounded by a vast void that echoed with unspoken conversations and missed opportunities. There were countless apologies left unsaid, gestures of love withheld, and moments that lingered in the realms of what could have been. The depth of her confusion and the unexpressed appreciation for both family and partnership love cast a touching shadow over her.

Brandy's sudden death, a consequence of guilt and sorrow manifested in a fatal overdose, mirrored the tragic fate of her mother. Both succumbed to the same poison, seeking solace from internal pain at the ultimate cost of an eternal farewell. The repercussions of her actions reverberated, impacting everyone connected to her.

There were consequences to her actions, and collectively, we all were impacted by those decisions. But like Bobby, even in the wake of life's most brutal experiences, we validate our part in the pathways taken by those around us and express our unconditional love that remains stronger than the paths we each take.

After the funeral, Christina couldn't stop thinking about the strange man who had approached her with such a life-altering claim. She sat in her kitchen, the quiet of her home making the moment feel even more surreal. Among the various items she had been handed throughout the day, she found the envelope Brother Carl had given her.

Her hands trembled slightly as she opened the envelope. The first thing she pulled out was a stack of old photographs held together by a rubber band. Carefully removing the band, Christina looked at the top picture. It was of a woman who looked uncannily like the picture of her mother that Mama Lella May had given her years ago. Christina's mother had died in childbirth, so she had always had a fragmented understanding of who she was.

Curiosity grabbed Christina as she rushed to her bedroom closet and retrieved her keepsake box. She pulled out one precious photograph of her mother and placed it next to the one from Carl. A chill ran down her spine as she realized the two women looked nearly identical. Her heart raced with questions she didn't yet have answers to.

As she sifted through the remaining photographs, one caught her eye: a baby in a shopping cart, with a little girl standing next to it. The baby bore a striking resemblance to herself, and the girl looked a lot like Brandy. Standing beside them, smiling into the camera, was Carl. Another picture showed Carl playing the piano in a church, followed by one of him singing as a young man. "So, he was a musician and a singer," Christina thought, a light dawning in her mind. "That must be where I get my love for music."

But the most startling revelation came when she turned over the picture of the baby and the little girl in the grocery store. Written on the back in Mama-Lella-May's familiar handwriting were the words, "My two baby girls, Brandy and Christina, already hanging out together." Christina gasped, the words sinking in. "Oh my God," she whispered, "Brandy and I are sisters. And Carl... Carl is our father."

She continued to go through the photographs, each one revealing more about the man she never knew. One showed Carl and Mama-Lella-May standing together at church with her mother, the inscription reading, "Easter Sunday service." Another showed Carl standing behind a pulpit, the back labeled, "Carl's trial sermon." "Wait," Christina muttered to herself, "Carl was a preacher?"

Then, there was a picture of Carl holding her as a baby, the inscription simply saying, "My baby girl, so precious." The warmth of those words contrasted sharply with what she found next—a newspaper article tucked among the pictures. It detailed the conviction of a pastor for the sexual abuse of several boys in his church. The article listed the boys involved, and among them was Carl. The words blurred as Christina read the part where the pastor had been killed by one of the boys he had assaulted. "That explains so much," she thought, feeling a wave of sorrow for the man who had lived a troubled life.

Finally, buried at the bottom of the envelope was another, smaller envelope. Inside was a large sum of money—about half a million dollars—and a letter. With trembling hands, she could feel the weight of the paper, but it was nothing compared to the emotional weight she was about to bear. Slowly, she unfolded the letter and began to read, her breath catching in her throat as she took in Carl's words.

"My dearest Christina,

I've carried this burden for so long, and now it's time you knew the truth. It's hard for me to even begin this letter because I know the pain it might bring you. But you deserve to know everything—about me, about your mother, and about Brandy.

You and Brandy are my daughters, my precious girls. I wish I could have been there to tell you that in person, to hold you both and be the father you deserved. But I wasn't. And for that, I'm deeply, deeply sorry.

I've made so many mistakes, Christina. Unforgivable mistakes. I let the horrors of my past consume me. When I was a child, the things that the pastor did to me and the other boys in the church broke something inside of me. I was just a kid, and I didn't know how to handle the shame, the anger, the confusion. Instead of facing it, I ran. I ran straight into the arms of drugs, thinking they could numb the pain. But all they did was turn me into a monster—a dopefiernd who lost control of everything good in his life.

I became a man I never wanted to be, a man who hurt the people he loved the most. I failed Brandy, and I failed you. The drugs made me do terrible things, things that haunt me to this day. I had no right to put that weight on Brandy, and I'm so sorry for the suffering I caused her. My heart aches every day knowing that she's gone and that I'll never be able to make it right with her. I'll carry that guilt with me until the day I die.

Your mother, though we didn't have much time together, was the love of my life. She had a way of seeing the good in me, even when I couldn't see it in myself. When she passed, I was lost, and I didn't know how to raise you alone. One of those things was arranging for you both to stay with my sister Caroline, who ultimately became your foster mother. She kept me informed about the two of you as you grew up. After she died in the car accident, I lost some of my ability to keep an eye on you, but I've always been here, behind the scenes.

James, your foster father, didn't know about me or my sister, but I knew he would be a great father to you both. I understand this must be shocking, and I'm sorry if it hurts you to learn this now, but I have loved you all my life.

I know this letter is probably overwhelming, and I don't expect you to forgive me. But I want you to understand that I never stopped loving you. Every day in this prison, I think about you and Brandy. Watching you both from afar was the only thing that kept me going. I knew I had to make sure you had a fighting chance in this world, even if I couldn't be there with you.

The money I'm leaving you is my way of trying to make amends, and it's not illegal money; it's from my organization, the Nation of Islam, where I currently hold a very high office, though I know no amount of money can fix what I've done. Use it to further your life, Christina, to chase your dreams as the lead in "One Woman's Trash." You have a gift, just like your mother, and I'll be watching over you from wherever I am, wishing I could be there in the front row, cheering you on.

Please know that you and Brandy were my light in the darkness, even if I wasn't there to show it the way a father should. I'm so sorry for all the pain I caused. I hope that one day you can find it in your heart to forgive me, but if you can't, I understand.

"I love you, Christina. I've loved you all my life."

Your father, Carl.

Tears blurred Christina's vision as she finished reading. The raw honesty in Carl's words cut through her, filling her with a mix of emotions she couldn't yet untangle. The man who had given her life had also brought her so much pain, but in his final words, she could feel the depth of his regret and the love he had tried, in his own broken way, to express.

"The Harmony of Destiny and Poem of Departure"

It was the grand opening night, a theatrical debut that stirred anticipation in the hearts of the audience. The theater, a tapestry of eager faces, brimming with excitement, ready to witness a performance of "One Woman's Trash" that had garnered rave reviews during its off-Broadway tours. Those fortunate enough to have caught glimpses of this play in its earlier incarnations spoke with fervor, particularly praising the past star of earlier productions, Brandy Pope.

As playbills passed through the hands of attendees, a murmur of discovery rippled through the crowd. Whispers traveled like a secret shared in confidence—Brandy Pope, the original lead, was absent due to undisclosed health issues. In her place, however, emerged a new force: Brandy's sister, poised to claim the spotlight. The debate over whether the newcomer could surpass Brandy's brilliance lingered in the air, heightening the anticipation of the impending spectacle.

Christina, the new lead, stood in the wings, a bittersweet shadow cast by the absence of family. Her parents long departed, left a void in the cheering section. However, with the resilience of a true artist, she steeled herself for the performance that awaited. The curtain rose, and the stage embraced her with its luminescent glow—a rendezvous with her own purpose.

Taking center stage, Christina commenced with the opening notes of the inaugural song, a melody that echoed with promise. The audience, a sea of attentive eyes, was enthralled by her presence. Amidst the applause and cheers, Christina's gaze descended to the first row, where a familiar face awaited: Meeka, a friend and a beacon of support. A shared smile and a blown kiss forged a connection across the footlights, providing comfort in the absence of familial presence.

In the midst of her performance, a radiant moment transpired. A play of light and shadows cast Christina's eyes into a brief dazzle, and within that luminous embrace, she believed she glimpsed the spectral figures from her past—the ladies from the church adorned with their resplendent hats. Their smiles, undiminished by time, conveyed approval and pride, reminiscent of a time when Christina was a prodigious young girl brimming with talent and potential. The convergence of past and present created a harmonic resonance, a symphony of destiny playing out on the stage of Christina's life. As the performance closed out and Christina took a bow before the standing ovation crowd, she looked up with tears in her eyes and said Thank you, Momma Maybelline and Thank you God. Blowing a kiss up in the air.

Christina's journey unfolded on the grand stage, was a journey marked by moving performances and relentless dedication. In the ensuing years, she ascended to the role of the show's lead, navigating the complex tapestry of emotions that wove through the narrative. Her artistry, a beacon of brilliance, resonated with audiences, leaving a lasting imprint on the theatrical landscape.

As the curtains rose and fell, Christina's name became synonymous with excellence. Her portrayal garnered acclaim, and her mastery of the craft reached its high point. The culmination of her efforts was marked by a defining moment—an accolade that crowned her artistry. The prestigious Tony Award, a symbol of theatrical prowess, found its way into Christina's hands, a testament to her unparalleled contribution to the production.

During the award ceremony, Christina stood at the microphone, her voice steady but filled with emotion. "I would like to thank those who supported me and pushed me to become worthy of this award," she began. "First and foremost, I want to thank my mother, whom we lovingly called 'Mother Lella May.' She is one of the primary reasons I stand before you all tonight to receive this honor."

Christina paused, gathering her thoughts as she continued, "I also want to thank a special friend who always worked behind the scenes to support me and push me, even when I didn't know he was pushing me: my brother and dear friend, Mr. Bobby Pope."

Her voice wavered slightly as she spoke her next words. "But I would be remiss tonight if I didn't take the time to thank my departed big sister, my true blood sister in life and the wind beneath my wings, Brandy Pope. Brandy, I know you can hear me tonight. I love you so much, and I miss you with everything in me."

Christina's eyes glistened with tears as she continued, "When I was a little girl, I remember you coming into my room and speaking to me with the most wonderful peace I had ever felt. Up until that time, I wasn't speaking to anyone because I felt such a deep sense of loss when I lost Momma Maybelline. But you gave me that peace that day, and it rebirthed me into this world. I know that if it hadn't been for you, I wouldn't be here today."

She looked out at the audience, many of whom had known Brandy, heard her sing, and witnessed her perform at the highest level. "You, Brandy, are my reason for breathing, and every day of my life, I will breathe knowing that each breath happens because you have pushed it out of me."

Most people didn't know that my big sister loved to write poetry. As her little sister, I often got in trouble for sneaking peeks at her poems when we were kids. Once, I told her that one of her poems sounded stupid, and she beat me up that day. But when I cried, she kept saying she was sorry and held me like I was her baby, and we'd fall asleep together. After that first time, I'd intentionally sneak a look at her poems just so she would hold me when I cried. Of course, the little beating came with that as well, but it was never anything big, just two sisters at each other.

Her poems reflected the things she felt and experienced in her life. She once told me that writing poetry made her feel relieved and that it was a way of speaking to our mother. One day, I took one of her poems that she wrote as a young adult just before heading to college. Here's what it said:

There is a mystery I seek to solve that seems like an equation with no answer.

It encompasses places I yearn to go and things I hope I'll be able to do.

"Accomplishments I dream I will attain, and wishes I declare will come true."

The mystery is not in the attainment of these things; it is in the journey I must travel to achieve them.

A journey I realize will be filled with streets with names I can't recognize, cities I can't find on my map, and highways that have no exits.

A journey that's built like a Ferris wheel, where you go around to go up, down to go left or right, and you have to wait for others to get off while you hang in the balance before getting your turn for the ride to be over.

A journey that has a mandatory destination with unlimited roads you can travel until you get there, only to discover that the roads you chose to travel provide you with a combination to a gate that, if not correct, will not open to you when you arrive. afforded going back is not an affordable option.

A journey where the partners who sometimes accompany you change as often as the sun rises in the morning, only to ensure that it's not wise to over-expect from those you see beside you.

But the mystery doesn't end with the journey or the destination.

It lies within the traveler: the doubts, the fears, the hopes, and the dreams.

That shifts and changes with every step taken, every road chosen, and every gate passed or missed.

The real mystery is how you grow and how you change.

And how you find yourself transformed by the very path you didn't recognize.

The map you couldn't read and the exits you couldn't find.

And perhaps, when the journey ends,

The mystery isn't in solving the equation.

But in realizing that the journey itself was the answer all along.

"Thank you all for this award."

With that, Christina walked off the stage, tears of joy rolling down her face—a tribute to the love and support that had carried her to this moment.

The reflection of her life captures the transformative journey of a performer who transcended the shadows of uncertainty. Each note sung, every emotion portrayed, and every step taken on the stage was a testament to Christina's resilience and unwavering commitment to her art and a symbol of risks taken, consequences lived, and change that came without notice. The award stood as a luminous trophy, dispelling the shadows of doubt and illuminating a path that heralded a new chapter in Christina's illustrious career.

"Unfinished Business and Echoes of Unspoken Words"

Christina felt the weight of the past few days pressing heavily on her heart as she made her way to the rehab facility. Brandy's funeral had left her feeling adrift, searching for a sense of belonging, of family. Bobby was the closest thing she had left, and she needed to see him, to feel connected again.

As she entered the facility and took the elevator to the third floor, Christina tried to steady herself. When she reached room 206 and pushed the door open, she was surprised to find it empty, except for a nurse tidying up.

"Hello, I'm looking for the patient who was in room 206. Can you tell me what the status is on that patient, please?" Christina asked, a hint of concern in her voice.

The nurse looked up and smiled kindly. "Oh yes, ma'am. Mr. Pope checked out yesterday. He'll be completing his rehabilitation at home."

Christina felt a wave of relief wash over her. "Oh, well, that's great news! Did he leave a forwarding address?"

"I'm sorry, ma'am, we can't give out addresses unless you're family."

Christina hesitated for a moment before replying, "Well, then give it to me because I am his sister."

The nurse nodded and checked her records. "Yes, ma'am, let me see here. He's listed as being at the Lincoln Complex Condominium Place in downtown Chicago."

Christina frowned slightly. "Really? That's the old address. I thought he would have moved from there." She remembered that the condo had been foreclosed on. Why would Bobby be headed back there?

Leaving the facility, Christina's thoughts raced as she made her way to the Lincoln Complex. The memories of the condo flooded back—she had been there with Brandy so many times. The entrance code came back to her effortlessly, a relic from better days when they would visit Bobby together.

As she stepped out of the elevator and walked down the familiar hallway, her heart began to pound. The door to the condo was slightly ajar, and a sense of anxiety gripped her, mingling with the painful memory of Brandy's final moments in her arms.

"Hello, is anyone here?" Christina called out, her voice shaky.

Suddenly, Bobby appeared from the back of the condo, catching her by surprise. "Hey, how are you?" he said, his voice warm, his movements fluid and strong as if the shooting had never happened. He hurried to her and pulled her into a long embrace.

Christina felt a rush of emotions—admiration, affection, and that old, hidden passion she had buried deep inside. She quickly composed herself. "Hello, Bobby. My, you look like your old self."

"Yeah, I finally feel like my old self," Bobby replied, smiling. "It's been a little while. The doctors said if the bullet had been just a centimeter to the left, it would've penetrated my heart. I might not have lived. So, thank God for that, right? But I'm on the mend, and barring any unforeseen issues, I'll be making a full recovery."

"That's great to hear, Bobby. I've really missed seeing you," Christina said, her voice softening with sincerity. "Listen, do you want to talk about everything that's happened? Sometimes things happen, and we don't really get a chance to fully deal with them, you know?"

Bobby's expression grew serious for a moment. Then he shrugged it off. "I've had a lot of time to think things over, and I've decided to put it all to rest. I finished my novel—cleaned it up for the publisher, and it's set to be released next week. I'm doing a book signing, and I'd love for you to come and support me."

Christina's face lit up with genuine happiness. "Oh, really, Bobby? I would love to do that."

As they stood there in the dimly lit condo, surrounded by the echoes of their past, Christina realized that despite everything that had happened, they still had each other. And in that moment, it was enough.

Bobby's phone rang, breaking the silence. He answered, "Hey, Bobby, this is Greg from Genesis Global. I hope you remember me."

"Oh yes, Greg, I sure do," Bobby replied, though his mind flashed back to the intense encounter with Jay Willabee. "But you should know, I'm not with the company anymore. If something didn't work out, you'd be better off reaching out to them directly."

Greg's voice softened. "I heard about your situation, and we've all been praying for your recovery. I don't want to take up too much of your time, but I wanted to let you know that the advice you gave us during COVID really paid off. The company and I are incredibly grateful for your guidance during that challenging time."

A smile touched Bobby's lips, a rare moment of warmth in

the cold reality of his recent life. "Well, you're welcome, Greg. I'm glad I could have a positive impact on your investments."

The call reminded Bobby of the fleeting nature of success and the lasting impressions one could make, even when life takes unexpected turns. It was a brief yet meaningful acknowledgment of the legacy he was still capable of leaving behind despite everything he had been through.

"You sure did. Anyway, when we talked during those tough times, I made a commitment to you. I know the company you were with went through some issues, and we're no longer doing business with them, but we definitely wanted to reach out to you and do two things. First, we wanted to keep our word and give you a small percentage of our earnings. Secondly, I want to present a proposal to you."

Greg continued, "We know about your ambitions as a writer and producer, and we know you're working on your novel—or novels. We don't want to interrupt that, but we also recognize your talent and believe both pursuits can coexist. We want you to consider working with us as a consultant, which would free you from the day-to-day grind of corporate America so you can stay creative. Additionally, we want to invest in your novel and potentially become an executive sponsor for your upcoming movie."

"Wow, that's a lot, Greg. Are you guys sure you want to do this?"

"Absolutely, Bobby. Take a week or two to think about it. We'll make it worth your while. Oh, and by the way, Sarah, your former secretary, now works for us. She'll be calling to get your address and will personally drop off your commission check."

"Commission check?" Bobby asked, surprised.

"Yes, a check for $2 million. Bobby, when I say you hit the nail on the head, I mean you really hit the nail on the head. We are eternally grateful."

Bobby ended the call and placed his phone down gently, the

weight of the conversation still lingering in the air. Christina, noticing the shift in his demeanor, asked softly, "Is everything okay?"

"Yes," Bobby replied, his voice steady but laced with emotion.

Christina, sensing something in his tone, asked, "Why do you look like that? Are you okay?"

Bobby nodded, though his expression remained reflective. "Yes, I'm fine." "I just got a call from one of the companies I worked with years ago during the COVID epidemic." At first, I thought it was yet another investor looking to blame me for decisions that didn't turn out right, and I got really panicky because of the last experience. But then, Greg—the guy who called—started to talk, and it just changed my life. "They're sending me a check for some advice I gave them at the time." He promised that if things worked out, the company would take care of me. Well, they're having a check dropped off by my former secretary for $2 million."

Christina's eyes widened in disbelief. "What did you just say? Two million dollars?"

Bobby nodded, a smile breaking through his serious demeanor. "Yes, two million dollars. And they want me to work for them as a consultant, so the work won't interfere with my writing. They also want to be the executive producer of my movie based on the book, funding the whole thing."

Without thinking, Christina and Bobby started jumping for joy. The reality of the situation, the sudden windfall, and the new opportunities overwhelmed them both. They grabbed each other in a tight, supportive hug, their shared excitement tangible.

Just then, the phone rang again, and Bobby, still catching his breath from the excitement, answered, "Hello?"

"Hello, Mr. Pope," came the voice from Willow Creek Cemetery. "All has been secured for you and your wife with the plots. We received the final payment, and the gravestones have arrived. They will be installed next week, ready for your arrival and visit with your wife, as requested."

Bobby's voice softened. "Thank you so much."

He turned back to Christina, his tone shifting to something more solemn. "I was just securing the gravestones and finishing the payments for the plots at Willow Creek Cemetery. I wanted the stone done a specific way, and you know me; I'm very meticulous about how I want things done."

Christina nodded, a gentle smile forming on her lips. "Yeah, I know that about you, Bobby," she said, her eyes reflecting a shared understanding. But as she watched him, she noticed a single tear rolling down his cheek, a tear that seemed to emerge from the deepest parts of his soul, unbidden and raw.

Bobby paused, his voice catching as he stopped speaking. The tear was a silent testament to the pain that still lingered, the deep wound that Brandy's loss had left in his heart. It was clear that, despite his composed exterior, Bobby missed Brandy dearly, and the pain of everything that had transpired was still fresh and unhealed.

Sensing the need to shift the mood, Christina gently changed the subject. "Hey, I'm hoping you'll be at my opening night here in downtown Chicago for the new play 'One Woman's Trash,'" she said, her tone light but hopeful.

"Of course, I'll be there," Bobby replied, nodding. "I'm moving around now, and I really want to get out and be more mobile. I also plan on getting over to the gravesite. I couldn't attend the funeral because of the pain I was dealing with, but now that I'm feeling a lot better, I want to pay my respects."

Christina's expression softened with empathy. "Would you like me to go with you?" she offered.

"That would be nice, Christina," Bobby said, his voice warm but resolute. "But for this first time, I'd like to go by myself. I hope you understand."

"Absolutely, Bobby, I really do," Christina assured him, her tone full of understanding.

"Oh, and by the way, my novel just arrived from the printers. The publishing company is really excited about it—they've even increased the promotional budget to really push it out."

"Wow, Bobby, can you say 'New York Times Best Seller'?" Christina replied, her eyes sparkling with excitement for him.

Bobby chuckled, a modest smile forming on his lips. "Well, I don't know about that, but anything's possible, right?"

"Right, it's definitely possible!" Christina affirmed, her enthusiasm contagious.

Bobby smiled, gratitude evident in his expression. "Christina, I want you to know that in the absence of my sister, I'm going to need to lean on you. And I pray that you'll do the same."

"Without question, Bobby," Christina said softly, her voice filled with sincerity. "We'll lean on each other."

In that moment, there was a shared understanding between them, a bond that had been strengthened by loss and the shared burden of moving forward. Together, they would find a way to navigate the pain, the memories, and the new paths their lives were taking.

Once again, Bobby's phone rang. "I've got to take this, Christina," he said, stepping away to answer the call.

"No problem," Christina replied, watching him leave the room. She began to wander around, her eyes scanning the room filled with mementos and memories. As she approached a small table in the corner, something glowing caught her attention. Intrigued, she moved closer and noticed a beautiful, large gold coin resting on the table. It was polished and well-kept, its surface gleaming under the soft light. She picked it up, turning it over in her hand and admiring its craftsmanship.

Bobby reentered the room and noticed her examining the coin. "It's beautiful, isn't it?"

"Yes, it is," Christina replied, still captivated by the coin's luster. "You know, I remember Brandy telling me a story a long time ago about you and a lady with sky-blue eyes. She said the woman asked you for money, but you told her you didn't have any, even though you'd just been paid. Brandy said you drove away but then felt guilty and went back to where you saw her, only to find she was gone—and in her place was a gold coin. Don't tell me that's a true story, Bobby. I mean, really?"

Bobby smiled, a mix of nostalgia and wonder in his eyes. "Yes, it's true. And that is the coin I found, clear as day. When I had it appraised back then, it was worth five hundred dollars. I recently had it reappraised, and now it's valued at ten thousand dollars. It turns out it's made from a special kind of gold that comes from Israel, and the coin is hundreds of years old."

Christina's eyes widened in disbelief. "No way."

Bobby continued, "The night I was shot, I was carrying it like I always do. But that night, I was wearing one of those new suits with straight-leg pants, and carrying it in my pocket wasn't working, so I put it in my suit jacket pocket—right over my heart. The doctors told me I should have died that night, but the bullet hit the coin instead. It didn't penetrate because of the strength of the gold; it just pushed it aside enough to redirect the bullet. It passed straight through my body without hitting anything vital."

Christina stared at him, her face a mix of awe and disbelief. "Shut up, Bobby. You're freaking me out. I mean, really?"

Bobby nodded, his expression serious. "Yeah, I know. It's strange, but I believe that everything that happened that evening was just part of the journey we took. It was already mapped out in advance."

Christina looked at the coin again, now seeing it as more than just a beautiful object. It was a symbol of something greater—fate, protection, and the mysterious ways life unfolds. She handed the coin back to Bobby, her mind buzzing with the weight of his story.

Bobby, who navigated life's harshest ordeals, demonstrated that even amid the brutality of experiences, there exists a profound validation of our roles in shaping the paths of those around us. The enduring strength of unconditional love emerges as a force more resilient than the divergent paths chosen by each individual.

"Farewell to My Queen"

Days later, Bobby stood at the entrance of the cemetery, his heart heavy with emotions he had tried to bury deep inside. The air was still, and the sun was low in the sky, casting a soft orange glow over the rows of headstones. For a moment, Bobby hesitated, unsure if he was ready for this. But he knew he had to do it. He had to say goodbye to Brandy.

He walked slowly, his footsteps crunching on the gravel path as he made his way to Brandy's grave. It was the first time he had come here since the night of the incident with Fleet and Timmoreia. That night had changed everything. It was the night he was shot, the night Brandy had slipped away from him forever.

As he approached the grave, Bobby's breath caught in his throat. The sight of Brandy's name etched into the stone brought a fresh wave of pain. He knelt beside the grave, his hands trembling as he traced the letters with his fingers. "Brandy," he whispered, his voice breaking. "My queen... my best friend."

Tears welled up in his eyes as memories of their time together flooded his mind. He remembered the laughter they shared, the quiet moments of comfort, and the countless challenges they faced. Their relationship had its ups and downs, but through it all, Brandy had been his rock, his partner, his love.

"I know we went through a lot," Bobby said, his voice choked with emotion. "We had our struggles, our fights... but we also had so many good times. We traveled, we dreamed, we built something together. And even though it wasn't always easy, I wouldn't trade it for anything."

Bobby took a deep breath, trying to steady himself. "What happened to you... it wasn't just your fault," he said, his voice barely above a whisper. "I know you carried so much weight, so much pain. But I should have been there for you more. I should have seen what was happening and done something. I'm so sorry, Brandy. I wish I could have saved you from all of it."

He placed a hand on the cold stone, feeling the rough surface under his fingers. "The drugs... the things you went through... they weren't your fault. You were exposed to so much trauma, so many bad influences when you were just a kid. It wasn't fair. You didn't deserve any of it."

Bobby reached into his jacket pocket and pulled out a folded piece of paper. It was the poem he had written for Brandy, the words that had come to him late at night when he couldn't sleep, when the pain of losing her was too much to bear.

He unfolded the paper and began to read aloud:
"It will always be like you never left me."
"Like time never passed and left you and us behind."
"Like the questions you asked me in the morning:
"How do I look in this? Is my hair okay?"
"Is my body still to your liking?"
"It will always be like you never left me."
Because there is no key to the door for your exit,
And there is no exit from the door of my heart.
"You are with me always."
In the quiet moments and the loud,

In the laughter and the tears.
"You live on in my memories."
In every corner of my soul.
And though you're gone,
You will never be forgotten.
For you, my queen,
"Are forever a part of me."

Bobby's voice cracked as he finished the poem, tears streaming down his face. He folded the paper and placed it gently on Brandy's grave. "The stones are really beautiful, baby," he said softly. "I know you would be pleased with them. I made sure my plot was right next to yours. We'll have matching stones, side by side, just like we always were. They've already been placed, so one day... one day, we'll rest together, eternally."

He looked down at his black outfit, the one Brandy always loved him in. "Oh, I'm wearing black today, my favorite color. You always loved me in black," he whispered with a faint smile, remembering how she would tease him about it.

"I finished my novel," Bobby continued, his voice filled with a mix of pride and sorrow. "I dedicated it to you. I know we had some challenges with how you felt about it, but I think... I think you would have loved reading it. You were the star, after all."

Bobby stayed there for a long time, kneeling by the grave, lost in his memories of Brandy. He remembered the good times, the laughter, and the love they shared. But he also acknowledged the pain, the struggles, and the things they couldn't fix. It was a bittersweet farewell, but Bobby knew it was time to let go.

"I promise I'll keep living," he said softly. "I'll keep going for both of us. And I'll carry you with me, always. I'll see you soon, Brandy. One day, we'll rest side by side together."

With one last look at the grave, Bobby stood up, his heart heavy but a little lighter than before. He knew Brandy would always have a special place in his life, in his heart. As he walked away, the sun dipped below the horizon, casting long shadows across the cemetery. Bobby didn't look back. He didn't need to. Brandy was with him, and she always would be.

Bobby, Bobby, Yes, Mother, it's time to leave for the show. If we don't leave now, we'll be late, and you know Christina won't like that. The narrative seamlessly transitions to a moment of urgency as Bobby, torn between finishing the last chapter and attending the show, responds to his mother's call. Seated at his desk, a smile plays on Bobby's lips as he gazes at a picture of Brandy. The lingering validation of the Christmas bonus, endorsed by his attorney Meeka, becomes a testament to a lasting financial legacy.

The scene shifts to Bobby's current reality, living in a high-rise in the heart of Downtown Chicago, caring for his elderly mother. His success as a writer becomes a blessing shared with those in his orbit. As he closes his computer, a substantial sense of relief accompanies the completion of the last piece. Yet, amid the closure, a casual inquiry to his mother about car keys introduces a note of continuity, reminding us that life's journey perpetually moves forward.

Ultimately, Brandy departed from this world not due to health-related reasons but as a consequence of the risks she daringly embraced and the subsequent fallout of those choices. Within the realm of narratives, it becomes evident that countless untold stories and unrealized cinematic creations populate the graveyard of unrealized potential. However, in a stroke of fortune for Bobby, who ultimately survived his encounter with death, his tombstone will bear witness to a narrative contrary to this trend. His tale will stand as a testament to a life fully lived, a story penned with bold decisions that defied the common fate of languishing in the cemetery of unwritten novels and unrealized films.

Christina sat in her dressing room, bathed in the warm, golden glow of the makeup lights, a sanctuary from the bustling energy outside. The room hummed with life—flowers sent by well-wishers filled the air with their sweet scent, and the distant murmur of the audience created a symphony of anticipation. Each element of this moment seemed to resonate with the culmination of her life's journey.

The worn edges of her script, lying gently on the vanity, were physical reminders of the countless hours she had poured into this role. It wasn't just the script, though—it was the journey: the countless auditions, the late-night rehearsals, the days when she questioned her path, and the exhilarating moments when she knew this was what she was meant to do. Yet, all those memories converged on a singular, bittersweet moment: the day she lost her mother, Lella-May.

That memory had become a cornerstone of her resolve. As the first cue for her entrance echoed faintly through the walls, Christina felt her focus sharpen, pulling her back to the present. The reflections in the mirror weren't just images of herself—they were reflections of every step, every lesson, and every piece of advice her mother had given her. Tonight, each memory was another patch in the quilt of her life, now coming together in a spectacular display.

The thought that Broadway directors might be in the audience added a layer of pressure, but it was the kind that exhilarated rather than overwhelmed. Her heart raced, driven by a mixture of anticipation and fear, but underneath it all was a quiet confidence. She thought of herself as a young girl, performing in school plays, dreaming of one day commanding a stage like this in a role that truly mattered—like the one she was about to perform tonight.

As she delicately touched up her makeup, Christina allowed a moment of pride to seep in. For too long, she had followed in Brandy's footsteps, but tonight was different. She wasn't just Brandy's sister anymore; she was Christina, an actress in her own right with her own story to tell. The reflection in the mirror revealed a woman who had been transformed by her journey—

no longer tentative but poised, confident, and ready to conquer the world beyond the dressing room doors.

"Here's to making dreams a reality," she whispered to herself, her voice steady and filled with determination. The character she was about to bring to life wasn't just a role; it was a declaration, a statement to the world that Christina had arrived —not just as an actress and a singer, but as a force of nature.

As she stood, the stage manager's earlier words, "Break a leg," rang in her ears. Christina smiled at her reflection one last time before heading toward the stage. This performance was more than just an act; it was her moment to inspire, to captivate, to shine. The curtain was about to rise, and in that split second before stepping into the spotlight, she heard her mother's voice in her mind: "It's time to come out now, baby."

And with that, Christina stepped into the spotlight, ready to embrace whatever came next, fully knowing she had everything it took to make "One Woman's Trash..." not just a success but a monumental triumph.

"Echoes of Unwritten Stories"

After paying their respects at Grandmother June's grave, Clara and Amelia made their way slowly back through the peaceful rows of the cemetery. The atmosphere, laden with memories and whispers of lives past, seemed to hold them in a gentle embrace. Amelia's thoughts, however, lingered on the two beautiful gravestones they had encountered earlier—those of Bobby and Brandy Pope.

"Mommy, can we stop by those stones again on the way back? I think there was more written on them that I didn't get to read," Amelia asked, her curiosity rekindled by the mysteries those stones hinted at.

"Of course, baby. We can stop," Clara replied, smiling gently at her daughter's burgeoning interest in stories, even those set in stone.

As they approached the twin gravestones again, Amelia rushed ahead with youthful eagerness. "Look, Mommy, someone was just here. They left a note on Brandy's grave." Before her mother had time to stop her, Amelia grabbed the note and opened it. "It's a poem, Mommy."

"Yes, baby, but it shouldn't be read. I'm sure it's from someone," Clara said gently. Amelia frowned slightly as she continued, "But on the bottom, it says it's from Bobby Pope. How could that be? I thought they were both buried here?"

"I'm not sure, baby," Clara replied, her voice tinged with confusion. Suddenly, she felt the presence of someone behind them. Turning slowly, she saw a woman—older but well-preserved, with the most beautiful sky-blue eyes she had ever seen.

"Hello, how are you?" Clara asked, feeling a bit unsettled. "Please excuse us; my daughter and I are just visiting the gravesites."

"Well, that's wonderful," the woman said kindly. "These two here are very special and lovely people." Clara listened as the woman continued to speak, her voice soft and reverent as she looked at the stones.

But when Clara turned around to respond, the woman was gone—vanished into thin air as if she had never been there at all.

"Look, Mommy, this is so beautiful," Amilia said as she touched the stone with her hand. Amilia, now even more curious, knelt down beside Bobby's gravestone first. This time, she noticed something peculiar about the dates inscribed on it. "November 3, 1990, to..." The inscription trailed off into a blank space where the end date should have been.

"Mother, what does that mean?" Amelia asked, looking up at Clara with puzzled eyes.

"It means that Bobby is still living, sweetheart. He isn't here yet. This is a placeholder for when he eventually joins Brandy," Clara explained, her voice soft, trying to simplify the concept of a reserved grave space for her young daughter.

Amelia then turned her attention to Brandy's stone, which read, "October 10, 1990, to July 7, 2022." The finality of the dates struck a chord in her, a somber reminder of the story's end. "Why does she have a number, Mommy?"

"Brandy, unfortunately, has passed away, like your grandmother. That's why her dates are complete," Clara said, touching Amelia's shoulder gently.

Amelia nodded slowly. "I bet she was a pretty girl," she murmured, almost to herself.

"I'm sure she was," Clara agreed, her gaze lingering on the intricately carved flowers on the stone.

Excitedly, Amelia pointed to another part of the stone. "Look, Mommy! Bobby wrote something else here." She traced her fingers over the additional inscription. "What does it say, baby?"

Amelia read aloud, "There are many novels in the graveyard that have never been written, but not this one: 'Brandy and Bobby: The Risks of Consequences.' Mommy, what does that mean?"

Clara knelt beside her, her eyes reflective. "It means that Bobby wrote a novel about his life with Brandy so that anyone who wants to can read about their love and the choices they made. It's a way of ensuring their story lives on, even if they cannot."

"Wow, Mommy, can we read about them?" Amelia's eyes were wide with wonder, a spark of excitement dancing in them.

"Well, I'm sure we can. When we get home, I'll look for the novel," Clara promised, touched by her daughter's interest.

"Oh, great, Mommy! I can't wait to read it!" Amelia clapped her hands in delight, her imagination already weaving images of Brandy and Bobby's life together.

As they walked back to the car, the cemetery seemed less a place of endings and more a repository of stories waiting to be discovered, each gravestone a silent sentinel guarding the tales of lives woven with love, loss, and the imprints they leave behind.

Clara's heart skipped a beat as she took in the strange scene. The poem, the mysterious woman, and now the blank space on Bobby's gravestone—it was all too much to take in at once.

Amelia, still holding the note, stared at the blank space on the stone with wide, curious eyes. "Mother, what does that mean?" she asked, her small voice trembling slightly.

Her mind raced, trying to make sense of it all. Bobby Pope—the name on the note, the man who was supposed to be resting here beside Brandy, his queen. But why was the end date missing? And who was that woman with the sky-blue eyes who had appeared so suddenly, only to vanish just as quickly?

Clara looked around the cemetery, searching for any sign of the woman, but there was nothing—only the quiet rustle of leaves in the gentle breeze and the distant sound of birds singing. It was as if the woman had never been there at all.

"Mommy, look," Amelia said, her voice full of wonder as she pointed to the ground where the woman had stood. Clara followed her daughter's gaze and saw the gold coin gleaming in the sunlight. It looked ancient, untouched as if it had been waiting there for centuries.

Clara reached down and picked up the coin, feeling its weight in her hand. It was warm, almost as if it were alive. The intricate designs on the surface were unlike anything she had ever seen—symbols that seemed to shift and change as she looked at them.

"Where do you think this came from?" Amelia asked, her eyes wide with fascination.

Clara shook her head, still holding the coin. "I don't know, sweetheart. But it's beautiful, isn't it?" She looked at the grave-stones again, then back at the coin. Something about the whole situation felt otherworldly as if they had stepped into a place where the lines between the living and the dead, the past and the present, had blurred.

"Mommy," Amelia said, her voice quieter now, "do you think the woman left this for us?"

Clara thought for a moment, then nodded slowly. "Maybe she did, baby. Maybe she wanted us to find it." She took

Amelia's hand, squeezing it gently. "Let's keep it safe. It feels... important."

As they stood there, a sense of calm washed over Clara. She didn't have all the answers, but something in her heart told her that everything was as it should be. Bobby's unfinished date, the mysterious woman, the gold coin—they were all connected in ways she couldn't yet understand.

But one thing was clear: Bobby and Brandy's story wasn't over—not yet.

"Come on, sweetheart," Clara said softly, standing up and leading Amelia away from the gravestones. "Let's go home."

As they walked back to the car, the poem slipped from Amelia's hand, fluttering gently to the ground beside Brandy's grave. The words, carried by the wind, seemed to linger in the air:

"It will always be like you never left me..."

Clara didn't look back, but she felt the presence of the woman, of Bobby and Brandy, with her as they left the cemetery. And though she couldn't explain it, she knew that their story, like the poem, would live on—forever etched in time.

The End

A Novel by Dr. Freddie Lee Thomas Jr.

"Risk of Consequences"

The Risk of Consequences tells the intertwined stories of characters navigating their paths through life's uncertainties. Each of them is like a thread in a vast and intricate fabric, representing their pursuit of happiness, acceptance, and belonging in a world full of unpredictability. Every decision they make is a delicate balance between possibilities, holding the potential to either build or break their lives, to give them joy or take it away.

Throughout the novel, we see these characters embark on personal and collective journeys, each searching for meaning and connection. They face doors of opportunity, each one leading to new adventures or unknown challenges. As they navigate these paths, they shine as individual lights in a world filled with endless possibilities, where every risk they take leads to consequences that are often shaped by their past experiences.

As the characters approach the end of their journeys, they reflect on everything they've gone through—their successes, failures, hopes, and regrets. This novel isn't just a collection of separate stories; it's a shared narrative that offers lessons from the lives of its characters. It serves as a guide for others who are on their own journeys, showing the results of the risks taken in the darkness of the past. **The Risk of Consequences** invites readers to reflect on the intricate connections between people and how the choices we make can profoundly affect not only our lives but also the lives of those around us.

The book, "The Risk of Consequences," revolves around the intricate interplay between choices, risks, and the inevitable outcomes. At its core, the novel explores how each decision we make can lead to a cascade of consequences that not only impact our own lives but also the lives of those around us. This philosophy is grounded in several key themes:

1. Interconnectedness of Lives:

The novel emphasizes that no life is lived in isolation. Every action and every choice creates ripples that affect others, often in ways we cannot predict. This interconnectedness is symbolized by the metaphor of lives as threads in a large, intricate fabric. Each character's decisions weave together, creating a tapestry that tells a collective story, illustrating how deeply our lives are intertwined.

2. The Dance of Possibilities:

Life is portrayed as a series of possibilities, where every choice is a step in a dance that can lead to different outcomes. This dance is delicate and requires careful consideration, but it is also unpredictable and filled with unknowns that can lead to either fulfillment or regret. The philosophy here suggests that while we may try to control our destinies, much of life's journey is about navigating uncertainty and making peace with the unknown.

3. The Weight of the Past:

The novel explores how the shadows of the past influence present decisions and future outcomes. Characters often find themselves grappling with the consequences of earlier actions, realizing that the past is not just a distant memory but a powerful force that shapes the present. This theme underscores the idea that our past choices, whether good or bad, have lasting impacts that we must confront and learn from.

4. The Search for Belonging and Acceptance:

Throughout the novel, characters are depicted as searching for a place where they feel they belong, where they are accepted for who they are. This search is fraught with challenges as the characters navigate their own insecurities, desires, and the expectations of others. The philosophy here is that true belonging and acceptance are not just about finding the right place or people but about understanding and accepting oneself.

5. Hope Amidst Uncertainty:

Despite the uncertainties and risks inherent in life, the novel carries a message of hope. The characters, through their struggles and triumphs, demonstrate that even in the darkest moments, there is the possibility of light. This hope is not about avoiding risks but about embracing them with the understanding that every step forward is an opportunity for growth and change.

6. Consequences as Life Lessons:

The title itself, **"The Risk of Consequences,"** suggests that the consequences we face are not just results of our actions but are also valuable life lessons. The philosophy here is that every consequence, whether positive or negative, provides an opportunity to learn, grow, and become more self-aware. The novel encourages readers to view consequences not as punishments but as part of the natural progression of life, where every experience, no matter how challenging, contributes to personal development.

7. Reflection and Growth:

As the characters reach the end of their journeys, they engage in deep reflection, considering the paths they've taken and the lessons learned. This reflection is a crucial part of the novel's philosophy, suggesting that true growth comes from understanding where we've been and how our choices have shaped our present. The book encourages a reflective mindset, urging readers to look back on their own lives with a sense of curiosity and a willingness to learn from the past.

In essence, **"The Risk of Consequences"** is a philosophical exploration of the human experience, focusing on the complexities of choice, the inevitability of consequences, and the potential for growth and understanding that comes from facing life's challenges head-on. It invites readers to consider their own lives in the context of these themes, offering a narrative that is both introspective and deeply connected to the broader human condition.

FREDDIE L. THOMAS'S
SPECIAL PREVIEW

"Echoes from the Corner of Redemption"

There he sat at the corner of W Monroe and Pine, amidst the bustling streets of Chicago, an observer and participant in the ebb and flow of city life. Known among the street natives in the hood simply as "Gee Easy," he was a figure of multifaceted character: a comedian with a quick wit, a philosopher pondering the mysteries of life, a wino without a care, and a voice of warning to those who would listen. To many, he appeared as a bum, a man shaped and subdued by his choices, yet his presence on that corner spoke of a deeper story, a narrative that intertwined his current existence with fragments of a once notable past.

Once, Gee Easy was not merely a fixture of the streets but a man of stature and influence—Bishop George Evan Davidson, renowned across Chicago as one of the city's most successful preachers during his time. Now, his corner served as both home and pulpit, a solitary testament to a life once filled with promise and now marred by regret. Life's temptations, symbolized by the metaphorical apple, had stripped him of his recognizable identity, leaving behind only the essence of the man he once was.

His once recognizable features had been gradually obscured, a visage now camouflaged by the ravages of drug and alcohol abuse, coupled with the relentless advance of age. This transformation rendered him nearly unrecognizable to the casual observer, his face a living postcard from a life marred by excess and moral abandonment. Only those who had navigated through the turbulent narrative of his journey—a saga punctuated by episodes of immorality and self-indulgence—could truly discern the man he once was beneath the mask that his existence had become.

These changes in Gee Easy's appearance were not merely physical; they symbolized the profound impact of his choices, each line and scar a testament to the trials he had endured. His story, once marked by the potential for greatness and spiritual leadership, had deviated into a cautionary tale, showcasing the stark realities of a life surrendered to momentary pleasures and the avoidance of deeper truths.

Yet, within this drapery of loss and transformation, there remained a thread of resilience. Despite the physical alterations that concealed his former identity, Gee Easy's spirit, though battered, persisted. It was this enduring essence that continued to draw people to him, compelling them to listen and, perhaps, to learn from the hard-earned lessons he shared. His ability to connect with others, to offer wisdom distilled from the depths of his own fall from grace, spoke to the indomitable nature of the human spirit.

In this way, Gee Easy's marked visage became a symbol of both warning and wisdom, a beacon for those who found themselves adrift in their own lives. Through him, the harsh consequences of certain paths were laid bare, yet so too was the possibility of insight and understanding born from adversity. His story, etched into his very skin, stood as a vivid reminder that, even in our lowest moments, there exists the potential for redemption and the opportunity to alter the course of our narrative.

As he sat, projecting his thoughts and instructions to anyone within earshot, his presence occasionally became a source of irritation to Tom Chang, the owner of the liquor store in front of which Gee Easy made his stand. Tom and his family owned most of the block, a stretch of land that had once been a beacon of black-owned businesses and aspiring stars. "Look, Easy, now I done told your old ass to get away from my store entrance. You go now, you go now," Tom would say, trying to reclaim some peace for his establishment.

Despite such confrontations, Gee Easy was seldom alone. Drawn by his words and charisma, other homeless individuals and friends would often join him. His philosophical musings sometimes earned him a few dollars, which he would use to buy a bottle of wine for communal sharing, a modern-day act of communion in memory of higher teachings, though he never partook in the drinking himself. His income, however modest, was carefully hidden away, saved from the prying eyes of the world.

Gee Easy's unique standing in the community attracted a diverse following. From churchgoers to business professionals and even gang members and drug dealers, many would contribute to his makeshift offering box. Despite his inability to walk well, necessitating his leaning against walls for support, he was known to mysteriously disappear each night, leaving many to wonder about his whereabouts. Unlike other homeless individuals who stayed put, Gee Easy would vanish, only to reappear each morning as if by magic. This peculiar habit intrigued those who knew him, though his status as a community fixture meant that few delved deeper into the mystery of his nightly absences.

His unusual character and the paradoxes that defined his life made Gee Easy a beloved figure in the neighborhood. Outsiders and return visitors alike sought him out, drawn by his unique perspective and memorable sayings, such as "Truth to the pimp, pimp to the truth." Despite the appearance of impropriety, Gee Easy lived outside the consequences typically associated with such a life, embodying a complexity that endeared him to people from all walks of life.

Though Gee Easy seldom delved into the details of his past, it was clear he saw his current state not just as a consequence of his actions but as a form of atonement. He had once been a guiding light, leading many toward faith and God,he now believed he had been placed among the people, on this very corner, as a living testament to his own failures. His leadership, while once revered, had also led him down paths that strayed from the teachings he professed, steering both himself and his followers toward metaphorical "conditions of hell." This realization weighed heavily on him, transforming his existence into a cautionary tale.

Embracing his circumstances, Gee Easy perceived his life as a penalty for the disparity between the man he was and the God he preached. He acknowledged that in following the man—himself—his followers had overlooked the divine guidance that should have been at the forefront of their journey. This dissonance between his actions and the spiritual ideals he was supposed to embody haunted him, a constant reminder of the pain and suffering his misguidance inflicted on others.

In his interactions, Gee Easy took on the mantle of a teacher, albeit one whose classroom was the harsh realities of street life. His message was not one of redemption for himself but a dire warning for others. He sought to instruct those around him to avoid the pitfalls that had ensnared him, to learn from the errors that had cost him everything. "It's me, your future you," he would often say, a stark warning that the path he trod could be theirs if they were not careful. This phrase encapsulated his message: a life lesson born from personal downfall, serving as a beacon for those willing to heed his advice.

In this way, Gee Easy transformed his own miseries into a powerful tool for guidance. Despite the remnants of his crumbled past and the reality of his present, his words carried the weight of lived experience, offering a unique perspective that resonated with many. Through his daily presence and the wisdom he shared, Gee Easy became more than just a fixture of the neighborhood; he was a voice of warning, a mirror reflecting the potential consequences of one's actions, urging others to choose a path different from his own.

On a particularly dreary day, as the rain poured down in sheets, a chilling scene unfolded at the corner of W. Monroe and Pine. The usual bustle was muted, the heavy rain dissuading most from venturing out, leaving only a handful of onlookers to witness what was about to occur. Without warning, a man approached Gee Easy, rage contorting his features. The confrontation escalated rapidly as the man unleashed a torrent of blows upon Gee Easy, each punch and kick delivered with a ferocity that seemed to draw from a deep well of personal anguish. "There you are, you motherfucker! You ruined my damn life. You took from me my dreams and my future," he yelled, articulating each word with a strike that seemed to echo through the empty streets.

The assault was brutal, each hit threatening to be the last for Gee Easy. As the assailant raised his hand for what could have been the fatal blow, Gee Easy, through swollen eyes and a face marred by the violence inflicted upon him, locked eyes with his attacker. At that moment, a flash of something profound and indefinable shone through Gee Easy's gaze—his eyes, pure white and glaring, a stark contrast to the chaos around him seemed to be the last vestiges of his spiritual connection to God. "Forgive me, please forgive me," Gee Easy implored, his voice barely above a whisper yet carrying an immense weight.

The effect was immediate and startling. The fury that had propelled the man's actions seemed to evaporate, replaced by a torrent of tears. The realization of what he was doing, spurred by Gee Easy's plea, broke through his anger, and with a cry of anguish, he retreated to his still-running car by the curb and drove away, leaving behind a silence punctuated only by the sound of the falling rain.

Gee Easy, battered and bruised, managed to rise. With the rain pouring down, masking his injuries and mingling with his blood, he slipped away around a corner, disappearing from the lives of those who had come to know him as a constant presence. He would not return for several months, his absence marking a somber period for the corner of W. Monroe and Pine.

The aftermath of the beating left a visible mark on the corner, a stain of blood that Tom Chang, despite his best efforts, could not remove. The blood, strangely, remained a vivid red, untouched by the passage of time, serving as a haunting reminder of that day's violence. This persistent stain became more than just a physical reminder; it was a testament to the intensity of the encounter and the profound impact of Gee

Easy's words. In the face of such aggression, his plea for forgiveness not only spared his life but also left an indelible mark on the conscience of the community, symbolizing the lasting effects of violence, the power of forgiveness, and the enduring spirit of Gee Easy.